Python Data Structures and Algorithms

Improve the performance and speed of your applications

Benjamin Baka

BIRMINGHAM - MUMBAI

Python Data Structures and Algorithms

Copyright © 2017 Packt Publishing

First published: May 2017

Production reference: 1260517

Published by Packt Publishing Ltd.
Livery Place
35 Livery Street
Birmingham
B3 2PB, UK.
ISBN 978-1-78646-735-5

www.packtpub.com

Credits

Author

Benjamin Baka

Reviewer

David Julian

Commissioning Editor

Kunal Parikh

Acquisition Editor

Denim Pinto

Content Development Editor

Zeeyan Pinheiro

Technical Editors

Pavan Ramchandani
Ketan Kamble

Copy Editor

Safis Editing

Project Coordinator

Vaidehi Sawant

Proofreader

Safis Editing

Indexer

Tejal Daruwale Soni

Graphics

Abhinash Sahu

Production Coordinator

Melwyn Dsa

About the Author

Benjamin Baka works as a software developer and has over 10 years, experience in programming. He is a graduate of Kwame Nkrumah University of Science and Technology and a member of the Linux Accra User Group. Notable in his language toolset are C, C++, Java, Python, and Ruby. He has a huge interest in algorithms and finds them a good intellectual exercise.

He is a technology strategist and software engineer at mPedigree Network, weaving together a dizzying array of technologies in combating counterfeiting activities, empowering consumers in Ghana, Nigeria, and Kenya to name a few.

In his spare time, he enjoys playing the bass guitar and listening to silence. You can find him on his blog.

Many thanks to the team at Packt who have played a major part in bringing this book to light. I would also like to thank David Julian, the reviewer on this book, for all the assistance he extended through diverse means in preparing this book.

I am forever indebted to Lorenzo E. Danielson and Guido Sohne for their immense help in ways I can never repay.

About the Reviewer

David Julian has over 30 years of experience as an IT educator and consultant.

He has worked on a diverse range of projects, including assisting with the design of a machine learning system used to optimize agricultural crop production in controlled environments and numerous backend web development and data analysis projects.

He has authored the book *Designing Machine Learning Systems with Python* and worked as a technical reviewer on Sebastian Raschka's book *Python Machine Learning*, both by Packt Publishing.

www.PacktPub.com

For support files and downloads related to your book, please visit www.PacktPub.com.

Did you know that Packt offers eBook versions of every book published, with PDF and ePub files available? You can upgrade to the eBook version at www.PacktPub.com and as a print book customer, you are entitled to a discount on the eBook copy. Get in touch with us at service@packtpub.com for more details.

At www.PacktPub.com, you can also read a collection of free technical articles, sign up for a range of free newsletters and receive exclusive discounts and offers on Packt books and eBooks.

https://www.packtpub.com/mapt

Get the most in-demand software skills with Mapt. Mapt gives you full access to all Packt books and video courses, as well as industry-leading tools to help you plan your personal development and advance your career.

Why subscribe?

- Fully searchable across every book published by Packt
- Copy and paste, print, and bookmark content
- On demand and accessible via a web browser

Customer Feedback

Thanks for purchasing this Packt book. At Packt, quality is at the heart of our editorial process. To help us improve, please leave us an honest review on this book's Amazon page at https://www.amazon.com/dp/1786467356.

If you'd like to join our team of regular reviewers, you can e-mail us at customerreviews@packtpub.com. We award our regular reviewers with free eBooks and videos in exchange for their valuable feedback. Help us be relentless in improving our products!

Table of Contents

Preface

A knowledge of data structures and the algorithms that bring them to life is the key to building successful data applications. With this knowledge, we have a powerful way to unlock the secrets buried in large amounts of data. This skill is becoming more important in a data-saturated world, where the amount of data being produced dwarfs our ability to analyze it. In this book, you will learn the essential Python data structures and the most common algorithms. This book will provide basic knowledge of Python and an insight into the exciting world of data algorithms. We will look at algorithms that provide solutions to the most common problems in data analysis, including sorting and searching data, as well as being able to extract important statistics from data. With this easy-to-read book, you will learn how to create complex data structures such as linked lists, stacks, and queues, as well as sorting algorithms such as bubble sort and insertion sort. You will learn the common techniques and structures used in tasks such as preprocessing, modeling, and transforming data. We will also discuss how to organize your code in a manageable, consistent, and extendable way. You will learn how to build components that are easy to understand, debug, and use in different applications.

A good understanding of data structures and algorithms cannot be overemphasized. It is an important arsenal to have in being able to understand new problems and find elegant solutions to them. By gaining a deeper understanding of algorithms and data structures, you may find uses for them in many more ways than originally intended. You will develop a consideration for the code you write and how it affects the amount of memory and CPU cycles to say the least. Code will not be written for the sake of it, but rather with a mindset to do more using minimal resources. When programs that have been thoroughly analyzed and scrutinized are used in a real-life setting, the performance is a delight to experience. Sloppy code is always a recipe for poor performance. Whether you like algorithms purely from the standpoint of them being an intellectual exercise or them serving as a source of inspiration in solving a problem, it is an engagement worthy of pursuit.

The Python language has further opened the door for many professionals and students to come to appreciate programming. The language is fun to work with and concise in its description of problems. We leverage the language's mass appeal to examine a number of widely studied and standardized data structures and algorithms.

The book begins with a concise tour of the Python programming language. As such, it is not required that you know Python before picking up this book.

What this book covers

Chapter 1, *Python Objects, Types, and Expressions*, introduces you to the basic types and objects of Python. We will give an overview of the language features, execution environment, and programming styles. We will also review the common programming techniques and language functionality.

Chapter 2, *Python Data Types and Structures*, explains each of the five numeric and five sequence data types, as well as one mapping and two set data types, and examine the operations and expressions applicable to each type. We will also give examples of typical use cases.

Chapter 3, *Principles of Algorithm Design*, covers how we can build additional structures with specific capabilities using the existing Python data structures. In general, the data structures we create need to conform to a number of principles. These principles include robustness, adaptability, reusability, and separating the structure from a function. We look at the role iteration plays and introduce recursive data structures.

Chapter 4, *Lists and Pointer Structures*, covers linked lists, which are one of the most common data structures and are often used to implement other structures, such as stacks and queues. In this chapter, we describe their operation and implementation. We compare their behavior to arrays and discuss the relative advantages and disadvantages of each.

Chapter 5, *Stacks and Queues*, discusses the behavior and demonstrates some implementations of these linear data structures. We give examples of typical applications.

Chapter 6, *Trees*, will look at how to implement a binary tree. Trees form the basis of many of the most important advanced data structures. We will examine how to traverse trees and retrieve and insert values. We will also look at how to create structures such as heaps.

Chapter 7, *Hashing and Symbol Tables*, describes symbol tables, gives some typical implementations, and discusses various applications. We will look at the process of hashing, give an implementation of a hash table, and discuss the various design considerations.

Chapter 8, *Graphs and Other Algorithms*, looks at some of the more specialized structures, including graphs and spatial structures. Representing data as a set of nodes and vertices is convenient in a number of applications, and from this, we can create structures such as directed and undirected graphs. We will also introduce some other structures and concepts such as priority queues, heaps, and selection algorithms.

Chapter 9, *Searching*, discusses the most common searching algorithms and gives examples of their use for various data structures. Searching a data structure is a fundamental task and there are a number of approaches.

Chapter 10, *Sorting*, looks at the most common approaches to sorting. This will include bubble sort, insertion sort, and selection sort.

Chapter 11, *Selection Algorithms*, covers algorithms that involve finding statistics, such as the minimum, maximum, or median elements in a list. There are a number of approaches and one of the most common approaches is to first apply a sort operation. Other approaches include partition and linear selection.

Chapter 12, *Design Techniques and Strategies*, relates to how we look for solutions for similar problems when we are trying to solve a new problem. Understanding how we can classify algorithms and the types of problem that they most naturally solve is a key aspect of algorithm design. There are many ways in which we can classify algorithms, but the most useful classifications tend to revolve around either the implementation method or the design method.

Chapter 13, *Implementations, Applications, and Tools*, discusses a variety of real-world applications. These include data analysis, machine learning, prediction, and visualization. In addition, there are libraries and tools that make our work with algorithms more productive and enjoyable.

What you need for this book

The code in this book will require you to run Python 2.7.x or higher. Python's default interactive environment can also be used to run the snippets of code. In order to use other third-party libraries, pip should be installed on your system.

Who this book is for

This book would appeal to Python developers. Basic knowledge of Python is preferred but is not a requirement. No previous knowledge of computer concepts is assumed. Most of the concepts are explained with everyday scenarios to make it very easy to understand.

Conventions

In this book, you will find a number of text styles that distinguish between different kinds of information. Here are some examples of these styles and an explanation of their meaning.

Code words in text, database table names, folder names, filenames, file extensions, pathnames, dummy URLs, user input, and Twitter handles are shown as follows: "This repetitive construct could be a simple `while` loop or any other kind of loop."

A block of code is set as follows:

```
def dequeue(self):
    if not self.outbound_stack:
        while self.inbound_stack:
            self.outbound_stack.append(self.inbound_stack.pop())
    return self.outbound_stack.pop()
```

When we wish to draw your attention to a particular part of a code block, the relevant lines or items are set in bold:

```
def dequeue(self):
    if not self.outbound_stack:
        while self.inbound_stack:
            self.outbound_stack.append(self.inbound_stack.pop())
    return self.outbound_stack.pop()
```

Any command-line input or output is written as follows:

```
% python bubble.py
```

New terms and **important words** are shown in bold. Words that you see on the screen, for example, in menus or dialog boxes, appear in the text like this: "Clicking the **Next** button moves you to the next screen."

Warnings or important notes appear in a box like this.

Tips and tricks appear like this.

Reader feedback

Feedback from our readers is always welcome. Let us know what you think about this book-what you liked or disliked. Reader feedback is important for us as it helps us develop titles that you will really get the most out of.

To send us general feedback, simply e-mail feedback@packtpub.com, and mention the book's title in the subject of your message.

If there is a topic that you have expertise in and you are interested in either writing or contributing to a book, see our author guide at www.packtpub.com/authors.

Customer support

Now that you are the proud owner of a Packt book, we have a number of things to help you to get the most from your purchase.

Downloading the example code

You can download the example code files for this book from your account at http://www.packtpub.com. If you purchased this book elsewhere, you can visit http://www.packtpub.com/support and register to have the files e-mailed directly to you.

You can download the code files by following these steps:

1. Log in or register to our website using your e-mail address and password.
2. Hover the mouse pointer on the **SUPPORT** tab at the top.
3. Click on **Code Downloads & Errata**.
4. Enter the name of the book in the **Search** box.
5. Select the book for which you're looking to download the code files.
6. Choose from the drop-down menu where you purchased this book from.
7. Click on **Code Download**.

Once the file is downloaded, please make sure that you unzip or extract the folder using the latest version of:

- WinRAR / 7-Zip for Windows
- Zipeg / iZip / UnRarX for Mac
- 7-Zip / PeaZip for Linux

The code bundle for the book is also hosted on GitHub at `https://github.com/PacktPubl ishing/Python-Data-Structures-and-Algorithma`. We also have other code bundles from our rich catalog of books and videos available at `https://github.com/PacktPublish ing/`. Check them out!

Errata

Although we have taken every care to ensure the accuracy of our content, mistakes do happen. If you find a mistake in one of our books-maybe a mistake in the text or the code-we would be grateful if you could report this to us. By doing so, you can save other readers from frustration and help us improve subsequent versions of this book. If you find any errata, please report them by visiting `http://www.packtpub.com/submit-errata`, selecting your book, clicking on the **Errata Submission Form** link, and entering the details of your errata. Once your errata are verified, your submission will be accepted and the errata will be uploaded to our website or added to any list of existing errata under the Errata section of that title.

To view the previously submitted errata, go to `https://www.packtpub.com/books/conten t/support` and enter the name of the book in the search field. The required information will appear under the **Errata** section.

Piracy

Piracy of copyrighted material on the Internet is an ongoing problem across all media. At Packt, we take the protection of our copyright and licenses very seriously. If you come across any illegal copies of our works in any form on the Internet, please provide us with the location address or website name immediately so that we can pursue a remedy.

Please contact us at `copyright@packtpub.com` with a link to the suspected pirated material.

We appreciate your help in protecting our authors and our ability to bring you valuable content.

Questions

If you have a problem with any aspect of this book, you can contact us at `questions@packtpub.com`, and we will do our best to address the problem.

1
Python Objects, Types, and Expressions

Python is the language of choice for many advanced data tasks for a very good reason. Python is one of the easiest advanced programming languages to learn. Intuitive structures and semantics mean that for people who are not computer scientists, but maybe biologists, statisticians, or the directors of a start-up, Python is a straightforward way to perform a wide variety of data tasks. It is not just a scripting language, but a full-featured object-oriented programming language.

In Python, there are many useful data structures and algorithms built in to the language. Also, because Python is an object-based language, it is relatively easy to create custom data objects. In this book, we will examine both Python internal libraries, some of the external libraries, as well as learning how to build your own data objects from first principles.

This book does assume that you know Python. However, if you are a bit rusty, coming from another language, or do not know Python at all, don't worry, this first chapter should get you quickly up to speed. If not, then visit `https://docs.python.org/3/tutorial/index.html`, and also you can find the documentation at `https://www.python.org/doc/`. These are all excellent resources to easily learn this programming language.

In this chapter, we will look at the following topics:

- Obtaining a general working knowledge of data structures and algorithms
- Understanding core data types and their functions
- Exploring the object-oriented aspects of the Python programming language

Understanding data structures and algorithms

Algorithms and data structures are the most fundamental concepts in computing. They are the building blocks from which complex software is built. Having an understanding of these foundation concepts is hugely important in software design and this involves the following three characteristics:

- How algorithms manipulate information contained within data structures
- How data is arranged in memory
- What the performance characteristics of particular data structures are

In this book, we will examine this topic from several perspectives. Firstly, we will look at the fundamentals of the Python programming language from the perspective of data structures and algorithms. Secondly, it is important that we have the correct mathematical tools. We need to understand some fundamental concepts of computer science and for this we need mathematics. By taking a heuristics approach, developing some guiding principles means that, in general, we do not need any more than high school mathematics to understand the principles of these key ideas.

Another important aspect is evaluation. Measuring an algorithms performance involves understanding how each increase in data size affects operations on that data. When we are working on large datasets or real-time applications, it is essential that our algorithms and structures are as efficient as they can be.

Finally, we need a sound experimental design strategy. Being able to conceptually translate a real-world problem into the algorithms and data structures of a programming language involves being able to understand the important elements of a problem and a methodology for mapping these elements to programming structures.

To give us some insight into algorithmic thinking, let's consider a real-world example. Imagine we are at an unfamiliar market and we are given the task of purchasing a list of items. We assume that the market is laid out randomly, and each vendor sells a random subset of items, some of which may be on our list. Our aim is to minimize the price we pay for each item as well as minimize the time spent at the market. One way to approach this is to write an algorithm like the following:

Repeat for each vendor:

1. Does the vendor have items on my list and is the cost less than a predicted cost for the item?
2. If yes, buy and remove from list; if no, move on to the next vendor.
3. If no more vendors, end.

This is a simple iterator, with a decision and an action. If we were to implement this, we would need data structures to define both the list of items we want to buy as well as the list of items of each vendor. We would need to determine the best way of matching items in each list and we need some sort of logic to decide whether to purchase or not.

There are several observations that we can make regarding this algorithm. Firstly, since the cost calculation is based on a prediction, we don't know what the real average cost is; if we underpredict the cost of an item, we come to the end of the market with items remaining on our list. Therefore, we need an efficient way to backtrack to the vendor with the lowest cost.

Also, we need to understand what happens to the time it takes to compare items on our shopping list with items sold by each vendor as the number of items on our shopping list, or the number of items sold by each vendor, increases. The order in which we search through items and the shape of the data structures can make a big difference to the time it takes to do a search. Clearly, we would like to arrange our list, as well as the order we visit each vendor, in such a way that we minimize search time.

Also, consider what happens when we change the buy condition to purchase at the *cheapest* price, not just the below average price. This changes the problem entirely. Instead of sequentially going from one vendor to the next, we need to traverse the market once and, with this knowledge, we can order our shopping list with regards to the vendors we want to visit.

Obviously, there are many more subtleties involved in translating a real-world problem into an abstract construct such as a programming language. For example, as we progress through the market, our knowledge of the cost of a product improves, so our predicted average price variable becomes more accurate until, by the last stall, our knowledge of the market is perfect. Assuming any kind of backtracking algorithm incurs a cost, we can see cause to review our entire strategy. Conditions such as high price variability, the size and shape of our data structures, and the cost of backtracking all determine the most appropriate solution.

Python for data

Python has several built-in data structures, including lists, dictionaries, and sets, that we use to build customized objects. In addition, there are a number of internal libraries, such as collections and the `math` object, which allow us to create more advanced structures as well as perform calculations on those structures. Finally, there are the external libraries such as those found in the `SciPy` packages. These allow us to perform a range of advanced data tasks such as logistic and linear regression, visualization, and mathematical calculations such as operations on matrixes and vectors. External libraries can be very useful for an *out-of-the-box* solution. However, we must also be aware that there is often a performance penalty compared to building customized objects from the ground up. By learning how to code these objects ourselves, we can target them to specific tasks, making them more efficient. This is not to exclude the role of external libraries and we will look at this in `Chapter 12`, *Design Techniques and Strategies.*

To begin, we will take an overview of some of the key language features that make Python such a great choice for data programming.

The Python environment

A feature of the Python environment is its interactive console allowing you to both use Python as a desktop programmable calculator and also as an environment to write and test snippets of code. The **read-evaluate-print** loop of the console is a very convenient way to interact with a larger code base, such as to run functions and methods or to create instances of classes. This is one of the major advantages of Python over compiled languages such as C/C++ or Java, where the **write-compile-test-recompile** cycle can increase development time considerably compared to Python's read - evaluate - print loop. Being able to type in expressions and get an immediate response can greatly speed up data science tasks.

There are some excellent distributions of Python apart from the official CPython version. Two of the most popular are Anaconda (`https://www.continuum.io/downloads`) and Canopy (`https://www.enthought.com/products/canopy/`). Most distributions come with their own developer environments. Both Canopy and Anaconda include libraries for scientific, machine learning, and other data applications. Most distributions come with an editor.

There are also a number of implementations of the Python console, apart from the CPython version. Most notable amongst these is the Ipython/Jupyter platform that includes a web-based computational environment.

Variables and expressions

To translate a real-world problem into one that can be solved by an algorithm, there are two interrelated tasks. Firstly, select the variables, and secondly, find the expressions that relate to these variables. Variables are labels attached to objects; they are not the object itself. They are not containers for objects either. A variable does not contain the object, rather it acts as a pointer or reference to an object. For example, consider the following code:

```
In [1]: a=[2,4,6]

In [2]: b=a

In [3]: a.append(8)

In [4]: b
Out[4]: [2, 4, 6, 8]
```

Here we have created a variable, a, which points to a list object. We create another variable, b, which points to this same list object. When we append an element to this list object, this change is reflected in both a and b.

Python is a dynamically typed language. Variable names can be bound to different values and types during program execution. Each value is of a type, a string, or integer for example; however, the name that points to this value does not have a specific type. This is different from many languages such as C and Java where a name represents a fixed size, type, and location in memory. This means when we initialize variables in Python, we do not need to declare a type. Also, variables, or more specifically the objects they point to, can change type depending on the values assigned to them, for example:

```
In [1]: a=1

In [2]: type(a)
Out[2]: int

In [3]: a=a+0.1

In [4]: type(a)
Out[4]: float
```

Variable scope

It is important to understand the scoping rules of variables inside functions. Each time a function executes, a new local namespace is created. This represents a local environment that contains the names of the parameters and variables that are assigned by the function. To resolve a namespace when a function is called, the Python interpreter first searches the local namespace (that is, the function itself) and if no match is found, it searches the global namespace. This global namespace is the module in which the function was defined. If the name is still not found, it searches the built-in namespace. Finally, if this fails then the interpreter raises a `NameError` exception. Consider the following code:

```
a=10; b=20
def my_function():
    global a
    a=11; b=21
my_function()
print(a) #prints 11
print(b) #prints 20
```

Here is the output of the preceding code:

```
>>> print(a) #prints 11
10
>>> print(b) #prints 20
20
```

In the preceding code, we define two global variables. We need to tell the interpreter, using the keyword `global`, that inside the function, we are referring to a global variable. When we change this variable to `11`, these changes are reflected in the global scope. However, the variable b we set to `21` is local to the function, and any changes made to it inside the function are not reflected in the global scope. When we run the function and print b, we see that it retains its global value.

Flow control and iteration

Python programs consist of a sequence of statements. The interpreter executes each statement in order until there are no more statements. This is true if both files run as the main program as well as files that are loaded via `import`. All statements, including variable assignment, function definitions, class definitions, and module imports, have equal status. There are no special statements that have higher priority than any other and every statement can be placed anywhere in a program. There are two main ways of controlling the flow of program execution, conditional statements and loops.

The if, else, and elif statements control the conditional execution of statements. The general format is a series of if and elif statements followed by a final else statement:

```
x='one'
if x==0:
    print ('False')
elif x==1:
    print ('True')
else: print ('Something else')
#prints 'Something else'
```

Note the use of the == operator to test for the same values. This returns true if the values are equal; it returns false otherwise. Note also that setting x to a string will return *something else* rather than generate a type error as may happen in languages that are not dynamically typed. Dynamically typed languages such as Python allow flexible assignment of objects with different types.

The other way of controlling program flow is with loops. They are created using the while or for statements, for example:

```
In [5]: x=0

In [6]: while x < 3 : print(x); x +=1
0
1
2
```

Overview of data types and objects

Python contains 12 built-in data types. These include four numeric types (int, float, complex, bool), four sequence types (str, list, tuple, range), one mapping type (dict), and two set types. It is also possible to create user-defined objects such as functions or classes. We will look at the string and the list data types in this chapter and the remaining built-in types in the next chapter.

All data types in Python are **objects**. In fact, pretty much everything is an object in Python, including modules, classes, and functions, as well as literals such as strings and integers. Each object in Python has a **type**, a **value,** and an **identity**. When we write greet = "hello world" we are creating an instance of a string object with the value "hello world" and the identity of greet. The identity of an object acts as a pointer to the object's location in memory. The type of an object, also known as the object's class, describes the object's internal representation as well as the methods and operations it supports. Once an instance of an object is created, its identity and type cannot be changed.

We can get the identity of an object by using the built-in function id(). This returns an identifying integer and on most systems this refers to its memory location, although you should not rely on this in any of your code.

Also, there are a number of ways to compare objects, for example:

```
if a== b: #a and b have the same value

if a is b: # if a and b are the same object
if type(a) is type(b): # a and b are the same type
```

An important distinction needs to be made between **mutable** and **immutable** objects. Mutable object's such as lists can have their values changed. They have methods, such as insert() or append(), that change an objects value. Immutable objects, such as strings, cannot have their values changed, so when we run their methods, they simply return a value rather than change the value of an underlying object. We can, of course, use this value by assigning it to a variable or using it as an argument in a function.

Strings

Strings are immutable sequence objects, with each character representing an element in the sequence. As with all objects, we use methods to perform operations. Strings, being immutable, do not change the instance; each method simply returns a value. This value can be stored as another variable or given as an argument to a function or method.

The following table is a list of some of the most commonly used string methods and their descriptions:

Methods	Descriptions
s.count(substring, [start,end])	Counts the occurrences of a substring with optional start and end parameters.
s.expandtabs([tabsize])	Replaces tabs with spaces.
s.find(substring, [start, end])	Returns the index of the first occurrence of a substring or returns -1 if the substring is not found.
s.isalnum()	Returns True if all characters are alphanumeric, returns False otherwise.
s.isalpha()	Returns True if all characters are alphabetic, returns False otherwise.
s.isdigit()	Returns True if all characters are digits, returns False otherwise.
s.join(t)	Joins the strings in sequence t.
s.lower()	Converts the string to all lowercase.
s.replace(old, new [maxreplace])	Replaces old substring with new substring.
s.strip([characters])	Removes whitespace or optional characters.
s.split([separator], [maxsplit])	Splits a string separated by whitespace or an optional separator. Returns a list.

Strings, like all sequence types, support indexing and slicing. We can retrieve any character from a string by using its index s[i]. We can retrieve a slice of a string by using s[i:j], where i and j are the start and end points of the slice. We can return an extended slice by using a stride, as in the following: s[i:j:stride]. The following code should make this clear:

```
In [19]: greet = 'hello world'

In [20]: greet[1]
Out[20]: 'e'

In [21]: greet[0:8]
Out[21]: 'hello wo'

In [22]: greet[0:8:2]
Out[22]: 'hlow'

In [23]: greet[0::2]
Out[23]: 'hlowrd'
```

The first two examples are pretty straightforward, returning the character located at index 1 and the first seven characters of the string, respectively. Notice that indexing begins at 0. In the third example, we are using a stride of 2. This results in every second character being returned. In the final example, we omit the end index and the slice returns every second character in the entire string.

You can use any expression, variable, or operator as an index as long as the value is an integer, for example:

```
In [9]: greet[1+2]
Out[9]: 'l'

In [10]: greet[len(greet)-1]
Out[10]: 'd'
```

Another common operation is traversing through a string with a loop, for example:

```
In [24]: for i in enumerate(greet[0:5]): print(i)
(0, 'h')
(1, 'e')
(2, 'l')
(3, 'l')
(4, 'o')
```

Given that strings are immutable, a common question that arises is how we perform operations such inserting values. Rather than changing a string, we need to think of ways to build new string objects for the results we need. For example, if we wanted to insert a word into our greeting, we could assign a variable to the following:

```
In [19]: greet[:5] + ' wonderful' + greet[5:]
Out[19]: 'hello wonderful world'
```

As this code shows, we use the slice operator to split the string at index position 5 and use + to concatenate. Python never interprets the contents of a string as a number. If we need to perform mathematical operations on a string, we need to first convert them to a numeric type, for example:

```
In [15]: x='3'; y='2'

In [16]: x + y #concatenation
Out[16]: '32'

In [17]: int(x) + int(y) #addition
Out[17]: 5
```

Lists

Lists are probably the most used built-in data structures in Python because they can be composed of any number of other data types. They are a simple representation of arbitrary objects. Like strings, they are indexed by integers starting with zero. The following table contains the most commonly used list methods and their descriptions:

Method	Description
list(s)	Returns a list of the sequence s.
s.append(x)	Appends element x to the end of s.
s.extend(x)	Appends the list x to s.
s.count(x)	Counts the occurrence of x in s.
s.index(x, [start], [stop])	Returns the smallest index, i, where s[i] ==x. Can include optional start and stop index for the search.

`s.insert(i,e)`	Inserts x at index `i`.
`s.pop(i)`	Returns the element `i` and removes it from the list.
`s.remove(x)`	Removes x from `s`.
`s.reverse()`	Reverses the order of `s`.
`s.sort(key ,[reverse])`	Sorts `s` with optional key and reverse.

When we are working with lists, and other *container* objects, it is important to understand the internal mechanism that Python uses to copy them. Python creates real copies only if it has to. When we assign the value of a variable to another variable, both of these variables point to the same memory location. A new slot in memory will only be allocated if one of the variables changes. This has important consequences for mutable compound objects such as lists. Consider the following code:

```
In [8]: x=1;y=2;z=3
In [9]: list1 =[x,y,z]
In [10]: list2 = list1
In [11]: list2[1] = 4
In [12]: list1
Out[12]: [1, 4, 3]
```

Here, both the `list1` and `list2` variables point to the same slot in memory. When we change the `y` variable to `4`, we are changing the same `y` variable that `list1` is pointing to.

An important feature of list's is that they can contain nested structures, that is, other lists, for example:

```
In [5]: items = [["rice",2.4, 8 ],["flour", 1.9, 5], ["Corn", 4.7, 6] ]
In [6]: for item in items:
   ...:     print("Product: %s Price: %.2f Quality: %i" % (item[0], item[1], item[2]))
   ...:
Product: rice Price: 2.40 Quality: 8
Product: flour Price: 1.90 Quality: 5
Product: Corn Price: 4.70 Quality: 6
```

We can access the lists values using the bracket operators and since lists are mutable, they are copied in place. The following example demonstrates how we can use this to update elements; for example, here we are raising the price of flour by 20 percent:

```
In [26]: items[1][1] = items[1][1] * 1.2

In [27]: items[1][1]
Out[27]: 2.28
```

A common and very intuitive way to create lists from expressions is using **list comprehensions.** This allows us to create a list by writing an expression directly into the list, for example:

```
In [27]: l= [2,4,8,16]

In [28]: [i**3 for i in l]
Out[28]: [8, 64, 512, 4096]
```

List comprehensions can be quite flexible; for example, consider the following code. It essentially shows two different ways to performs a function composition, where we apply one function (x * 4) to another (x * 2). The following code prints out two lists representing the function composition of f1 and f2 calculated first using a for loop and then using a list comprehension:

```
def f1(x): return x*2
def f2(x): return x*4

lst = []
for i in range(16):
    lst.append(f1(f2(i)))

print(lst)

print([f1(x)  for x in range(64) if x in [f2(j) for j in range(16)]])
```

The first line of output is from the for loop construct. The second is from the list comprehension expression:

```
[0, 8, 16, 24, 32, 40, 48, 56, 64, 72, 80, 88, 96, 104, 112, 120]
[0, 8, 16, 24, 32, 40, 48, 56, 64, 72, 80, 88, 96, 104, 112, 120]
```

List comprehensions can also be used to replicate the action of nested loops in a more compact form. For example, we multiply each of the elements contained within `list1` with each other:

```
In [13]: list1= [[1,2,3], [4,5,6]]

In [14]: [i * j for i in list1[0] for j in list1[1]]
Out[14]: [4, 5, 6, 8, 10, 12, 12, 15, 18]
```

We can also use list comprehensions with other objects such as strings, to build more complex structures. For example, the following code creates a list of words and their letter count:

```
In [20]: words = 'here is a sentence'.split()

In [21]: [[word, len(word)] for word in words]
Out[21]: [['here', 4], ['is', 2], ['a', 1], ['sentence', 8]]
```

As we will see, lists form the foundation of many of the data structures we will look at. Their versatility, ease of creation, and use enables them to build more specialized and complex data structures.

Functions as first class objects

In Python, it is not only data types that are treated as objects. Both functions and classes are what are known as first class objects, allowing them to be manipulated in the same ways as built-in data types. By definition, first class objects are:

- Created at runtime
- Assigned as a variable or in a data structure
- Passed as an argument to a function
- Returned as the result of a function

In Python, the term **first class object** is a bit of a misnomer since it implies some sort of hierarchy, whereas all Python objects are essentially first class.

To have a look at how this works, let's define a simple function:

```
def greeting(language):
if language== 'eng':
        return 'hello world'
    if language  == 'fr'
        return 'Bonjour le monde'
    else: return 'language not supported'
```

Since user-defined functions are objects, we can do things such as include them in other objects, such as lists:

```
In [9]: l=[greeting('eng'), greeting('fr'), greeting('ger')]

In [10]: l[1]
Out[10]: ' Bonjour le monde'
```

Functions can also be used as arguments for other functions. For example, we can define the following function:

```
In [14]: def callf(f):
   ...:         lang='eng'
   ...:         return (f(lang))
   ...:

In [15]: callf(greeting)
Out[15]: 'hello world'
```

Here, `callf()` takes a function as an argument, sets a language variable to `'eng'`, and then calls the function with the language variable as its argument. We could see how this would be useful if, for example, we wanted to produce a program that returns specific sentences in a variety of languages, perhaps for some sort of natural language application. Here we have a central place to set the language. As well as our `greeting` function, we could create similar functions that return different sentences. By having one point where we set the language, the rest of the program logic does not have to worry about this. If we want to change the language, we simply change the language variable and we can keep everything else the same.

Higher order functions

Functions that take other functions as arguments, or that return functions, are called **higher order functions**. Python 3 contains two built-in higher order functions, `filter()` and `map()`. Note that in earlier versions of Python, these functions returned lists; in Python 3, they return an iterator, making them much more efficient. The `map()` function provides an easy way to transform each item into an iterable object. For example, here is an efficient, compact way to perform an operation on a sequence. Note the use of the `lambda` anonymous function:

```
In [40]: lst=[1,2,3,4]

In [41]: list(map(lambda x: x**3, lst))
Out[41]: [1, 8, 27, 64]
```

Similarly, we can use the `filter` built-in function to filter items in a list:

```
In [43]: list(filter((lambda x: x<3),lst))
Out[43]: [1, 2]
```

Note that both `map` and `filter` perform the identical function as to what can be achieved by list comprehensions. There does not seem to be a great deal of difference in the performance characteristics apart from a slight performance advantage when using the in built functions `map` and `filter` without the `lambda` operator, compared to list comprehensions. Despite this, most style guides recommend the use of list comprehensions over built-in functions, possibly because they tend to be easier to read.

Creating our own higher order functions is one of the hallmarks of functional programming style. A practical example of how higher order functions can be useful is demonstrated by the following. Here we are passing the `len` function as the key to the `sort` function. This way, we can sort a list of words by length:

```
In [19]: words=str.split('The longest word in this sentence')

In [20]: sorted(words, key=len)
Out[20]: ['in', 'The', 'word', 'this', 'longest', 'sentence']
```

Here is another example for case-insensitive sorting:

```
In [84]: sl=['A','b','a', 'C', 'c']

In [85]: sl.sort(key=str.lower)

In [86]: sl
Out[86]: ['A', 'a', 'b', 'C', 'c']

In [87]: sl.sort()

In [88]: sl
Out[88]: ['A', 'C', 'a', 'b', 'c']
```

Note the difference between the `list.sort()` method and the `sorted` built-in function. `list.sort()`, a method of the `list` object, sorts the existing instance of a list without copying it. This method changes the target object and returns `None`. It is an important convention in Python that functions or methods that change the object return `None` to make it clear that no new object was created and that the object itself was changed.

On the other hand, the sorted built-in function returns a new list. It actually accepts any iterable object as an argument, but it will always return a list. Both `list sort` and `sorted` take two optional keyword arguments as key.

A simple way to sort more complex structures is to use the index of the element to sort using the `lambda` operator, for example:

```
In [92]: items.sort(key=lambda item: item[1])

In [93]: items
Out[93]: [['flour', 1.9, 5], ['rice', 2.4, 8], ['Corn', 4.7, 6]]
```

Here we have sorted the items by price.

Recursive functions

Recursion is one of the most fundamental concepts of computer science. In Python, we can implement a recursive function simply by calling it within its own function body. To stop a recursive function turning into an infinite loop, we need at least one argument that tests for a terminating case to end the recursion. This is sometimes called the base case. It should be pointed out that recursion is different from iteration. Although both involve repetition, iteration loops through a sequence of operations, whereas recursion repeatedly calls a function. Both need a selection statement to end. Technically, recursion is a special case of iteration known as tail iteration, and it is usually always possible to convert an iterative function to a recursive function and vice versa. The interesting thing about recursive functions is that they are able to describe an infinite object within a finite statement.

The following code should demonstrate the difference between recursion and iteration. Both these functions simply print out numbers between `low` and `high`, the first one using iteration and the second using recursion:

```
def iterTest(low,high):
    while low <= high:
        print(low)
        low=low+1

def recurTest(low,high):
    if low <= high:
        print(low)
        recurTest(low+1, high)
```

Notice, `iterTest`, the iteration example, we use a `while` statement to test for the condition, then call the `print` method, and finally increment the `low` value. The recursive example tests for the condition, prints, then calls itself, incrementing the `low` variable in its argument. In general, iteration is more efficient; however, recursive functions are often easier to understand and write. Recursive functions are also useful for manipulating recursive data structures such as linked lists and trees, as we will see.

Generators and co-routines

We can create functions that do not just return one result, but rather an entire sequence of results, by using the `yield` statement. These functions are called **generators.** Python contains generator functions, which are an easy way to create iterators and they are especially useful as a replacement for unworkably long lists. A generator yields items rather than build lists. For example, the following code shows why we might choose to use a generator as opposed to creating a list:

```
# compares the running time of a list compared to a generator
import time
#generator function creates an iterator of odd numbers between n and m
def oddGen(n, m):
    while n < m:
        yield n
        n += 2
#builds a list of odd numbers between n and m
def oddLst(n,m):
    lst=[]
    while n<m:
        lst.append(n)
        n +=2
    return lst
#the time it takes to perform sum on an iterator
t1=time.time()
sum(oddGen(1,1000000))
print("Time to sum an iterator: %f" % (time.time() - t1))

#the time it takes to build and sum a list
t1=time.time()
sum(oddLst(1,1000000))
print("Time to build and sum a list: %f" % (time.time() - t1))
```

This prints out the following:

```
Time to sum an iterator: 0.133119
Time to build and sum a list: 0.191172
```

As we can see, building a list to do this calculation takes significantly longer. The performance improvement as a result of using generators is because the values are generated on demand, rather than saved as a list in memory. A calculation can begin before all the elements have been generated and elements are generated only when they are needed.

In the preceding example, the sum method loads each number into memory when it is needed for the calculation. This is achieved by the generator object repeatedly calling the __next__() special method. Generators never return a value other than None.

Typically, generator objects are used in for loops. For example, we can make use of the oddcount generator function created in the preceding code to print out odd integers between 1 and 10:

```
for i in oddcount(1,10):print(i)
```

We can also create a **generator expression,** which, apart from replacing square brackets with parentheses, uses the same syntax and carries out the same operation as list comprehensions. Generator expressions, however, do not create a list, they create a **generator object**. This object does not create the data, but rather creates that data on demand. This means that generator objects do not support sequence methods such as `append()` and `insert()`. You can, however, change a generator into a list using the `list()` function:

```
In [5]: lst1= [1,2,3,4]

In [6]: gen1 = (10**i for i in lst1)

In [7]: gen1
Out[7]: <generator object <genexpr> at 0x000001B981504C50>

In [8]: for x in gen1: print(x)
10
100
1000
10000
```

Classes and object programming

Classes are a way to create new kinds of objects and they are central to object-oriented programming. A class defines a set of attributes that are shared across instances of that class. Typically, classes are sets of functions, variables, and properties.

The object-oriented paradigm is compelling because it gives us a concrete way to think about and represent the core functionality of our programs. By organizing our programs around objects and data rather than actions and logic, we have a robust and flexible way to build complex applications. The actions and logic are still present of course, but by embodying them in objects, we have a way to encapsulate functionality, allowing objects to change in very specific ways. This makes our code less error-prone, easier to extend and maintain, and able to model real-world objects.

Classes are created in Python using the `class` statement. This defines a set of shared attributes associated with a collection of class instances. A class usually consists of a number of methods, class variables, and computed properties. It is important to understand that defining a class does not, by itself, create any instances of that class. To create an instance, a variable must be assigned to a class. The class body consists of a series of statements that execute during the class definition. The functions defined inside a class are called **instance methods.** They apply some operations to the class instance by passing an instance of that class as the first argument. This argument is called `self` by convention, but it can be any legal identifier. Here is a simple example:

```
class Employee(object):
    numEmployee = 0
    def __init__(self, name, rate):
        self.owed = 0
        self.name = name
        self.rate=rate
        Employee.numEmployee += 1

    def __del__(self):
        Employee.numEmployee -= 1

    def hours(self, numHours):
        self.owed += numHours * self.rate
        return("%.2f hours worked" % numHours)

    def pay(self):
        self.owed = 0
        return("payed %s " % self.name)
```

Class variables, such as numEmployee, share values among all the instances of the class. In this example, numEmployee is used to count the number of employee instances. Note that the Employee class implements the __init__ and __del__ special methods, which we will discuss in the next section.

We can create instances of the Employee objects, run methods, and return class and instance variables by doing the following:

```
In [3]: emp1=Employee("Jill", 18.50)

In [4]: emp2=Employee("Jack", 15.50)

In [5]: Employee.numEmployee
Out[5]: 2

In [6]: emp1.hours(20)
Out[6]: '20.00 hours worked'

In [7]: emp1.owed
Out[7]: 370.0

In [8]: emp1.pay()
Out[8]: 'payed Jill '
```

Special methods

We can use the `dir(object)` function to get a list of attributes of a particular object. The methods that begin and end with two underscores are called **special methods.** Apart from the following exception, special method, are generally called by the Python interpreter rather than the programmer; for example, when we use the + operator, we are actually invoking a call to __add__(). For example, rather than using `my_object.__len__()` we can use `len(my_object)` using `len()` on a string object is actually much faster because it returns the value representing the object's size in memory, rather than making a call to the object's __len__ method. The only special method we actually call in our programs, as common practice, is the __init__ method, to invoke the initializer of the superclass in our own class definitions. It is strongly advised not to use the double underscore syntax for your own objects because of potential current or future conflicts with Python's own special methods.

We may, however, want to implement special methods in custom objects, to give them some of the behavior of built-in types. In the following code, we create a class that implements the __repr__ method. This method creates a string representation of our object that is useful for inspection purposes:

```
class my_class():
    def __init__(self, greet):
        self.greet = greet
    def __repr__(self):
        return 'a custom object (%r)' % (self.greet)
```

When we create an instance of this object and inspect it, we can see we get our customized string representation. Notice the use of the `%r` format placeholder to return the standard representation of the object. This is useful and best practice, because, in this case, it shows us that the `greet` object is a string indicated by the quotation marks:

```
In [13]: a=my_class('giday')

In [14]: a
Out[14]: a custom object ('giday')
```

Inheritance

It is possible to create a new class that modifies the behavior of an existing class through inheritance. This is done by passing the inherited class as an argument in the class definition. It is often used to modify the behavior of existing methods, for example:

```
class specialEmployee(Employee):
    def hours(self, numHours):
        self.owed += numHours * self.rate * 2
        return("%.2f hours worked" % numHours)
```

An instance of the `specialEmployee` class is identical to an `Employee` instance except for the changed `hours()` method.

For a subclass to define new class variables, it needs to define an __init__() method, as follows:

```
class specialEmployee(Employee):
    def __init__(self,name,rate, bonus):
        Employee.__init__(self, name, rate) #calls the base classes
        self.bonus = bonus

    def hours(self, numHours):
        self.owed += numHours * self.rate + self.bonus
        return("%.2f hours worked" % numHours)
```

Notice that the methods of the base class are not automatically invoked and it is necessary for the derived class to call them. We can test for class membership using the built-in function `isintance(obj1, obj2)`. This returns true if `obj1` belongs to the class of `obj2` or any class derived from `obj2`.

Within a class definition, it is assumed that all methods operate on the instance, but this is not a requirement. There are, however, other types of methods: **static methods** and **class methods**. A static method is just an ordinary function that just happens to be defined in a class. It does not perform any operations on the instance and it is defined using the `@staticmethod` class decorator. Static methods cannot access the attributes of an instance, so their most common usage is as a convenience to group utility functions together.

Class methods operate on the class itself, not the instance, in the same way that class variables are associated with the classes rather than instances of that class. They are defined using the `@classmethod` decorator, and are distinguished from instance methods in that the class is passed as the first argument. This is named `cls` by convention.

```
class Aexp(object):
    base=2
    @classmethod
    def exp(cls,x):
        return(cls.base**x)

class Bexp(Aexp):
    base=3
```

The class `Bexp` inherits from the `Aexp` class and changes the base class variable to 3. We can run the parent class's `exp()` method as follows:

```
In [4]: BxSqr.sqr(3)
Out[4]: 27
```

Although this example is a little contrived, there are several reasons why class methods may be useful. For example, because a subclass inherits all the same features of its parent, there is the potential for it to break inherited methods. Using class methods is a way to define exactly what methods are run.

Data encapsulation and properties

Unless otherwise specified, all attributes and methods are accessible without restriction. This also means that everything defined in a base class is accessible from a derived class. This may cause problems when we are building object-oriented applications where we may want to hide the internal implementation of an object. This can lead to namespace conflicts between objects defined in derived classes with the base class. To prevent this, the methods we define private attributes with have a double underscore, such as `__privateMethod()`. These method names are automatically changed to `_Classname__privateMethod()` to prevent name conflicts with methods defined in base classes. Be aware that this does not strictly hide private attributes, rather it just provides a mechanism for preventing name conflicts.

It is recommended to use private attributes when using a class **property** to define mutable attributes. A property is a kind of attribute that rather than returning a stored value, computes its value when called. For example, we could redefine the `exp()` property with the following:

```
class Bexp(Aexp):
    __base=3
    def __exp(self):
        return(x**cls.base)
```

In this chapter, we have looked at some of the fundamentals of the Python programming language, from basic operations to functions, classes, and objects in Python. In the next chapter, we will examine, in detail, the built-in data structures of Python.

Summary

This chapter has given us a good foundation and introduction into Python programming. We covered the use of variables, lists, a couple of control structures, and learned how to use conditionals statement. The various kinds of objects were discussed, together with some materials on the object-oriented aspects of the Python language. We created our own objects and inherited from them.

There is still more that Python offers. As we prepare to examine the later chapters on some implementations of algorithms, the next chapter will focus on numbers, sequences, maps, and sets. These are also data types in Python that prove useful when organizing data for a series of operations.

2
Python Data Types and Structures

In this chapter, we are going to examine the Python data types in detail. We have already been introduced to two data types, the string, `str()`, and `list()`. It is often the case where we want more specialized objects to represent our data. In addition to the built-in types, there are several internal modules that allow us to address common issues when working with data structures. First, we are going to review some operations and expressions that are common to all data types.

Operations and expressions

There are a number of operations that are common to all data types. For example, all data types, and generally all objects, can be tested for a truth value in some way. The following are values that Python considers `False`:

- The `None` type
- `False`
- An integer, float, or complex zero
- An empty sequence or mapping
- An instance of a user-defined class that defines a `__len__()` or `__bool__()` method that returns zero or `False`

All other values are considered `True`.

Boolean operations

A Boolean operation returns a value of eighter `True` or `False`. Boolean operations are ordered in priority, so if more than one Boolean operation occurs in an expression, the operation with the highest priority will occur first. The following table outlines the three Boolean operators in descending order of priority:

Operator	Example
not x	Returns `True` if x is `False`; returns `False` otherwise.
x and y	Returns `True` if both x and y are `True`; returns `False` otherwise.
x or y	Returns `True` if either x or y is `True`; returns `False` otherwise.

Both the `and` operator and the `or` operator use "short-circuiting" when evaluating an expression. This means Python will only evaluate an operator if it needs to. For example, if x is `True` then in an expression x or y, the y does not get evaluated since the expression is obviously `True`. In a similar way, in an expression x and y where x is `False`, the interpreter will simply evaluate x and return `False`, without evaluating y.

Comparison and Arithmetic operators

The standard arithmetic operators (+, −, *, /) work with all Python numeric types. The // operator gives an integer quotient, (for example, 3 // 2 returns 1), the exponent operator is x ** y, and the modulus operator, given by a % b, returns the remainder of the division a/b. The comparison operators (<, <=, >, >=, ==, and !=) work with numbers, strings, lists, and other collection objects and return `True` if the condition holds. For collection objects, these operators compare the number of elements and the equivalence operator == b returns `True` if each collection object is structurally equivalent, and the value of each element is identical.

Membership, identity, and logical operations

Membership operators (`in`, `not in`) test for variables in sequences, such as lists or strings do what you would expect, x in y returns `True` if a variable x is found in y. The `is` operator compares object identity. For example, the following snippet shows contrast equivalence with object identity:

```
In [11]: x =[1,2,3] ; y=[1,2,3]

In [12]: x == y #equivalence
Out[12]: True

In [13]: x is y #object identity
Out[13]: False

In [14]: x = y #assignment

In [15]: x is y
Out[15]: True
```

Built-in data types

Python data types can be divided into three categories: numeric, sequence, and mapping. There is also the `None` object that represents a `Null`, or absence of a value. It should not be forgotten either that other objects such as classes, files, and exceptions can also properly be considered *types*; however, they will not be considered here.

Every value in Python has a data type. Unlike many programming languages, in Python you do not need to explicitly declare the type of a variable. Python keeps track of object types internally.

Python built-in data types are outlined in the following table:

Category	Name	Description
None	None	The null object.
Numeric	int	Integer.
	float	Floating point number.
	complex	Complex number.
	bool	Boolean (True, False).
Sequences	str	String of characters.
	list	List of arbitrary objects.
	Tuple	Group of arbitrary items.
	range	Creates a range of integers.
Mapping	dict	Dictionary of key-value pairs.

	`set`	Mutable, unordered collection of unique items.
	`frozenset`	Immutable set.

None type

The None type is immutable and has one value, `None`. It is used to represent the absence of a value. It is returned by objects that do not explicitly return a value and evaluates to `False` in Boolean expressions. It is often used as the default value in optional arguments to allow the function to detect whether the caller has passed a value.

Numeric Types

All numeric types, apart from `bool`, are signed and they are all immutable. Booleans have two possible values, `True` and `False`. These values are mapped to 1 and 0, respectively. The integer type, `int`, represents whole numbers of unlimited range. Floating point numbers are represented by the native double precision floating point representation of the machine. Complex numbers are represented by two floating point numbers. They are assigned using the `j` operator to signify the imaginary part of the complex number, for example:

```
a = 2+3j
```

We can access the real and imaginary parts with `a.real` and `a.imag`, respectively.

Representation error

It should be noted that the native double precision representation of floating point numbers leads to some unexpected results. For example, consider the following:

```
In [14]: 1-0.9
Out[14]: 0.09999999999999998

In [15]: 1-0.9 ==0.1
Out[15]: False
```

This is a result of the fact that most decimal fractions are not exactly representable as a binary fraction, which is how most underlying hardware represents floating point numbers. For algorithms or applications where this may be an issue, Python provides a `decimal` module. This module allows for the exact representation of decimal numbers and facilitates greater control properties such as rounding behavior, number of significant digits, and precision. It defines two objects, a `Decimal` type, representing decimal numbers, and a `Context` type, representing various computational parameters such as precision, rounding, and error handling. An example of its usage can be seen in the following snippet:

```
In [1]: import decimal

In [2]: x = decimal.Decimal(3.14); y= decimal.Decimal(2.74)

In [3]: x * y
Out[3]: Decimal('8.6036000000000001010036498883')

In [4]: decimal.getcontext().prec = 4

In [5]: x * y
Out[5]: Decimal('8.604')
```

Here we have created a global context and set the precision to 4. The `Decimal` object can be treated pretty much as you would treat an `int` or a `float`. They are subject to all the same mathematical operations and can be used as dictionary keys, placed in sets, and so on. In addition, `Decimal` objects also have several methods for mathematical operations, such as natural exponents, `x.exp()`, natural logarithms, `x.ln()`, and base 10 logarithms, `x.log10()`.

Python also has a `fractions` module that implements a rational number type. The following example shows several ways to create fractions:

```
In [62]: import fractions

In [63]: fractions.Fraction(3,4) # creates the fraction 3/4
Out[63]: Fraction(3, 4)

In [64]: fractions.Fraction(0.5) #creates a fraction from a float
Out[64]: Fraction(1, 2)

In [65]: fractions.Fraction(".25") #creates a fraction from a string
Out[65]: Fraction(1, 4)
```

It is also worth mentioning here the `NumPy` extension. This has types for mathematical objects such as arrays, vectors, and matrixes, and capabilities for linear algebra, calculation of Fourier transforms, eigenvectors, logical operations, and much more.

Sequences

Sequences are ordered sets of objects indexed by non-negative integers. Lists and tuples are sequences of arbitrary objects, strings are sequences of characters. String, tuple, and range objects are immutable. All sequence types have a number of operations in common. For all sequences, the indexing and slicing operators apply as described in the previous chapter. Note that for the immutable types, any operation will only return a value rather than actually change the value.

All sequences have the following methods:

Method	Description
`len(s)`	Number of elements in `s`
`min(s, [,default=obj, key=func])`	The minimum value in `s` (alphabetically for strings)
`max(s, [,default=obj, key=func])`	Maximum value in `s` (alphabetically for strings)
`sum(s, [,start=0])`	The sum of the elements (returns `TypeError` if `s` is not numeric)
`all(s)`	Returns `True` if all elements in `s` are True (that is, not 0, `False`, or `Null`)
`any(s)`	Checks whether any item in `s` is `True`

In addition, all sequences support the following operations:

Operation	Description
`s + r`	Concatenates two sequences of the same type
`s * n`	Make n copies of `s`, where n is an integer
`v1, v2 ..., vn = s`	Unpacks n variables from s to v1, v2, and so on
`s[i]`	Indexing-returns element i of `s`
`s[i:j:stride]`	Slicing returns elements between i and j with optional stride
`x in s`	Returns `True` if element x is in `s`
`x not in s`	Returns true if element x is not in `s`

Tuples

Tuples are immutable sequences of arbitrary objects. They are indexed by integers greater than zero. Tuples are **hashable**, which means we can sort lists of them and they can be used as keys to dictionaries. Syntactically, tuples are just a comma-separated sequence of values; however, it is common practice to enclose them in parentheses:

```
tpl= ('a', 'b', 'c')
```

It is important to remember to use a trailing comma when creating a tuple with one element, for example:

```
t = ('a',)
```

Without the trailing comma, this would be interpreted as a string.

We can also create a tuple using the built-in function `tuple()`. With no argument, this creates an empty tuple. If the argument to `tuple()` is a sequence then this creates a tuple of elements of that sequence, for example:

```
In [10]: tuple('sequence')
Out[10]: ('s', 'e', 'q', 'u', 'e', 'n', 'c', 'e')
```

Most operators, such as those for slicing and indexing, work as they do on lists. However, because tuples are immutable, trying to modify an element of a tuple will give you a `TypeError`. We can compare tuples in the same way that we compare other sequences, using the ==, > and < operators.

An important use of tuples is to allow us to assign more than one variable at a time by placing a tuple on the left-hand side of an assignment, for example:

```
In [21]: l=['one', 'two']
In [22]: x,y = l # assigns x and y to 'one' and 'two' respectively
```

We can actually use this multiple assignment to swap values in a tuple, for example:

```
In [25]: x,y = y,x #x = 'two' and y = 'one'
```

A `ValueError` will be thrown if the number of values on each side of the assignment are not the same.

Dictionaries

Dictionaries are arbitrary collections of objects indexed by numbers, strings, or other immutable objects. Dictionaries themselves are mutable; however, their index keys must be immutable. The following table contains all the dictionary methods and their descriptions:

Method	Description
`len(d)`	Number of items in d.
`d.clear()`	Removes all items from d.
`d.copy()`	Makes a shallow copy of d.
`d.fromkeys(s [,value])`	Returns a new dictionary with keys from sequence s and values set to `value`.
`d.get(k [,v])`	Returns d[k] if found, or else returns v, or None if v is not given.
`d.items()`	Returns a sequence of key:value pairs in d.
`d.keys()`	Returns a sequence of keys in d.
`d.pop(k [,default])`	Returns d[k] and removes it from d. If d[k] is not found, it returns default or raises `KeyError`.
`d.popitem()`	Removes a random key:value pair from d and returns it as a tuple.
`d.setdefault(k [,v])`	Returns d[k]. If d[k] is not found, it returns v and sets d[k] to v.
`d.update(b)`	Adds all objects from b to d.
`d.values()`	Returns a sequence of values in d.

Python dictionaries are the only built-in mapping type and they are similar to hash tables or associative arrays found in other languages. They can be thought of as a mapping from a set of keys to a set of values. They are created using the syntax `{key:value}`. For example, the following creates a dictionary mapping words to numerals:

```
d ={'one': 1 , 'two': 2, 'three': 3 } # creates a dictionary
```

We can add keys and values as follows:

```
d['four']=4 #add an item
```

Or update multiple values using the following:

```
d.update({'five': 5, 'six': 6}) #add multiple items
```

When we inspect d, we get the following:

```
In [2]: d
Out[2]: {'five': 5, 'four': 4, 'one': 1, 'six': 6, 'three': 3, 'two': 2}
```

We can test for the occurrence of a value using the in operator, for example:

```
In [10]: 'five' in d
Out[10]: True
```

It should be noted that the in operator, when applied to dictionaries, works in a slightly different way to when it is applied to a list. When we use the in operator on a list, the relationship between the time it takes to find an element and the size of the list is considered linear. That is, as the size of the list gets bigger, the corresponding time it takes to find an element grows, at most, linearly. The relationship between the time an algorithm takes to run compared to the size of its input is often referred to as its time complexity. We will talk more about this important topic in the next (and subsequent) chapters.

In contrast to the list object, when the in operator is applied to dictionaries, it uses a hashing algorithm and this has the effect of the increase in time for each lookup almost independent of the size of the dictionary. This makes dictionaries extremely useful as a way to work with large amounts of indexed data. We will talk more about this important topic of rates of growth hashing in Chapter 4, *Lists and pointer structures*, and Chapter 13, *Implementations, applications and tools*.

Notice when we print out the key:value pairs of the dictionary it does so in no particular order. This is not a problem since we use specified keys to look up each dictionary value rather than an ordered sequence of integers as is the case for strings and lists.

Sorting dictionaries

If we want to do a simple sort on either the keys or values of a dictionary, we can do the following:

```
In [4]: sorted(list(d)) #sorts keys
Out[4]: ['five', 'four', 'one', 'six', 'three', 'two']

In [5]: sorted(list(d.values())) #sorts values
Out[5]: [1, 2, 3, 4, 5, 6]
```

Note that the first line in the preceding code sorts the keys according to alphabetical order, and the second line sorts the values in order of integer value.

The `sorted()` method has two optional arguments that are of interest: `key` and `reverse`. The key argument has nothing to do with the dictionary keys, but rather is a way of passing a function to the sort algorithm to determine the sort order. For example, in the following code, we use the `__getitem__` special method to sort the dictionary keys according to the dictionary values:

```
sorted(list(d), key = d.__getitem__)
['one', 'two', 'three', 'four', 'five', 'six']
```

Essentially, what the preceding code is doing is for every `key` in d to use the corresponding value to sort. We can also sort the values according to the sorted order of the dictionary keys. However, since dictionaries do not have a method to return a `key` by using its value, the equivalent of the `list.index` method for lists, using the optional `key` argument to do this is a little tricky. An alternative approach is to use a list comprehension, as the following example demonstrates:

```
In [7]: [value for (key, value) in sorted(d.items())]
Out[7]: [5, 4, 1, 6, 3, 2]
```

The `sorted()` method also has an optional reverse argument, and unsurprisingly, this does exactly what it says, reverses the order of the sorted list, for example:

```
In [11]: sorted(list(d), key = d.__getitem__ , reverse=True)
Out[11]: ['six', 'five', 'four', 'three', 'two', 'one']
```

Now, let's say we are given the following dictionary, English words as keys and French words as values. Our task is to place these string values in correct numerical order:

```
d2 ={'one':'uno' , 'two':'deux', 'three':'trois', 'four': 'quatre', 'five':
'cinq', 'six':'six'}
```

Of course, when we print this dictionary out, it will be unlikely to print in the correct order. Because all keys and values are strings, we have no context for numerical ordering. To place these items in correct order, we need to use the first dictionary we created, mapping words to numerals as a way to order our English to French dictionary:

```
In [15]: sorted(d2, key=d.__getitem__)
Out[15]: ['one', 'two', 'three', 'four', 'five', 'six']
```

Notice we are using the values of the first dictionary, d, to sort the keys of the second dictionary, d2. Since our keys in both dictionaries are the same, we can use a list comprehension to sort the values of the French to English dictionary:

```
In [16]: [d2[i] for i in sorted(d2, key=d.__getitem__)]
Out[16]: ['uno', 'deux', 'trois', 'quatre', 'cinq', 'six']
```

We can, of course, define our own custom method that we can use as the key argument to the sorted method. For example, here we define a function that simply returns the last letter of a string:

```
def corder(string):

    return(string[len(string)-1])
```

We can then use this as the key to our sorted function to sort each element by its last letter:

```
sorted(d2.values(), key=corder)
['quatre', 'uno', 'cinq', 'trois', 'deux', 'six']
```

Dictionaries for text analysis

A common use of dictionaries is to count the occurrences of like items in a sequence; a typical example is counting the occurrences of words in a body of text. The following code creates a dictionary where each word in the text is used as a key and the number of occurrences as its value. This uses a very common idiom of nested loops. Here we are using it to traverse the lines in a file in an outer loop and the keys of a dictionary on the inner loop:

```
def wordcount(fname):
    try:
        fhand=open(fname)
    except:
        print('File cannot be opened')
        exit()

    count= dict()
    for line in fhand:
        words = line.split()
        for word in words:
            if word not in count:
                count[word] = 1
            else:
                count[word] += 1
    return(count)
```

This will return a dictionary with an element for each unique word in the text file. A common task is to filter items such as these into subsets we are interested in. You will need a text file saved in the same directory as you run the code. Here we have used `alice.txt`, a short excerpt from *Alice in Wonderland*. To obtain the same results, you can download `alice.txt` from davejulian.net/bo5630, or use a text file of your own. In the following code, we create another dictionary, `filtered`, containing a subset of items from `count`:

```
count=wordcount('alice.txt')
filtered = { key:value for key, value in count.items() if value  < 20 and
value > 15 }
```

When we print the filtered dictionary, we get the following:

```
In [6]: filtered
Out[6]: {'Alice': 19, 'but': 16, 'for': 17, 'had': 19, 'very': 19, 'you': 17}
```

Note the use of the **dictionary comprehension** used to construct the filtered dictionary. Dictionary comprehensions work in an identical way to the list comprehensions we looked at in Chapter 1, *Python Objects, Types, and Expressions*.

Sets

Sets are unordered collections of unique items. Sets are themselves mutable, we can add and remove items from them; however, the items themselves must be immutable. An important distinction with sets is that they cannot contain duplicate items. Sets are typically used to perform mathematical operations such as intersection, union, difference, and complement.

Unlike sequence types, set types do not provide any indexing or slicing operations. There are also no keys associated with values, as is the case with dictionaries. There are two types of set objects in Python, the mutable set object and the immutable frozenset object. Sets are created using comma-separated values within curly braces. By the way, we cannot create an empty set using a={}, because this will create a dictionary. To create an empty set, we write either a=set() or a=frozenset().

Methods and operations of sets are described in the following table:

Method	Operators	Description
len(s)		Returns the number of elements in s
s.copy()		Returns a shallow copy of s
s.difference(t)	s - t- t2 - ...	Returns a set of all items in s but not in t
s.intersection(t)		Returns a set of all items in both t and s
s.isdisjoint(t)		Returns True if s and t have no items in common
s.issubset(t)	s <= t s < t (s != t)	Returns True if all items in s are also in t
s.issuperset(t)	s >= t s > t (s != t)	Returns True if all items in t are also in s

`s.symmetric_difference(t)`	`s ^ t`	Returns a set of all items that are in `s` or `t`, but not both
`s.union(t)`	`s | t1 | t2 | ...`	Returns a set of all items in `s` or `t`

In the preceding table, the parameter `t` can be any Python object that supports iteration and all methods are available to both `set` and `frozenset` objects. It is important to be aware that the operator versions of these methods require their arguments to be sets, whereas the methods themselves can accept any iterable type. For example, `s - [1,2,3]`, for any set `s`, will generate an unsupported operand type. Using the equivalent `s.difference([1,2,3])` will return a result.

Mutable set objects have additional methods, described in the following table:

Method	Description
`s.add(item)`	Adds item to `s`. Has no effect if `item` is already present.
`s.clear()`	Removes all items from `s`.
`s.difference_update(t)`	Removes all items in `s` that are also in `t`.
`s.discard(item)`	Removes `item` from `s`.
`s.intersection_update(t)`	Removes all items from `s` that are not in the intersection of `s` and `t`.
`s.pop()`	Returns and removes an arbitrary item from `s`.
`s.remove(item)`	Removes item from `s`.
`s.symetric_difference_update(t)`	Removes all items from `s` that are not in the symmetric difference of `s` and `t`.
`s.update(t)`	Adds all the items in an iterable object `t` to `s`.

The following example demonstrates some simple set operations and their results:

```
In [1]: s1={'ab',3,4,(5,6)}

In [2]: s2={'ab',7,(7,6)}

In [3]: s1-s2 # same as s1.difference(s2)
Out[3]: {(5, 6), 3, 4}

In [4]: s1.intersection(s2)
Out[4]: {'ab'}

In [5]: s1.union(s2)
Out[5]: {3, 4, 'ab', 7, (5, 6), (7, 6)}
```

Notice that the set object does not care that its members are not all of the same type, as long as they are all immutable. If you try to use a mutable object such as a list or dictionaries in a set, you will receive an unhashable type error. Hashable types all have a hash value that does not change throughout the lifetime of the instance. All built-in immutable types are hashable. All built-in mutable types are not hashable, so they cannot be used as elements of sets or keys to dictionaries.

Notice also in the preceding code that when we print out the union of s1 and s2, there is only one element with the value 'ab'. This is a natural property of sets in that they do not include duplicates.

In addition to these built-in methods there are a number of other operations that we can perform on sets. For example, to test for membership of a set, use the following:

```
In [6]: 'ab' in s1
Out[6]: True

In [7]: 'ab' not in s1
Out[7]: False
```

We can loop through elements in a set using the following:

```
In [8]: for element in s1: print(element)
(5, 6)
ab
3
4
```

Immutable sets

Python has an immutable set type called `frozenset`. It works pretty much exactly like `set` apart from not allowing methods or operations that change values such as the `add()` or `clear()` methods. There are several ways that this immutability can be useful. For example, since normal sets are mutable and therefore not hashable, they cannot be used as members of other sets. The `frozenset`, on the other hand, is immutable and therefore able to be used as a member of a set:

```
In [26]: s1.add(s2)
Traceback (most recent call last):

  File "<ipython-input-26-05d7ba45d78a>", line 1, in <module>
    s1.add(s2)

TypeError: unhashable type: 'set'

In [27]: s1.add(frozenset(s2))

In [28]: s1
Out[28]: {(5, 6), 'ab', 3, 4, frozenset({(7, 6), 'ab', 7})}
```

Also the immutable property of `frozenset` means we can use it for a `key` to a dictionary, for example:

```
In [38]: fs1 = frozenset(s1)

In [39]: fs2 = frozenset(s2)

In [40]: {fs1: 'fs1' , fs2: 'fs2'}
Out[40]: {frozenset({(7, 6), 'ab', 7}): 'fs2', frozenset({(5, 6), 'ab', 3, 4}): 'fs1'}
```

Modules for data structures and algorithms

In addition to the built-in types, there are several Python modules that we can use to extend these built-in types and functions. In many cases, these Python modules may offer efficiency and programming advantages that allow us to simplify our code.

So far, we have looked at the built-in datatypes of strings, lists, sets, and dictionaries as well as the `decimal` and `fractions` modules. They are often described by the term **abstract data types** (**ADTs**). ADTs can be considered as mathematical specifications for the set of operations that can be performed on data. They are defined by their behavior rather than their implementation. In addition to the ADTs that we have looked at, there are several Python libraries that provide extensions to the built-in datatypes. These will be discussed in the following section.

Collections

The `collections` module provides more specialized, high, performance alternatives for the built-in data types as well as a utility function to create named tuples. The following table lists the datatypes and operations of the collections module and their descriptions:

Datatype or operation	Description
`namedtuple()`	Creates tuple subclasses with named fields.
`deque`	Lists with fast appends and pops either end.
`ChainMap`	Dictionary like class to create a single view of multiple mappings.
`Counter`	Dictionary subclass for counting hashable objects.
`OrderedDict`	Dictionary subclass that remembers the entry order.
`defaultdict`	Dictionary subclass that calls a function to supply missing values.
`UserDict` `UserList` `UserString`	These three data types are simply wrappers for their underlying base classes. Their use has largely been supplanted by the ability to subclasas their respective base classes directly. Can be used to access the underlying object as an attribute.

Deques

Double-ended queues, or deques (usually pronounced *decks*), are list-like objects that support thread-safe, memory-efficient appends. Deques are mutable and support some of the operations of lists, such as indexing. Deques can be assigned by index, for example, `dq[1] = z`; however, we cannot directly slice deques. For example, `dq[1:2]` results in a `TypeError` (we will look at a way to return a slice from a `deque` as a list shortly).

The major advantage of deques over lists is that inserting items at the beginning of a deque is much faster than inserting items at the beginning of a list, although inserting items at the end of a `deque` is very slightly slower than the equivalent operation on a list. Deques are thread, safe and can be serialized using the `pickle` module.

A useful way of thinking about deques is in terms of populating and consuming items. Items in deques are usually populated and consumed sequentially from either end:

```
In [18]: from collections import deque

In [19]: dq = deque('abc') #creates deque(['a','b','c'])

In [20]: dq.append('d') #adds the value 'd' to the right

In [21]: dq.appendleft('z') #adds the value 'z' to the left

In [22]: dq.extend('efg') #adds multiple items to the right

In [23]: dq.extendleft('yxw') #adds multiple items to the left

In [24]: dq
Out[24]: deque(['w', 'x', 'y', 'z', 'a', 'b', 'c', 'd', 'e', 'f', 'g'])
```

We can use the `pop()` and `popleft()` methods for consuming items in the `deque`, for example:

```
In [25]: dq.pop() #returns and removes an item from the right
Out[25]: 'g'

In [26]: dq.popleft() #returns and removes an item from the left
Out[26]: 'w'

In [27]: dq
Out[27]: deque(['x', 'y', 'z', 'a', 'b', 'c', 'd', 'e', 'f'])
```

We can also use the `rotate(n)` method to move and rotate all items of *n* steps to the right for positive values of the integer *n*, or left for negative values of n the left, using positive integers as the argument, for example:

```
In [45]: dq.rotate(2) #rotates all items 2 steps to the right

In [46]: dq
Out[46]: deque(['e', 'f', 'x', 'y', 'z', 'a', 'b', 'c', 'd'])

In [47]: dq.rotate(-2) #rotates all items 2 steps to the left

In [48]: dq
Out[48]: deque(['x', 'y', 'z', 'a', 'b', 'c', 'd', 'e', 'f'])
```

Note that we can use the `rotate` and `pop` methods to delete selected elements. Also worth knowing is a simple way to return a slice of a deque, as a list, which can be done as follows:

```
In [14]: dq
Out[14]: deque(['x', 'y', 'z', 'a', 'b', 'c', 'd', 'e', 'f'])

In [15]: list(itertools.islice(dq,3,9))
Out[15]: ['a', 'b', 'c', 'd', 'e', 'f']
```

The `itertools.islice` method works in the same way that slice works on a list, except rather than taking a list for an argument, it takes an iterable and returns selected values, by start and stop indices, as a list.

A useful feature of deques is that they support a `maxlen` optional parameter that restricts the size of the `deque`. This makes it ideally suited to a data structure known as a **circular buffer**. This is a fixed-size structure that is effectively connected end to end and they are typically used for buffering data streams. The following is a basic example:

```
dq2=deque([],maxlen=3)
for i in range(6):
    dq2.append(i)
    print(dq2)
```

This prints out the following:

```
deque([0], maxlen=3)
deque([0, 1], maxlen=3)
deque([0, 1, 2], maxlen=3)
deque([1, 2, 3], maxlen=3)
deque([2, 3, 4], maxlen=3)
deque([3, 4, 5], maxlen=3)
```

In this example, we are populating from the right and consuming from the left. Notice that once the buffer is full, the oldest values are consumed first, and values are replaced from the right. We will look at circular buffers again in `Chapter 4`, *Lists and Pointer Structures*, by implementing circular lists.

ChainMaps

The `collections.chainmap` class was added in Python 3.2 and it provides a way to link a number of dictionaries, or other mappings, so that they can be treated as one object. In addition, there is a `maps` attribute, a `new_child()` method, and a `parents` property. The underlying mappings for `ChainMap` objects are stored in a list and are accessible using the `maps[i]` attribute to retrieve the `ith` dictionary. Note that even though dictionaries themselves are unordered, ChainMaps are an ordered list of dictionaries. `ChainMap` is useful in applications where we are using a number of dictionaries containing related data. The consuming application expects data in terms of a priority, where the same key in two dictionaries is given priority if it occurs at the beginning of the underlying list. `ChainMap` is typically used to simulate nested contexts such as when we have multiple overriding configuration settings. The following example demonstrates a possible use case for ChainMap:

```
In [22]: from collections import ChainMap
In [23]: defaults={'theme':'Default', 'language':'eng', 'showIndex':True, 'showFooter':True}
In [24]: cm=ChainMap(defaults) #creates a chainmap with the default configuration
In [25]: cm2 =cm.new_child({'theme':'bluesky'}) #creates a new chainmap with a child that overides the parent
In [26]: cm2['theme'] #returns the overidden theme
Out[26]: 'bluesky'
In [27]: cm2.pop('theme') #returns and removes child theme value
Out[27]: 'bluesky'
In [28]: cm2['theme'] #returns the default theme
Out[28]: 'Default'
```

The advantage of using ChainMaps, rather than just a dictionary, is that we retain previously set values. Adding a child context overrides values for the same key, but it does not remove it from the data structure. This can be useful for when we may need to keep a record of changes so that we can easily roll back to a previous setting.

We can retrieve and change any value in any of the dictionaries by providing the `map()` method with an appropriate index. This index represents a dictionary in the ChainMap. Also, we can retrieve the parent setting, that is, the default settings, by using the `parents()` method:

```
In [16]: from collections import ChainMap

In [17]: defaults={'theme':'Default', 'language':'eng', 'showIndex':True, 'showFooter':True}

In [18]: cm=ChainMap(defaults) #creates a chainmap with the default configuration

In [19]: cm2 =cm.new_child({'theme':'bluesky'}) #creates a new chainmap with a child that overides the parent

In [20]: cm2['theme'] #returns the overidden theme
Out[20]: 'bluesky'

In [21]: cm2.pop('theme') #returns and removes child theme value
Out[21]: 'bluesky'

In [22]: cm2['theme'] #returns the default theme
Out[22]: 'Default'

In [23]: cm2.maps[0] ={'theme':'desert', 'showIndex': False} # adds a 'root context' same as new_child

In [24]: cm2['showIndex']
Out[24]: False
```

Counter objects

Counter is a subclass of a dictionary where each dictionary `key` is a hashable object and the associated value is an integer count of that object. There are three ways to initialize a counter. We can pass it any sequence object, a dictionary of `key:value` pairs, or a tuple of the format `(object = value, ...)`, for example:

```
[42]: cm2.maps[0] ={'theme':'desert', 'showIndex': False} # adds a 'root context' same as new_child

[43]: cm2['showIndex'] #returns the overridden showIndex value
[43]: False

[44]: cm2.parents #returns defaults
[44]: ChainMap({'theme': 'Default', 'showFooter': True, 'language': 'eng', 'showIndex': True})
```

We can also create an empty counter object and populate it by passing its `update` method an iterable or a dictionary, for example:

```
In [55]: Counter('anysequence')
Out[55]: Counter({'a': 1, 'c': 1, 'e': 3, 'n': 2, 'q': 1, 's': 1, 'u': 1, 'y': 1})
```

Notice how the `update` method adds the counts rather than replacing them with new values. Once the counter is populated, we can access stored values in the same way we would for dictionaries, for example:

```
In [29]: from collections import Counter

In [30]: c1= Counter('anysequnece')

In [31]: c2 = Counter({'a':1,'c':1,'e':3})

In [32]: c3 = Counter(a=1,c=1,e=3)

In [33]: c1
Out[33]: Counter({'a': 1, 'c': 1, 'e': 3, 'n': 2, 'q': 1, 's': 1, 'u': 1, 'y': 1})
```

The most notable difference between counter objects and dictionaries is that counter objects return a zero count for missing items rather than raising a `key` error, for example:

```
In [1]: from collections import Counter

In [2]: ct = Counter() #creates an empty counter object

In [3]: ct.update('abca') #populates the object

In [4]: ct
Out[4]: Counter({'a': 2, 'b': 1, 'c': 1})

In [5]: ct.update({'a':3}) #updates the 'a' count

In [6]: ct
Out[6]: Counter({'a': 5, 'b': 1, 'c': 1})
```

We can create an iterator out of a `Counter` object by using its `elements()` method. This returns an iterator where counts below one are not included and the order is not guaranteed. In the following code, we perform some updates, create an iterator from `Counter` elements, and use `sorted()` to sort the keys alphabetically:

```
In [7]: for item in ct:
   ...:     print('%s : %d' % (item, ct[item]))
   ...:
a : 5
b : 1
c : 1
```

Two other Counter methods worth mentioning are `most_common()` and `subtract()`. The most common method takes a positive integer argument that determines the number of most common elements to return. Elements are returned as a list of (`key`, `value`) tuples. The `subtract` method works exactly like update except instead of adding values, it subtracts them, for example:

```
In [3]: ct['x']
Out[3]: 0
```

Ordered dictionaries

The important thing about ordered dictionaries is that they remember the insertion order, so when we iterate over them, they return values in the order they were inserted. This is in contrast to a normal dictionary, where the order is arbitrary. When we test to see whether two dictionaries are equal, this equality is only based on their keys and values; however, with an `OrderedDict`, the insertion order is also considered An equality test between two OrderedDicts with the same keys and values but a different insertion order will return `False`:

```
In [36]: ct.update({'a':-3, 'b':-2, 'd':3, 'e':2}) # perform an update

In [37]: sorted(ct.elements()) #returns a sorted list from the iterator
Out[37]: ['a', 'a', 'c', 'd', 'd', 'd', 'e', 'e']
```

Similarly, when we add values from a list using `update`, the `OrderedDict` will retain the same order as the list. This is the order that is returned when we iterate the values, for example:

```
In [42]: ct.most_common()
Out[42]: [('d', 3), ('a', 2), ('e', 2), ('c', 1), ('b', -1)]

In [43]: ct.subtract({'a':2})

In [44]: ct
Out[44]: Counter({'a': 0, 'b': -1, 'c': 1, 'd': 3, 'e': 2})
```

The `OrderedDict` is often used in conjunction with the sorted method to create a sorted dictionary. For example, in the following example we use a `lambda` function to sort on the values, here we use a numerical expression to sort the integer values:

```
In [36]: od1 = OrderedDict()

In [37]: od1['one'] = 1

In [38]: od1['two'] = 2

In [39]: od2 = OrderedDict()

In [40]: od2['two'] = 2

In [41]: od2['one'] = 1

In [42]: od1 == od2
Out[42]: False
```

defaultdict

The `defaultdict` object is a subclass of `dict` and therefore they share methods and operations. It acts as a convenient way to initialize dictionaries. With a `dict`, Python will throw a `KeyError` when attempting to access a key that is not already in the dictionary. The `defaultdict` overrides one method, `__missing__(key)`, and creates a new instance variable, `default_factory`. With `defaultdict`, rather than throw an error, it will run the function, supplied as the `default_factory` argument, which will generate a value. A simple use of `defaultdict` is to set `default_factory` to `int` and use it to quickly tally the counts of items in the dictionary, for example:

```
In [4]: kvs = [('three',3), ('four',4), ('five',5), ('six',6)]

In [5]: od1.update(kvs)

In [6]: for k, v in od1.items():print(k,v)
one 1
two 2
three 3
four 4
five 5
six 6
```

You will notice that if we tried to do this with an ordinary dictionary, we would get a key error when we tried to add the first key. The `int` we supplied as an argument to default `dict` is really the function `int()` that simply returns a zero. We can, of course, create a function that will determine the dictionary's values. For example, the following function returns `True` if the supplied argument is a primary color, that is red, green, or blue, or returns `False` otherwise:

```
def isprimary(c):
    if (c == 'red') or (c == 'blue') or (c == 'green'):
        return True
    else:
        return False
```

We can now create a new `defaultdict` object and use the `isprimary` function to populate it:

```
In [17]: od3 = OrderedDict(sorted(od1.items(), key = lambda t : (4*t[1]) - t[1]**2))

In [18]: od3.values()
Out[18]: odict_values([6, 5, 4, 1, 3, 2])
```

Named Tuples

The `namedtuple` method returns a tuple-like object that has fields accessible with named indexes as well as the integer indexes of normal tuples. This allows for code that is, to a certain extent, self-documenting and more readable. It can be especially useful in an application where there is a large number of tuples and we need to easily keep track of what each tuple represents. The `namedtuple` inherits methods from `tuple` and it is backward-compatible with `tuple`.

The field names are passed to the `namedtuple` method as comma and/or whitespace separated values. They can also be passed as a sequence of strings. Field names are single strings and they can be any legal Python identifier that does not begin with a digit or an underscore. A typical example is shown here:

```
In [1]: from collections import defaultdict

In [2]: dd = defaultdict(int)

In [3]: words=str.split('red blue green red yellow blue red green green red')

In [4]: for word in words: dd[word] += 1

In [5]: dd
Out[5]: defaultdict(int, {'blue': 2, 'green': 3, 'red': 4, 'yellow': 1})
```

The `namedtuple` method take two optional Boolean arguments, `verbose` and `rename`. When `verbose` is set to `True` then the class definition is printed when it is built. This argument is depreciated in favor of using the __source attribute. When the `rename` argument is set to `True` then any invalid field names will be automatically replaced with positional arguments. As an example, we attempt to use `def` as a field name. This would normally generate an error, but since we have assigned `rename` to `True`, the Python interpreter allows this. However, when we attempt to look up the `def` value, we get a syntax error, since `def` is a reserved keyword. The illegal field name has been replaced by a field name created by adding an underscore to the positional value:

```
In [43]: dd2 = defaultdict(bool)

In [44]: for word in words: dd2[word] = isprimary(word)

In [45]: dd2
Out[45]: defaultdict(bool, {'blue': True, 'green': True, 'red': True, 'yellow': False})
```

In addition to the inherited tuple methods, the named tuple also defines three methods of its own, `_make()` , `asdict()`, and `_replace`. These methods begin with an underscore to prevent potential conflicts with field names. The `_make()` method takes an iterable as an argument and turns it into a named tuple object, for example:

```
In [40]: from collections import namedtuple

In [41]: space = namedtuple('space' , 'x y z')

In [42]: s1 = space(x = 2.0, y = 4.0, z = 10) # we can also use space(2.0, 4.0, 10)

In [43]: s1.x * s1.y * s1.z # calculates the volume
Out[43]: 80.0
```

The _asdict method returns an OrderedDict with the field names mapped to index keys and the values mapped to the dictionary values, for example:

```
In [77]: space2 = namedtuple('space2' , 'x def z', rename = True)

In [78]: s1 =space2(3,4,5)

In [79]: s1.def
   File "<ipython-input-79-75c7c11b4596>", line 1
     s1.def
         ^
SyntaxError: invalid syntax


In [80]: s1._1
Out[80]: 4
```

The _replace method returns a new instance of the tuple, replacing the specified values, for example:

```
In [66]: sl = [4,5,6]

In [67]: space._make(sl)
Out[67]: space(x=4, y=5, z=6)
```

Arrays

The array module defines a datatype array that is similar to the list datatype except for the constraint that their contents must be of a single type of the underlying representation, as is determined by the machine architecture or underlying C implementation.

The type of an array is determined at creation time and it is indicated by one of the following type codes:

Code	C type	Python type	Minimum bytes
'b'	signed char	int	1
'B'	unsigned char	int	1
'u'	Py_UNICODE	Unicode character	2
'h'	signed short	int	2
'H'	unsigned short	int	2

'i'	signed int	int	2
'I'	unsigned int	int	2
'l'	signed long	int	4
'L'	unsigned long	int	8
'q'	signed long long	int	8
'Q'	unsigned lon long	int	8
'f'	float	float	4
'd'	double	float	8

The array objects support the following attributes and methods:

Attribute or method	Description
a.typecode	The typecode character used to create the array.
a.itemsize	Size, in bytes, of items stored in the array.
a.append(x)	Appends item x to the end of the array.
a.buffer_info()	Returns the memory location and length of the buffer used to store the array.
a.byteswap()	Swaps the byte order of each item. Used for writing to a machine or file with a different byte order.
a.count(x)	Returns the number of occurrences of x in a.
a.extend(b)	Appends any iterable, b, to the end of array a.
a.frombytes(s)	Appends items from a string, s, as an array of machine values.
a.fromfile(f, n)	Reads n items, as machine values, from a file object, f, and appends them to a. Raises an EOFError if there are fewer than n items in n.
a.fromlist(l)	Appends items from list l.
a.fromunicode(s)	Extends a with unicode string s. Array a must be of type u or else ValueError is raised.
index(x)	Returns the first (smallest) index of item x.
a.insert(i, x)	Inserts item x before index i.

`a.pop([i])`	Removes and returns items with index `i`. Defaults to the last item (`i = -1`) if not specified.
`a.remove(x)`	Removes the first occurrence of item `x`.
`a.reverse()`	Reverses the order of items.
`a.tobytes()`	Convert the array to machine values and returns the bytes representation.
`a.tofile(f)`	Writes all items, as machine values, to file object `f`.
`a.tolist()`	Converts the array to a list.
`a.tounicode()`	Convert an array to `unicode` string. The array type must be `'u'` or else a `ValueError` is raised.

Array objects support all the normal sequence operations such as indexing, slicing, concatenation, and multiplication.

Using arrays, as opposed to lists, is a much more efficient way of storing data that is all of the same type. In the following example, we have created an integer array of the digits from 0 to 1 million minus 1, and an identical list. Storing 1 million integers in an integer array requires around 45% of the memory of an equivalent list:

```
In [80]: s1._1
Out[80]: 4

In [81]: s1._asdict()
Out[81]: OrderedDict([('x', 3), ('_1', 4), ('z', 5)])
```

Because we are interested in saving space, that is, we are dealing with large datasets and limited memory size, we usually perform in-place operations on arrays, and only create copies when we need to. Typically, enumerate is used to perform an operation on each element. In the following snippet, we perform the simple operation of adding one to each item in the array:

```
In [82]: s1._replace(x =7, z=9)
Out[82]: space2(x=7, _1=4, z=9)
```

It should be noted that when performing operations on arrays that create lists, such as list comprehensions, the memory efficiency gains of using an array in the first place will be negated. When we need to create a new data object, a solution is to use a generator expression to perform the operation, for example:

```
In [69]: import array

In [70]: ba = array.array('i', range(10**6))

In [71]: bl = list(range(10**6))

In [72]: import sys

In [73]: 100 * sys.getsizeof(ba) / sys.getsizeof(bl)
Out[73]: 45.46534532014713
```

Arrays created with this module are unsuitable for work that requires a matrix of vector operations. In the next chapter, we will build our own abstract data type to deal with these operations. Also important for numerical work is the NumPy extension, available at www.numpy.org .

Summary

In the last two chapters, we have examined the language features and data types of Python. We have looked at the built-in data types and some internal Python modules, most notably the collections module. There are also several other Python modules that are relevant to the topic of this book, but rather than examining them separately, their use and functionality should become self-evident as we begin using them. There are also a number of external libraries such as the SciPy stack, and, likewise, I will attempt to explain their basic functionality as we begin to apply them.

In the next chapter, we will introduce the basic theory and techniques of algorithm design.

3
Principles of Algorithm Design

Why do we want to study algorithm design? There are of course many reasons, and our motivation for learning something is very much dependent on our own circumstances. There are without doubt important professional reasons for being interested in algorithm design. Algorithms are the foundations of all computing. We think of a computer as being a piece of hardware, a hard drive, memory chips, processors, and so on. However, the essential component, the thing that, if missing, would render modern technology impossible, is algorithms.

The theoretical foundation of algorithms, in the form of the Turing machine, was established several decades before digital logic circuits could actually implement such a machine. The Turing machine is essentially a mathematical model that, using a predefined set of rules, translates a set of inputs into a set of outputs. The first implementations of Turing machines were mechanical and the next generation may likely see digital logic circuits replaced by quantum circuits or something similar. Regardless of the platform, algorithms play a central predominant role.

Another aspect is the effect algorithms have in technological innovation. As an obvious example, consider the page rank search algorithm, a variation of which the Google search engine is based on. Using this and similar algorithms allows researchers, scientists, technicians, and others to quickly search through vast amounts of information extremely quickly. This has a massive effect on the rate at which new research can be carried out, new discoveries made, and new innovative technologies developed.

The study of algorithms is also important because it trains us to think very specifically about certain problems. It can serve to increase our mental and problem solving abilities by helping us isolate the components of a problem and define relationships between these components. In summary, there are four broad reasons for studying algorithms:

1. They are essential for computer science and *intelligent* systems.
2. They are important in many other domains (computational biology, economics, ecology, communications, ecology, physics, and so on).
3. They play a role in technology innovation.
4. They improve problem solving and analytical thinking.

Algorithms, in their simplest form, are just a sequence of actions, a list of instructions. It may just be a linear construct of the form do x, then do y, then do z, then finish. However, to make things more useful we add clauses to the effect of, x then do y, in Python the `if-else` statements. Here, the future course of action is dependent on some conditions; say the state of a data structure. To this we also add the operation, iteration, the while, and for statements. Expanding our algorithmic literacy further we add recursion. Recursion can often achieve the same result as iteration, however, they are fundamentally different. A recursive function calls itself, applying the same function to progressively smaller inputs. The input of any recursive step is the output of the previous recursive step.

Essentially, we can say that algorithms are composed of the following four elements:

- Sequential operations
- Actions based on the state of a data structure
- Iteration, repeating an action a number of times
- Recursion, calling itself on a subset of inputs

Algorithm design paradigms

In general, we can discern three broad approaches to algorithm design. They are:

- Divide and conquer
- Greedy algorithms
- Dynamic programming

As the name suggests, the divide and conquer paradigm involves breaking a problem into smaller sub problems, and then in some way combining the results to obtain a global solution. This is a very common and natural problem solving technique, and is, arguably, the most commonly used approach to algorithm design.

Greedy algorithms often involve optimization and combinatorial problems; the classic example is applying it to the traveling salesperson problem, where a greedy approach always chooses the closest destination first. This shortest path strategy involves finding the best solution to a local problem in the hope that this will lead to a global solution.

The dynamic programming approach is useful when our sub problems overlap. This is different from divide and conquer. Rather than break our problem into independent sub problems, with dynamic programming, intermediate results are cached and can be used in subsequent operations. Like divide and conquer it uses recursion; however, dynamic programming allows us to compare results at different stages. This can have a performance advantage over divide and conquer for some problems because it is often quicker to retrieve a previously calculated result from memory rather than having to recalculate it.

Recursion and backtracking

Recursion is particularly useful for divide and conquer problems; however, it can be difficult to understand exactly what is happening, since each recursive call is itself spinning off other recursive calls. At the core of a recursive function are two types of cases: base cases, which tell the recursion when to terminate, and recursive cases that call the function they are in. A simple problem that naturally lends itself to a recursive solution is calculating factorials. The recursive factorial algorithm defines two cases: the base case when n is zero, and the recursive case when n is greater than zero. A typical implementation is the following:

```
def factorial(n):
    #test for a base case
    if n==0:
        return 1
        # make a calculation and a recursive call
        f= n*factorial(n-1)
    print(f)
    return(f)
    factorial(4)
```

This code prints out the digits 1, 2, 4, 24. To calculate 4 requires four recursive calls plus the initial parent call. On each recursion, a copy of the methods variables is stored in memory. Once the method returns it is removed from memory. The following is a way we can visualize this process:

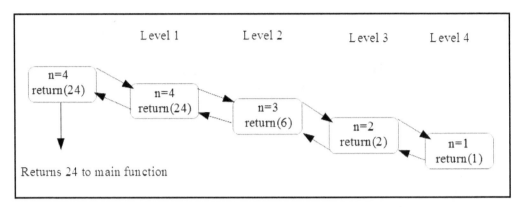

It may not necessarily be clear if recursion or iteration is a better solution to a particular problem; after all they both repeat a series of operations and both are very well suited to divide and conquer approaches to algorithm design. Iteration churns away until the problem is done. Recursion breaks the problem down into smaller and smaller chunks and then combines the results. Iteration is often easier for programmers, because control stays local to a loop, whereas recursion can more closely represent mathematical concepts such as factorials. Recursive calls are stored in memory, whereas iterations are not. This creates a trade off between processor cycles and memory usage, so choosing which one to use may depend on whether the task is processor or memory intensive. The following table outlines the key differences between recursion and iteration:

Recursion	Iteration
Terminates when a base case is reached	Terminates when a defined condition is met
Each recursive call requires space in memory	Each iteration is not stored in memory
An infinite recursion results in a stack overflow error	An infinite iteration will run while the hardware is powered
Some problems are naturally better suited to recursive solutions	Iterative solutions may not always be obvious

Backtracking

Backtracking is a form of recursion that is particularly useful for types of problems such as traversing tree structures, where we are presented with a number of options at each node, from which we must choose one. Subsequently we are presented with a different set of options, and depending on the series of choices made either a goal state or a dead end is reached. If it is the latter, we must backtrack to a previous node and traverse a different branch. Backtracking is a divide and conquer method for exhaustive search. Importantly backtracking **prunes** branches that cannot give a result.

An example of back tracking is given in the following example. Here, we have used a recursive approach to generating all the possible permutations of a given string, *s*, of a given length *n*:

```
def bitStr(n, s):

        if n == 1: return s
        return [ digit + bits for digit in bitStr(1,s)for bits in bitStr(n
- 1,s)]

    print (bitStr(3,'abc'))
```

This generates the following output:

```
['aaa', 'aab', 'aac', 'aba', 'abb', 'abc', 'aca', 'acb', 'acc', 'baa', 'bab', 'bac', 'bba',
'bbb', 'bbc', 'bca', 'bcb', 'bcc', 'caa', 'cab', 'cac', 'cba', 'cbb', 'cbc', 'cca', 'ccb', 'ccc']
```

Notice the double list compression and the two recursive calls within this comprehension. This recursively concatenates each element of the initial sequence, returned when $n = 1$, with each element of the string generated in the previous recursive call. In this sense it is *backtracking* to uncover previously ingenerated combinations. The final string that is returned is all *n* letter combinations of the initial string.

Divide and conquer - long multiplication

For recursion to be more than just a clever trick, we need to understand how to compare it to other approaches, such as iteration, and to understand when its use will lead to a faster algorithm. An iterative algorithm that we are all familiar with is the procedure we learned in primary math classes, used to multiply two large numbers. That is, long multiplication. If you remember, long multiplication involved iterative multiplying and carry operations followed by a shifting and addition operation.

Our aim here is to examine ways to measure how efficient this procedure is and attempt to answer the question; is this the most efficient procedure we can use for multiplying two large numbers together?

In the following figure, we can see that multiplying two 4 digit numbers together requires 16 multiplication operations, and we can generalize to say that an n digit number requires, approximately, n^2 multiplication operations:

```
                1   2   3   4
                3   4   5   6   x
            _____
                7   4   0   4
            6   1   7   0   0
        4   9   3   6   0   0        ≈ n² operations
    3   7   0   2   0   0   0
    4   2   6   4   7   0   4
```

$\approx n^2 \ operations$

This method of analyzing algorithms, in terms of the number of computational primitives such as multiplication and addition, is important because it gives us a way to understand the relationship between the time it takes to complete a certain computation and the size of the input to that computation. In particular, we want to know what happens when the input, the number of digits, n, is very large. This topic, called asymptotic analysis, or time complexity, is essential to our study of algorithms and we will revisit it often during this chapter and the rest of this book.

Can we do better? A recursive approach

It turns out that in the case of long multiplication the answer is yes, there are in fact several algorithms for multiplying large numbers that require less operations. One of the most well-known alternatives to long multiplication is the **Karatsuba algorithm**, first published in 1962. This takes a fundamentally different approach: rather than iteratively multiplying single digit numbers, it recursively carries out multiplication operations on progressively smaller inputs. Recursive programs call themselves on smaller subsets of the input. The first step in building a recursive algorithm is to decompose a large number into several smaller numbers. The most natural way to do this is to simply split the number in to two halves, the first half of most significant digits, and a second half of least significant digits. For example, our four-digit number, 2345, becomes a pair of two-digit numbers, 23 and 45. We can write a more general decomposition of any $2n$ digit numbers, x and y using the following, where m is any positive integer less than n:

$$x = 10^m a + b$$

$$y = 10^m c + d$$

So now we can rewrite our multiplication problem x, y as follows:

$$(10^m a + b)(10^m c + d)$$

When we expand and gather like terms we get the following:

$$10^m ac + 10^{2m}(ad + bc) + bd$$

More conveniently, we can write it like this:

$$10^{2m} z_2 + 10^m z_1 + z_0$$

Where:

$$z_2 = ac \;\; ; \;\; z_1 = ad + bc \;\; ; \;\; z_0 = bd$$

It should be pointed out that this suggests a recursive approach to multiplying two numbers since this procedure does itself involve multiplication. Specifically, the products $ac, ad, bc,$ and bd all involve numbers smaller than the input number and so it is conceivable that we could apply the same operation as a partial solution to the overall problem. This algorithm, so far, consists of four recursive multiplication steps and it is not immediately clear if it will be faster than the classic long multiplication approach.

What we have discussed so far in regards to the recursive approach to multiplication, has been well known to mathematicians since the late 19th century. The Karatsuba algorithm improves on this is by making the following observation. We really only need to know three quantities: $z_2 = ac$; $z_1 = ad + bc$, and $z_0 = bd$ to solve equation 3.1. We need to know the values of a, b, c, d only in so far as they contribute to the overall sum and products involved in calculating the quantities z_2, z_1, and z_0. This suggests the possibility that perhaps we can reduce the number of recursive steps. It turns out that this is indeed the situation.

Since the products ac and bd are already in their simplest form, it seems unlikely that we can eliminate these calculations. We can however make the following observation:

$$(a + b)(c + d) = ac + bd + ad + bc$$

When we subtract the quantities *ac* and *bd*, which we have calculated in the previous recursive step, we get the quantity we need, namely (*ad* + *bc*):

$$\boxed{ac + bd + ad + bc - ac - bd = ad + bc}$$

This shows that we can indeed compute the sum of *ad* + *bc* without separately computing each of the individual quantities. In summary, we can improve on equation 3.1 by reducing from four recursive steps to three. These three steps are as follows:

1. Recursively calculate *ac*.
2. Recursively calculate *bd*.
3. Recursively calculate (*a* +*b*)(*c* + *d*) and subtract *ac* and *bd*.

The following example shows a Python implementation of the Karatsuba algorithm:

```python
from math import log10
def karatsuba(x,y):

    # The base case for recursion
    if x < 10 or y < 10:
        return x*y

    #sets n, the number of digits in the highest input number
    n = max(int(log10(x)+1), int(log10(y)+1))

    # rounds up n/2
    n_2 = int(math.ceil(n / 2.0))
    #adds 1 if n is uneven
    n = n if n % 2 == 0 else n + 1

    #splits the input numbers
    a, b = divmod(x, 10**n_2)
    c, d = divmod(y, 10**n_2)

    #applies the three recursive steps
    ac = karatsuba(a,c)
    bd = karatsuba(b,d)
    ad_bc = karatsuba((a+b),(c+d)) - ac - bd

    #performs the multiplication
    return (((10**n)*ac) + bd + ((10**n_2)*(ad_bc)))
```

To satisfy ourselves that this does indeed work, we can run the following test function:

```
import random
def test():
    for i in range(1000):
        x = random.randint(1,10**5)
        y = random.randint(1,10**5)
        expected = x * y
        result = karatsuba(x, y)
        if result != expected:
            return("failed")
    return('ok')
```

Runtime analysis

It should be becoming clear that an important aspect to algorithm design is gauging the efficiency both in terms of space (memory) and time (number of operations). This second measure, called runtime performance, is the subject of this section. It should be mentioned that an identical metric is used to measure an algorithm's memory performance. There are a number of ways we could, conceivably, measure run time and probably the most obvious is simply to measure the time the algorithm takes to complete. The major problem with this approach is that the time it takes for an algorithm to run is very much dependent on the hardware it is run on. A platform-independent way to gauge an algorithm's runtime is to count the number of operations involved. However, this is also problematic in that there is no definitive way to quantify an operation. This is dependent on the programming language, the coding style, and how we decide to count operations. We can use this idea, though, of counting operations, if we combine it with the expectation that as the size of the input increases the runtime will increase in a specific way. That is, there is a mathematical relationship between n, the size of the input, and the time it takes for the algorithm to run.

Much of the discussion that follows will be framed by the following three guiding principles. The rational and importance of these principles should become clearer as we proceed. These principles are as follows:

- Worst case analysis. Make no assumptions on the input data.
- Ignore or suppress constant factors and lower order terms. At large inputs higher order terms dominate.
- Focus on problems with large input sizes.

Worst case analysis is useful because it gives us a tight upper bound that our algorithm is guaranteed not to exceed. Ignoring small constant factors, and lower order terms is really just about ignoring the things that, at large values of the input size, n, do not contribute, in a large degree, to the overall run time. Not only does it make our work mathematically easier, it also allows us to focus on the things that are having the most impact on performance.

We saw with the Karatsuba algorithm that the number of multiplication operations increased to the square of the size, n, of the input. If we have a four-digit number the number of multiplication operations is 16; an eight-digit number requires 64 operations. Typically, though, we are not really interested in the behavior of an algorithm at small values of n, so we most often ignore factors that increase at slower rates, say linearly with n. This is because at high values of n, the operations that increase the fastest as we increase n, will dominate.

We will explain this in more detail with an example, the merge sort algorithm. Sorting is the subject of `Chapter 10`, *Sorting*, however, as a precursor and as a useful way to learn about runtime performance, we will introduce merge sort here.

The merge sort algorithm is a classic algorithm developed over 60 years ago. It is still used widely in many of the most popular sorting libraries. It is relatively simple and efficient. It is a recursive algorithm that uses a divide and conquer approach. This involves breaking the problem into smaller sub problems, recursively solving them, and then somehow combining the results. Merge sort is one of the most obvious demonstrations of the divide and conquer paradigm.

The merge sort algorithm consists of three simple steps:

1. Recursively sort the left half of the input array.
2. Recursively sort the right half of the input array.
3. Merge two sorted sub arrays into one.

A typical problem is sorting a list of numbers into a numerical order. Merge sort works by splitting the input into two halves and working on each half in parallel. We can illustrate this process schematically with the following diagram:

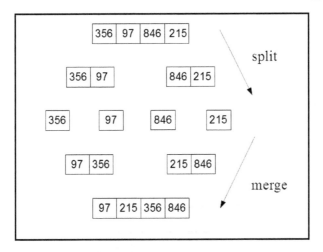

Here is the Python code for the merge sort algorithm:

```
def mergeSort(A):
    #base case if the input array is one or zero just return.
    if len(A) > 1:
        # splitting input array
        print('splitting ', A )
        mid = len(A)//2
        left = A[:mid]
        right = A[mid:]
        #recursive calls to mergeSort for left and right sub arrays
        mergeSort(left)
        mergeSort(right)
        #initalizes pointers for left (i) right (j) and output array
(k)
    # 3 initalization operations
        i = j = k = 0
        #Traverse and merges the sorted arrays
        while i <len(left) and j<len(right):
    # if left < right comparison operation
            if left[i] < right[j]:
    # if left < right Assignment operation
                A[k]=left[i]
                i=i+1
            else:
    #if right <= left assignment
                A[k]= right[j]
                j=j+1
            k=k+1

        while i<len(left):
```

```
#Assignment operation
        A[k]=left[i]
        i=i+1
        k=k+1

    while j<len(right):
#Assignment operation
        A[k]=right[j]
        j=j+1
        k=k+1
    print('merging ', A)
    return(A)
```

We run this program for the following results:

```
In [2]: mergeSort([356,97,846,215])
splitting  [356, 97, 846, 215]
splitting  [356, 97]
merging  [356]
merging  [97]
merging  [97, 356]
splitting  [846, 215]
merging  [846]
merging  [215]
merging  [215, 846]
merging  [97, 215, 356, 846]
Out[2]: [97, 215, 356, 846]
```

The problem that we are interested in is how we determine the running time performance, that is, what is the rate of growth in the time it takes for the algorithm to complete relative to the size of n. To understand this a bit better, we can map each recursive call onto a tree structure. Each node in the tree is a recursive call working on progressively smaller sub problems:

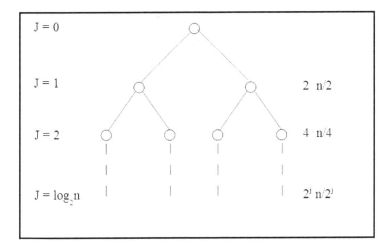

Each invocation of merge-sort subsequently creates two recursive calls, so we can represent this with a binary tree. Each of the child nodes receives a sub set of the input. Ultimately we want to know the total time it takes for the algorithm to complete relative to the size of n. To begin with we can calculate the amount of work and the number of operations at each level of the tree.

Focusing on the runtime analysis, at level 1, the problem is split into two $n/2$ sub problems, at level 2 there is four $n/4$ sub problems, and so on. The question is when does the recursion bottom out, that is, when does it reach its base case. This is simply when the array is either zero or one.

The number of recursive levels is exactly the number of times you need to divide n by 2 until you get a number that is at most 1. This is precisely the definition of log2. Since we are counting the initial recursive call as level 0, the total number of levels is $\log_2 n + 1$.

Let's just pause to refine our definitions. So far we have been describing the number of elements in our input by the letter n. This refers to the number of elements in the first level of the recursion, that is, the length of the initial input. We are going to need to differentiate between the size of the input at subsequent recursive levels. For this we will use the letter m or specifically m_j for the length of the input at recursive level j.

Also there are a few details we have overlooked, and I am sure you are beginning to wonder about. For example, what happens when $m/2$ is not an integer, or when we have duplicates in our input array. It turns out that this does not have an important impact on our analysis here; we will revisit some of the finer details of the merge sort algorithm in Chapter 12, *Design Techniques and Strategies*.

The advantage of using a recursion tree to analyze algorithms is that we can calculate the work done at each level of the recursion. How to define this work is simply as the total number of operations and this of course is related to the size of the input. It is important to measure and compare the performance of algorithms in a platform independent way. The actual run time will of course be dependent on the hardware on which it is run. Counting the number of operations is important because it gives us a metric that is directly related to an algorithm's performance, independent of the platform.

In general, since each invocation of merge sort is making two recursive calls, the number of calls is doubling at each level. At the same time each of these calls is working on an input that is half of its parents. We can formalize this and say that:

For level j , where j is an integer 0, 1, 2 ... $\log_2 n$, there are two^j sub problems each of size $n/2^j$.

To calculate the total number of operations, we need to know the number of operations encompassed by a single merge of two sub arrays. Let's count the number of operations in the previous Python code. What we are interested in is all the code after the two recursive calls have been made. Firstly, we have the three assignment operations. This is followed by three while loops. In the first loop we have an if else statement and within each of are two operations, a comparison followed by an assignment. Since there are only one of these sets of operations within the if else statements, we can count this block of code as two operations carried out m times. This is followed by two while loops with an assignment operation each. This makes a total of $4m + 3$ operations for each recursion of merge sort.

Since m must be at least 1, the upper bound for the number of operations is $7m$. It has to be said that this has no pretense at being an exact number. We could of course decide to count operations in a different way. We have not counted the increment operations or any of the housekeeping operations; however, this is not so important as we are more concerned with the rate of growth of the runtime with respect to n at high values of n.

This may seem a little daunting since each call of a recursive call itself spins off more recursive calls, and seemingly explodes exponentially. The key fact that makes this manageable is that as the number of recursive calls doubles, the size of each sub problem halves. These two opposing forces cancel out nicely as we can demonstrate.

To calculate the maximum number of operations at each level of the recursion tree we simply multiply the number of sub problems by the number of operations in each sub problem as follows:

$$2^j \times 7(n/2^j) = 7n$$

Importantly this shows that, because the 2^j cancels out the number of operations at each level is independent of the level. This gives us an upper bound to the number of operations carried out on each level, in this example, $7n$. It should be pointed out that this includes the number of operations performed by each recursive call on that level, not the recursive calls made on subsequent levels. This shows that the work done, as the number of recursive calls doubles with each level, is exactly counter balanced by the fact that the input size for each sub problem is halved.

To find the total number of operations for a complete merge sort we simply multiply the number of operations on each level by the number of levels. This gives us the following:

$$7n(\log_2 n + 1)$$

When we expand this out, we get the following:

$$7n\log_2 n + 7$$

The key point to take from this is that there is a logarithmic component to the relationship between the size of the input and the total running time. If you remember from school mathematics, the distinguishing characteristic of the logarithm function is that it flattens off very quickly. As an input variable, x, increases in size, the output variable, y increases by smaller and smaller amounts. For example, compare the log function to a linear function:

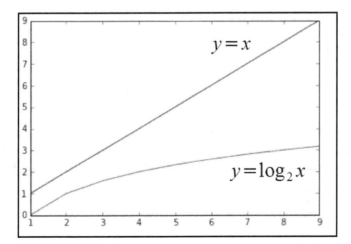

In the previous example, multiplying the $n\log_2 n$ component and comparing it to n^2.

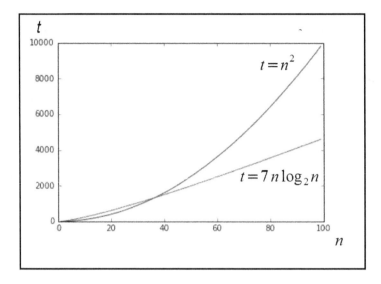

Notice how for very low values of n, the time to complete, t, is actually lower for an algorithm that runs in n^2 time. However, for values above about 40, the log function begins to dominate, flattening the output until at the comparatively moderate size $n = 100$, the performance is more than twice than that of an algorithm running in n^2 time. Notice also that the disappearance of the constant factor, + 7 is irrelevant at high values of n.

The code used to generate these graphs is as follows:

```
import matplotlib.pyplot as plt
import math
x=list(range(1,100))
l =[]; l2=[]; a = 1
plt.plot(x , [y * y for y in x] )
plt.plot(x, [(7 *y )* math.log(y, 2) for y in x])
plt.show()
```

You will need to install the matplotlib library, if it is not installed already, for this to work. Details can be found at the following address; I encourage you to experiment with this list comprehension expression used to generate the plots. For example, adding the following plot statement:

```
plt.plot(x, [(6 *y )* math.log(y, 2) for y in x])
```

Gives the following output:

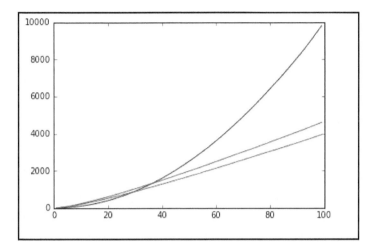

The preceding graph shows the difference between counting six operations or seven operations. We can see how the two cases diverge, and this is important when we are talking about the specifics of an application. However, what we are more interested in here is a way to characterize growth rates. We are not so much concerned with the absolute values, but how these values change as we increase n. In this way we can see that the two lower curves have similar growth rates, when compared to the top (x^2) curve. We say that these two lower curves have the same **complexity class**. This is a way to understand and describe different runtime behaviors. We will formalize this performance metric in the next section.

Asymptotic analysis

There are essentially three things that characterize an algorithm's runtime performance. They are:

- Worst case - Use an input that gives the slowest performance
- Best case - Use an input that give, the best results
- Average case - Assumes the input is random

To calculate each of these, we need to know the upper and lower bounds. We have seen a way to represent an algorithm's runtime using mathematical expressions, essentially adding and multiplying operations. To use asymptotic analyses, we simply create two expressions, one each for the best and worst cases.

Big O notation

The letter "O" in big O notation stands for order, in recognition that rates of growth are defined as the order of a function. We say that one function $T(n)$ is a big O of another function, $F(n)$, and we define this as follows:

$$T(n) = O(F(n)) \text{ iff there exists constants, } n_0 \text{ and } C \text{ such that:}$$
$$T(n) \leq C(F(n)) \text{ for all } n \geq n_0$$

The function, $g(n)$, of the input size, n, is based on the observation that for all sufficiently large values of n, $g(n)$ is bounded above by a constant multiple of $f(n)$. The objective is to find the smallest rate of growth that is less than or equal to $f(n)$. We only care what happens at higher values of n. The variable n_0 represents the threshold below which the rate of growth is not important, The function T(n) represents the **tight upper bound** F(n). In the following plot we see that $T(n) = n^2 + 500 = O(n^2)$ with $C = 2$ and n_0 is approximately 23:

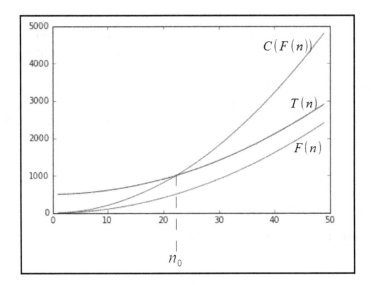

You will also see the notation $f(n) = O(g(n))$. This describes the fact that $O(g(n))$ is really a set of functions that include all functions with the same or smaller rates of growth than f(n). For example, $O(n^2)$ also includes the functions $O(n)$, $O(n\log n)$, and so on.

In the following table, we list the most common growth rates in order from lowest to highest. We sometimes call these growth rates the **time complexity** of a function, or the complexity class of a function:

Complexity Class	Name	Example operations
$O(1)$	Constant	append, get item, set item.
$O(\log n)$	Logarithmic	Finding an element in a sorted array.
$O(n)$	Linear	copy, insert, delete, iteration.
$n\text{Log}n$	Linear-Logarithmic	Sort a list, merge - sort.
n^2	Quadratic	Find the shortest path between two nodes in a graph. Nested loops.
n^3	Cubic	Matrix multiplication.
2^n	Exponential	'Towers of Hanoi' problem, backtracking.

Composing complexity classes

Normally, we need to find the total running time of a number of basic operations. It turns out that we can combine the complexity classes of simple operations to find the complexity class of more complex, combined operations. The goal is to analyze the combined statements in a function or method to understand the total time complexity of executing several operations. The simplest way to combine two complexity classes is to add them. This occurs when we have two sequential operations. For example, consider the two operations of inserting an element into a list and then sorting that list. We can see that inserting an item occurs in $O(n)$ time and sorting is $O(n\log n)$ time. We can write the total time complexity as $O(n + n\log n)$, that is, we bring the two functions inside the $O(...)$. We are only interested in the highest order term, so this leaves us with just $O(n\log n)$.

If we repeat an operation, for example, in a while loop, then we multiply the complexity class by the number of times the operation is carried out. If an operation with time complexity $O(f(n))$ is repeated $O(n)$ times then we multiply the two complexities:

$O(f(n) * O(n)) = O(nf(n))$.

For example, suppose the function f(...) has a time complexity of $O(n^2)$ and it is executed n times in a while loop as follows:

```
for i n range(n):
    f(...)
```

The time complexity of this loop then becomes $O(n^2) * O(n) = O(n * n^2) = O(n^3)$. Here we are simply multiplying the time complexity of the operation with the number of times this operation executes. The running time of a loop is at most the running time of the statements inside the loop multiplied by the number of iterations. A single nested loop, that is, one loop nested inside another loop, will run in n^2 time assuming both loops run n times. For example:

```
for i in range(0,n):
    for j in range(0,n)
        #statements
```

Each statement is a constant, c, executed nn times, so we can express the running time as ; $cn \, n = cn^2 = O(n2)$.

For consecutive statements within nested loops we add the time complexities of each statement and multiply by the number of times the statement executed. For example:

```
n = 500      #c0
#executes n times
for i in range(0,n):
    print(i)      #c1
#executes n times
for i in range(0,n):
    #executes n times
    for j in range(0,n):
    print(j)     #c2
```

This can be written as $c_0 + c_1 n + cn^2 = O(n^2)$.

We can define (base 2) logarithmic complexity, reducing the size of the problem by ½, in constant time. For example, consider the following snippet:

```
i = 1
while i <= n:
    i=i * 2
    print(i)
```

Notice that i is doubling on each iteration, if we run this with $n = 10$ we see that it prints out four numbers; 2, 4, 8, and 16. If we double n we see it prints out five numbers. With each subsequent doubling of n the number of iterations is only increased by 1. If we assume k iterations, we can write this as follows:

$$\log_2(2^k) = \log_2 n$$
$$k\log_2 = \log_2 n$$
$$k = \log n$$

From this we can conclude that the total time = **O**(*log(n)*).

Although Big O is the most used notation involved in asymptotic analysis, there are two other related notations that should be briefly mentioned. They are Omega notation and Theta notation.

Omega notation (Ω)

In a similar way that Big O notation describes the upper bound, Omega notation describes a **tight lower bound**. The definition is as follows:

$T(n) = \Omega(F(n))$ iff there exists positive constants, n_0 and C such that:
$$0 \le C(F(n)) \le T(n) \text{ for all } n \ge n_0$$

The objective is to give the largest rate of growth that is equal to or less than the given algorithms, T(*n*), rate of growth.

Theta notation (Θ)

It is often the case where both the upper and lower bounds of a given function are the same and the purpose of Theta notation is to determine if this is the case. The definition is as follows:

$T(n) = \Theta(F(n))$ iff there exists positive constants, n_0, C_1 and C_2 such that:
$$0 \le C_1(F(n)) \le T(n) \le C_2(F(n)) \text{ for all } n \ge n_0$$

Although Omega and Theta notations are required to completely describe growth rates, the most practically useful is Big O notation and this is the one you will see most often.

Amortized analysis

Often we are not so interested in the time complexity of individual operations, but rather the time averaged running time of sequences of operations. This is called amortized analysis. It is different from average case analysis, which we will discuss shortly, in that it makes no assumptions regarding the data distribution of input values. It does, however, take into account the state change of data structures. For example, if a list is sorted it should make any subsequent find operations quicker. Amortized analysis can take into account the state change of data structures because it analyzes sequences of operations, rather then simply aggregating single operations.

Amortized analysis finds an upper bound on runtime by imposing an artificial cost on each operation in a sequence of operations, and then combining each of these costs. The artificial cost of a sequence takes in to account that the initial expensive operations can make subsequent operations cheaper.

When we have a small number of expensive operations, such as sorting, and lots of cheaper operations such as lookups, standard worst case analysis can lead to overly pessimistic results, since it assumes that each lookup must compare each element in the list until a match is found. We should take into account that once we sort the list we can make subsequent find operations cheaper.

So far in our runtime analysis we have assumed that the input data was completely random and have only looked at the effect the size of the input has on the runtime. There are two other common approaches to algorithm analysis; they are:

- Average case analysis
- Benchmarking

Average case analysis finds the average running time based on some assumptions regarding the relative frequencies of various input values. Using real-world data, or data that replicates the distribution of real-world data, is many times on a particular data distribution and the average running time is calculated.

Benchmarking is simply having an agreed set of typical inputs that are used to measure performance. Both benchmarking and average time analysis rely on having some domain knowledge. We need to know what the typical or expected datasets are. Ultimately we will try to find ways to improve performance by fine-tuning to a very specific application setting.

Let's look at a straightforward way to benchmark an algorithm's runtime performance. This can be done by simply timing how long the algorithm takes to complete given various input sizes. As we mentioned earlier, this way of measuring runtime performance is dependent on the hardware that it is run on. Obviously faster processors will give better results, however, the relative growth rates as we increase the input size will retain characteristics of the algorithm itself rather than the hardware it is run on. The absolute time values will differ between hardware (and software) platforms; however, their relative growth will still be bound by the time complexity of the algorithm.

Let's take a simple example of a nested loop. It should be fairly obvious that the time complexity of this algorithm is $O(n^2)$ since for each n iterations in the outer loop there are also n iterations in the inter loop. For example, our simple nested for loop consists of a simple statement executed on the inner loop:

```
def nest(n):
    for i in range(n):
        for j in range(n):
            i+j
```

The following code is a simple test function that runs the nest function with increasing values of n. With each iteration we calculate the time this function takes to complete using the `timeit.timeit` function. The `timeit` function, in this example, takes three arguments, a string representation of the function to be timed, a setup function that imports the nest function, and an `int` parameter that indicates the number of times to execute the main statement. Since we are interested in the time the nest function takes to complete relative to the input size, n, it is sufficient, for our purposes, to call the nest function once on each iteration. The following function returns a list of the calculated runtimes for each value of n:

```
import timeit
def test2(n):
    ls=[]
    for n in range(n):
        t=timeit.timeit("nest(" + str(n) +")", setup="from __main__
import nest", number = 1)
        ls.append(t)
    return ls
```

In the following code we run the test2 function and graph the results, together with the appropriately scaled n^2 function for comparison, represented by the dashed line:

```
import matplotlib.pyplot as plt
n=1000
plt.plot(test2(n))
plt.plot([x*x/10000000 for x in range(n)])
```

This gives the following results:

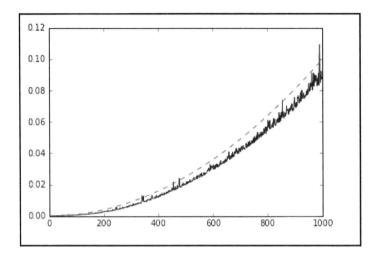

As we can see, this gives us pretty much what we expect. It should be remembered that this represents both the performance of the algorithm itself as well as the behavior of underlying software and hardware platforms, as indicated by both the variability in the measured runtime and the relative magnitude of the runtime. Obviously a faster processor will result in faster runtimes, and also performance will be affected by other running processes, memory constraints, clock speed, and so on.

Summary

In this chapter, we have taken a general overview of algorithm design. Importantly, we saw a platform independent way to measure an algorithm's performance. We looked at some different approaches to algorithmic problems. We looked at a way to recursively multiply large numbers and also a recursive approach for merge sort. We saw how to use backtracking for exhaustive search and generating strings. We also introduced the idea of benchmarking and a simple platform-dependent way to measure runtime. In the following chapters, we will revisit many of these ideas with reference to specific data structures. In the next chapter, we will discuss linked lists and other pointer structures.

4

Lists and Pointer Structures

You will have already seen lists in Python. They are convenient and powerful. Normally, any time you need to store something in a list, you use python's built-in list implementation. In this chapter, however, we are more interested in understanding how lists work. So we are going to study list internals. As you will notice, there are different types of lists.

Python's list implementation is designed to be powerful and to encompass several different use cases. We are going to be a bit more strict in our definition of what a list is.

The concept of a node is very important to lists. We shall discuss them in this chapter, but this concept will, in different forms, come back throughout the rest of the book.

The focus of this chapter will be the following:

- Understand pointers in Python
- Treating the concept of nodes
- Implementing singly, doubly, and circularly linked lists

In this chapter, we are going to deal quite a bit with pointers. So it may be useful to remind ourselves what these are. To begin with, imagine that you have a house that you want to sell. Lacking time, you contact an agent to find interested buyers. So you pick up your house and take it over to the agent, who will in turn carry the house to anybody who may want to buy it. Ludicrous, you say? Now imagine that you have a few Python functions that work with images. So you pass high-resolution image data between your functions.

Of course, you don't carry your house around. What you would do is write the address of the house down on a piece of scrap paper and hand it over to the agent. The house remains where it is, but the note containing the directions to the house is passed around. You might even write it down on several pieces of paper. Each one is small enough to fit in your wallet, but they all point to the same house.

As it turns out, things are not very different in Python land. Those large image files remain in one single place in memory. What you do is create variables that hold the locations of those images in memory. These variables are small and can easily be passed around between different functions.

That is the big benefit of pointers: they allow you to point to a potentially large segment of memory with just a simple memory address.

Support for pointers exists in your computer's hardware, where it is known as indirect addressing.

In Python, you don't manipulate pointers directly, unlike in some other languages, such as C or Pascal. This has led some people to think that pointers aren't used in Python. Nothing could be further from the truth. Consider this assignment in the Python interactive shell:

```
>>> s = set()
```

We would normally say that s is a variable of the type set. That is, s is a set. This is not strictly true, however. The variable s is rather a reference (a "safe" pointer) to a set. The set constructor creates a set somewhere in memory and returns the memory location where that set starts. This is what gets stored in s.

Python hides this complexity from us. We can safely assume that s is a set and that everything works fine.

Arrays

An array is a sequential list of data. Being sequential means that each element is stored right after the previous one in memory. If your array is really big and you are low on memory, it could be impossible to find large enough storage to fit your entire array. This will lead to problems.

Of course, the flip side of the coin is that arrays are very fast. Since each element follows from the previous one in memory, there is no need to jump around between different memory locations. This can be a very important point to take into consideration when choosing between a list and an array in your own real-world applications.

In the latter parts of Chapter 2, *Python Data Types and Structures*, we looked at the array data type and discovered the various operations that could be performed on it.

Pointer structures

Contrary to arrays, pointer structures are lists of items that can be spread out in memory. This is because each item contains one or more links to other items in the structure. What type of links these are dependent on the type of structure we have. If we are dealing with linked lists, then we will have links to the next (and possibly previous) items in the structure. In the case of a tree, we have parent-child links as well as sibling links. In a tile-based game where the game map is built up of hexes, each node will have links to up to six adjacent map cells.

There are several benefits with pointer structures. First of all, they don't require sequential storage space. Second, they can start small and grow arbitrarily as you add more nodes to the structure.

As noted in `Chapter 2`, *Python Data Types and Structures*, however, this comes at a cost. If you have a list of integers, each node is going to take up the space of an integer, as well as an additional integer for storing the pointer to the next node.

Nodes

At the heart of lists (and several other data structures) is the concept of a node. Before we go any further, let us consider this idea for a while.

To begin with, we shall create a few strings:

```
>>> a = "eggs"
>>> b = "ham"
>>> c = "spam"
```

Now you have three variables, each with a unique name, a type, and a value. What we do not have is a way of saying in which way the variables relate to each other. Nodes allow us to do this. A node is a container of data, together with one or more links to other nodes. A link is a pointer.

A simple type of node is one that only has a link to the next node.

Of course, knowing what we do about pointers, we realize that this is not entirely true. The string is not really stored in the node, but is rather a pointer to the actual string:

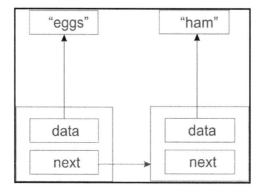

Thus the storage requirement for this simple node is two memory addresses. The data attribute of the nodes are pointers to the strings `eggs` and `ham`.

Finding endpoints

We have created three nodes: one containing **eggs**, one **ham**, and another **spam**. The **eggs** node points to the **ham** node, which in turn points to the **spam** node. But what does the **spam** node point to? Since this is the last element in the list, we need to make sure its next member has a value that makes this clear.

If we make the last element point to nothing then we make this fact clear. In python, we will use the special value `None` to denote nothing:

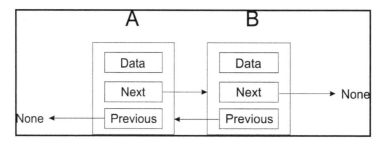

The last node has its next point pointing to None. As such it is the last node in the chain of nodes.

Node

Here is a simple node implementation of what we have discussed so far:

```
class Node:
    def __init__(self, data=None):
        self.data = data
        self.next = None
```

Do not confuse the concept of a node with Node.js, a server-side
technology implemented in JavaScript.

The `next` pointer is initialized to `None`, meaning that unless you change the value of `next`,
the node is going to be an end-point. This is a good idea, so that we do not forget to
terminate the list properly.

You can add other things to the `node` class as you see fit. Just make sure that you keep in
mind the distinction between node and data. If your node is going to contain customer data,
then create a `Customer` class and put all the data there.

One thing you may want to do is implement the __str__ method so that it calls the
__str__ method of the contained object is called when the node object is passed to print:

```
def __str__(self):
    return str(data)
```

Other node types

We have assumed nodes that have a pointer to the next node. This is probably the simplest
type of node. However, depending on our requirements, we can create a number of other
types of nodes.

Sometimes we want to go from A to B, but at the same time from B to A. In that case, we add a previous pointer in addition to the next pointer:

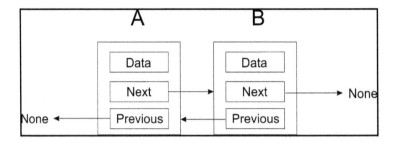

As you can see from the figure, we let both the last and the first nodes point to None, to indicate that we have reached they form the boundary of our list end-point. The first node's previous pointer points to None since it has no predecessor, just as the last item's next pointer points to None because it no successor node.

You might also be creating tiles for a tile-based game. In such a case, instead of previous and next, you might use north, south, east, and west. There are more types of pointers, but the principle is the same. Tiles at the end of the map will point to None:

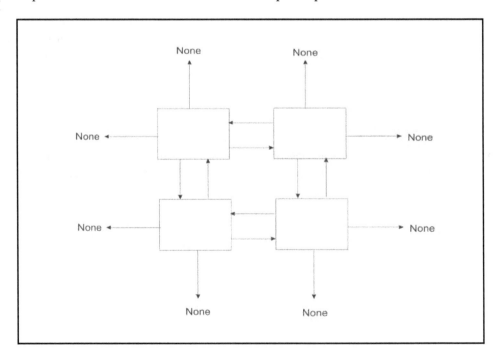

You can take this as far as you need to. If you need to be able to move north-west, north-east, south-east, and south-west as well, all you have to do is add these pointers to your `node` class.

Singly linked lists

A singly linked list is a list with only one pointer between two successive nodes. It can only be traversed in a single direction, that is, you can go from the first node in the list to the last node, but you cannot move from the last node to the first node.

We can actually use the `node` class that we created earlier to implement a very simple singly linked list:

```
>>> n1 = Node('eggs')
>>> n2 = Node('ham')
>>> n3 = Node('spam')
```

Next we link the nodes together so that they form a *chain*:

```
>>> n1.next = n2
>>> n2.next = n3
```

To traverse the list, you could do something like the following. We start by setting the variable `current` to the first item in the list:

```
current = n1
while current:
    print(current.data)
    current = current.next
```

In the loop we print out the current element after which we set current to point to the next element in the list. We keep doing this until we have reached the end of the list.

There are, however, several problems with this simplistic list implementation:

- It requires too much manual work by the programmer
- It is too error-prone (this is a consequence of the first point)
- Too much of the inner workings of the list is exposed to the programmer

We are going to address all these issues in the following sections.

Singly linked list class

A list is clearly a separate concept from a node. So we start by creating a very simple class to hold our list. We will start with a constructor that holds a reference to the very first node in the list. Since this list is initially empty, we will start by setting this reference to None:

```
class SinglyLinkedList:
    def __init__(self):
        self.tail = None
```

Append operation

The first operation that we need to perform is to append items to the list. This operation is sometimes called an insert operation. Here we get a chance to hide away the Node class. The user of our list class should really never have to interact with Node objects. These are purely for internal use.

A first shot at an append() method may look like this:

```
class SinglyLinkedList:
    # ...

    def append(self, data):
        # Encapsulate the data in a Node
        node = Node(data)

        if self.tail == None:
            self.tail = node
        else:
            current = self.tail
            while current.next:
                current = current.next
            current.next = node
```

We encapsulate data in a node, so that it now has the next pointer attribute. From here we check if there are any existing nodes in the list (that is, does self.tail point to a Node). If there is none, we make the new node the first node of the list; otherwise, find the insertion point by traversing the list to the last node, updating the next pointer of the last node to the new node.

We can append a few items:

```
>>> words = SinglyLinkedList()
>>> words.append('egg')
>>> words.append('ham')
>>> words.append('spam')
```

List traversal will work more or less like before. You will get the first element of the list from the list itself:

```
>>> current = words.tail
>>> while current:
        print(current.data)
        current = current.next
```

A faster append operation

There is a big problem with the append method in the previous section: it has to traverse the entire list to find the insertion point. This may not be a problem when there are just a few items in the list, but wait until you need to add thousands of items. Each append will be slightly slower than the previous one. A **O**(n) goes to prove how slow our current implementation of the append method will actually be.

To fix this, we will store, not only a reference to the first node in the list, but also a reference to the last node. That way, we can quickly append a new node at the end of the list. The worst case running time of the append operation is now reduced from **O**(n) to **O**(1). All we have to do is make sure the previous last node points to the new node, that is about to be appended to the list. Here is our updated code:

```
class SinglyLinkedList:
    def __init__(self):
        # ...
        self.tail = None

    def append(self, data):
        node = Node(data)
        if self.head:
            self.head.next = node
            self.head = node
        else:
            self.tail = node
            self.head = node
```

Take note of the convention being used. The point at which we append new nodes is through `self.head`. The `self.tail` variable points to the first node in the list.

Getting the size of the list

We would like to be able to get the size of the list by counting the number of nodes. One way we could do this is by traversing the entire list and increasing a counter as we go along:

```python
def size(self):
    count = 0
    current = self.tail
    while current:
        count += 1
        current = current.next
    return count
```

This works, but list traversal is potentially an expensive operation that we should avoid when we can. So instead, we shall opt for another rewrite of the method. We add a size member to the `SinglyLinkedList` class, initializing it to 0 in the constructor. Then we increment size by one in the `append` method:

```python
class SinglyLinkedList:
    def __init__(self):
        # ...
        self.size = 0

    def append(self, data):
        # ...
        self.size += 1
```

Because we are now only reading the size attribute of the node object, and not using a loop to count the number of nodes in the list, we get to reduce the worst case running time from **O**(n) to **O**(1).

Improving list traversal

If you notice how we traverse our list. That one place where we are still exposed to the `node` class. We need to use `node.data` to get the contents of the node and `node.next` to get the next node. But we mentioned earlier that client code should never need to interact with Node objects. We can achieve this by creating a method that returns a generator. It looks as follows:

```
def iter(self):
    current = self.tail
    while current:
        val = current.data
        current = current.next
        yield val
```

Now list traversal is much simpler and looks a lot better as well. We can completely ignore the fact that there is anything called a Node outside of the list:

```
for word in words.iter():
    print(word)
```

Notice that since the `iter()` method yields the data member of the node, our client code doesn't need to worry about that at all.

Deleting nodes

Another common operation that you would need to be able to do on a list is to delete nodes. This may seem simple, but we'd first have to decide how to select a node for deletion. Is it going to be by an index number or by the data the node contains? Here we will choose to delete a node by the data it contains.

The following is a figure of a special case considered when deleting a node from the list:

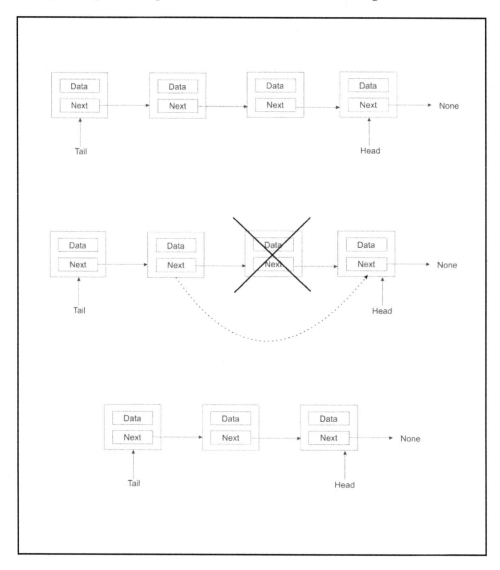

When we want to delete a node that is between two other nodes, all we have to do is make the previous node directly to the successor of its next node. That is, we simply cut the node to be deleted out of the chain as in the preceding image.

Here is the implementation of the `delete()` method may look like:

```
def delete(self, data):
    current = self.tail
    prev = self.tail
    while current:
        if current.data == data:
            if current == self.tail:
                self.tail = current.next
            else:
                prev.next = current.next
            self.size -= 1
            return
        prev = current
        current = current.next
```

It should take a **O**(n) to delete a node.

List search

We may also need a way to check whether a list contains an item. This method is fairly easy to implement thanks to the `iter()` method we previously wrote. Each pass of the loop compares the current data to the data being searched for. If a match is found, `True` is returned, or else `False` is returned:

```
def search(self, data):
    for node in self.iter():
        if data == node:
            return True
    return False
```

Clearing a list

We may want a quick way to clear a list. Fortunately for us, this is very simple. All we do is clear the pointers `head` and `tail` by setting them to `None`:

```
def clear(self):
    """ Clear the entire list. """
    self.tail = None
    self.head = None
```

In one fell swoop, we orphan all the nodes at the `tail` and `head` pointers of the list. This has a ripple effect of orphaning all the nodes in between.

Doubly linked lists

Now that we have a solid grounding on what a singly linked list is and the kind of operations that can be performed on it, we shall now turn our focus one notch higher to the topic of doubly linked lists.

A doubly linked list is somehow similar to a singly linked list in that we make use of the same fundamental idea of stringing nodes together. In a Singly linked list, there exists one link between each successive node. A node in a doubly linked list has two pointers: a pointer to the next node and a pointer to the previous node:

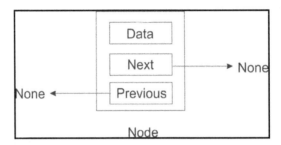

A node in a singly linked list can only determine the next node associated with it. But the referenced node or next node has no way of telling who is doing the referencing. The flow of direction is **only one way**.

In a doubly linked list, we add to each node the ability to not only reference the next node but also the previous node.

Let's examine the nature of the linkages that exist between two successive nodes for better understanding:

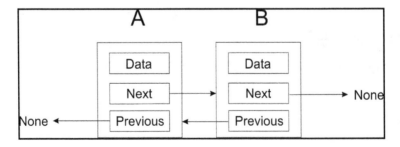

With the existence of two pointers that point to the next and previous nodes, doubly linked lists become equipped with certain capabilities.

Doubly linked lists can be traversed in any direction. Depending on the operation being performed, a node within a doubly linked list can easily refer to its previous node where necessary without having to designate a variable to keep track of that node. Because a Singly linked list can only be traversed in one direction it may sometimes mean moving to the start or beginning of the list in order to effect certain changes buried within the list.

Since there is immediate access to both next and previous nodes, deletion operations are much easier to perform, as you will see later on in this chapter.

A doubly linked list node

The Python code that creates a class to capture what a doubly linked list node is includes in its initializing method, the `prev`, `next`, and `data` instance variables. When a node is newly created, all these variables default to `None`:

```
class Node(object):
    def __init__(self, data=None, next=None, prev=None):
        self.data = data
        self.next = next
        self.prev = prev
```

The `prev` variable holds a reference to the previous node, while the `next` variable continues to hold a reference to the next node.

Doubly linked list

It is still important to create a class that captures the data that our functions will be operating on:

```
class DoublyLinkedList(object):
    def __init__(self):
        self.head = None
        self.tail = None
        self.count = 0
```

For the purposes of enhancing the `size` method, we also set the `count` instance variable to 0. `head` and `tail` will point to the head and tail of the list when we begin to insert nodes into the list.

We adopt a new convention where `self.head` points to the beginner node of the list and `self.tail` points to the latest node added to the list. This is contrary to the convention we used in the singly linked list. There are no fixed rules as to the naming of the head and tail node pointers.

Doubly linked lists also need to provide functions that return the size of the list, inserts into the list, and also deletes nodes from the list. We will be examining some of the code to do this. Let's commence with the `append` operation.

Append operation

During an `append` operation, it is important to check whether the `head` is `None`. If it is `None`, it means that the list is empty and should have the `head` set pointing to the just-created node. The `tail` of the list is also pointed at the new node through the head. By the end of these series of steps, `head` and `tail` will now be pointing to the same node:

```
def append(self, data):
    """ Append an item to the list. """

    new_node = Node(data, None, None)
    if self.head is None:
        self.head = new_node
        self.tail = self.head
    else:
        new_node.prev = self.tail
        self.tail.next = new_node
        self.tail = new_node

    self.count += 1
```

The following diagram illustrates the head and tail pointers of the doubly linked list when a new node is added to an empty list.

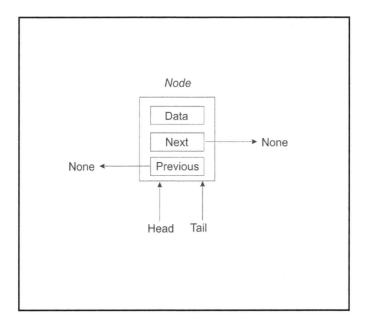

The else part of the algorithm is only executed if the list is not empty. The new node's previous variable is set to the tail of the list:

```
new_node.prev = self.tail
```

The tail's next pointer (or variable) is set to the new node:

```
self.tail.next = new_node
```

Lastly, we update the tail pointer to point to the new node:

```
self.tail = new_node
```

Since an append operation increases the number of nodes by one, we increase the counter by one:

```
self.count += 1
```

A visual representation of the `append` operation is as follows:

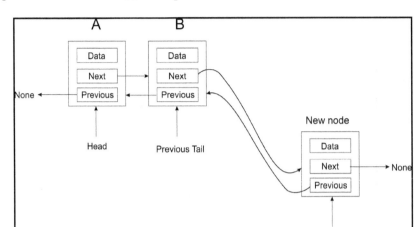

Delete operation

Unlike the singly linked list, where we needed to keep track of the previously encountered node anytime we traversed the whole length of the list, the doubly linked list avoids that whole step. This is made possible by the use of the previous pointer.

The algorithm for removing nodes from a doubly linked list caters for basically four scenarios before deletion of a node is completed. These are:

- When the search item is not found at all
- When the search item is found at the very beginning of the list
- When the search item is found at the tail end of the list
- When the search item is found somewhere in the middle of the list

The node to be removed is identified when its `data` instance variable matches the data that is passed to the method to be used in the search for the node. If a matching node is found and subsequently removed, the variable `node_deleted` is set to `True`. Any other outcome results in `node_deleted` being set to `False`:

```
def delete(self, data):
    current = self.head
    node_deleted = False
    ...
```

In the `delete` method, the `current` variable is set to the head of the list (that is, it points to the `self.head` of the list). A set of `if... else` statements are then used to search the various parts of the list to find the node with the specified data.

The `head` node is searched first. Since `current` is pointing at `head`, if `current` is None, it is presumed that the list has no nodes for a search to even begin to find the node to be removed:

```
if current is None:
    node_deleted = False
```

However, if `current` (which now points to head) contains the very data being searched for, then `self.head` is set to point to the `current` next node. Since there is no node behind head now, `self.head.prev` is set to `None`:

```
elif current.data == data:
    self.head = current.next
    self.head.prev = None
    node_deleted = True
```

A similar strategy is adopted if the node to be removed is located at the tail end of the list. This is the third statement that searches for the possibility that the node to be removed might be located at the end of the list:

```
elif self.tail.data == data:
    self.tail = self.tail.prev
    self.tail.next = None
    node_deleted = True
```

Lastly, the algorithm to find and remove a node loops through the list of nodes. If a matching node is found, `current`'s previous node is connected to current's next node. After that step, `current`'s next node is connected to previous node of `current`:

```
else
    while current:
        if current.data == data:
            current.prev.next = current.next
            current.next.prev = current.prev
            node_deleted = True
        current = current.next
```

The `node_delete` variable is then checked after all the `if-else` statements has been evaluated. If any of the `if-else` statements changed this variable, then it means a node has been deleted from the list. The count variable is therefore decremented by 1:

```
if node_deleted:
    self.count -= 1
```

As an example of deleting a node that is buried within a list, assume the existence of three nodes, A, B, and C. To delete node B in the middle of the list, we will essentially make A point to C as its next node, while making C point to A as its previous node:

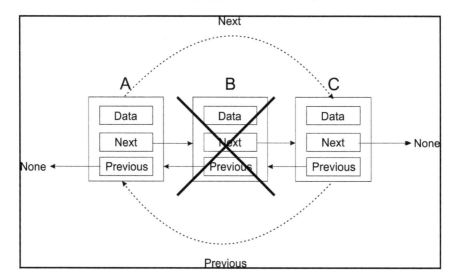

After such an operation, we end up with the following list:

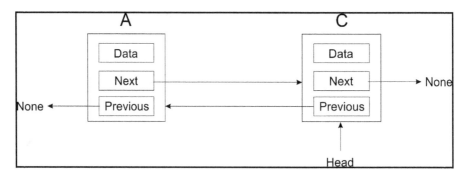

List search

The search algorithm is similar to that of the `search` method in a singly linked list. We call the internal method `iter()` to return the data in all the nodes. As we loop through the data, each is matched against the data passed into the `contain` method. If there is a match, we return `True`, or else we return `False` to symbolize that no match was found:

```
def contain(self, data):
    for node_data in self.iter():
        if data == node_data:
            return True
        return False
```

Our doubly linked list has a **O**(1) for the `append` operation and **O**(n) for the `delete` operation.

Circular lists

A circular list is a special case of a linked list. It is a list where the endpoints are connected. That is, the last node in the list points back to the first node. Circular lists can be based on both singly and doubly linked lists. In the case of a doubly linked circular list, the first node also needs to point to the last node.

Here we are going to look at an implementation of a singly linked circular list. It should be straightforward to implement a doubly linked circular list, once you have grasped the basic concepts.

We can reuse the `node` class that we created in the section on singly linked lists. As a matter of fact, we can reuse most parts of the `SinglyLinkedList` class as well. So we are going to focus on the methods where the circular list implementation differs from the normal singly linked list.

Appending elements

When we append an element to the circular list, we need to make sure that the new node points back to the tail node. This is demonstrated in the following code. There is one extra line as compared to the singly linked list implementation:

```
def append(self, data):
    node = Node(data)
    if self.head:
```

```
        self.head.next = node
        self.head = node
    else:
        self.head = node
        self.tail = node
    self.head.next = self.tail
    self.size += 1
```

Deleting an element

We may think that we can follow the same principle as for append and simply make sure the head points to the tail. This would give us the following implementation:

```
def delete(self, data):
    current = self.tail
    prev = self.tail
    while current:
        if current.data == data:
            if current == self.tail:
                self.tail = current.next
                self.head.next = self.tail
            else:
                prev.next = current.next
            self.size -= 1
            return
        prev = current
        current = current.next
```

As previously, there is just a single line that needs to change. It is only when we remove the tail node that we need to make sure that the head node is updated to point to the new tail node.

However, there is a serious problem with this code. In the case of a circular list, we cannot loop until current becomes None, since that will never happen. If you delete an existing node, you wouldn't see this, but try deleting a nonexistent node and you will get stuck in an indefinite loop.

We thus need to find a different way to control the `while` loop. We cannot check whether current has reached head, because then it will never check the last node. But we could use `prev`, since it lags behind current by one node. There is a special case, however. The very first loop iteration, `current` and `prev`, will point to the same node, namely the tail node. We want to ensure that the loop does run here, since we need to take the one node list into consideration. The updated `delete` method now looks as follows:

```
def delete(self, data):
        current = self.tail
        prev = self.tail
        while prev == current or prev != self.head:
            if current.data == data:
                if current == self.tail:
                    self.tail = current.next
                    self.head.next = self.tail
                else:
                    prev.next = current.next
                self.size -= 1
                return
            prev = current
            current = current.next
```

Iterating through a circular list

You do not need to modify the `iter()` method. It will work perfectly well for our circular list. But you do need to put in an exit condition when you are iterating through the circular list, otherwise your program will get stuck in a loop. Here is a way you could do this, by using a counter variable:

```
words = CircularList()
words.append('eggs')
words.append('ham')
words.append('spam')

counter = 0
for word in words.iter():
    print(word)
    counter += 1
    if counter > 1000:
        break
```

Once we have printed out 1,000 elements, we break out of the loop.

Summary

In this chapter, we have looked at linked lists. We have studied the concepts that underlie lists, such as nodes and pointers to other nodes. We implemented the major operations that occur on these types of list and saw how their worst case running times compare.

In the next chapter, we are going to look at two other data structures that are usually implemented using lists: stacks and queues.

5

Stacks and Queues

In this chapter, we are going to build upon the skills we learned in the last chapter in order to create special list implementations. We are still sticking to linear structures. We will get to more complex data structures in the coming chapters.

In this chapter, we are going to look at the following:

- Implementing stacks and queues
- Some applications of stacks and queues

Stacks

A stack is a data structure that is often likened to a stack of plates. If you have just washed a plate, you put it on top of the stack. When you need a plate, you take it off the top of the stack. So the last plate to be added to the stack will be the first to be removed from the stack. Thus, a stack is a **last in, first out** (**LIFO**) structure:

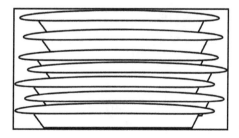

The preceding figure depicts a stack of plates. Adding a plate to the pile is only possible by leaving that plate on top of the pile. To remove a plate from the pile of plates means to remove the plate that is on top of the pile.

There are two primary operations that are done on stacks: `push` and `pop`. When an element is added to the top of the stack, it is pushed onto the stack. When an element is taken off the top of the stack, it is popped off the stack. Another operation which is used sometimes is `peek`, which makes it possible to see the element on the stack without popping it off.

Stacks are used for a number of things. One very common usage for stacks is to keep track of the return address during function calls. Let's imagine that we have the following little program:

```
def b():
    print('b')

def a():
    b()

a()
print("done")
```

When the program execution gets to the call to a(), it first pushes the address of the following instruction onto the stack, then jumps to a. Inside a, b() is called, but before that, the return address is pushed onto the stack. Once in b() and the function is done, the return address is popped off the stack, which takes us back to a(). When a has completed, the return address is popped off the stack, which takes us back to the `print` statement.

Stacks are actually also used to pass data between functions. Say you have the following function call somewhere in your code:

```
somefunc(14, 'eggs', 'ham', 'spam')
```

What is going to happen is that `14`, `'eggs'`, `'ham'` and `'spam'` will be pushed onto the stack, one at a time:

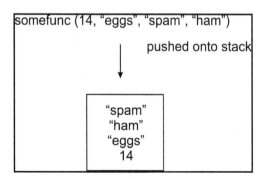

When the code jumps into the function, the values for a, b, c, d will be popped off the stack. The spam element will be popped off first and assigned to d, then "ham" will be assigned to c, and so on:

```
def somefunc(a, b, c, d):
    print("function executed")
```

Stack implementation

Now let us study an implementation of a stack in Python. We start off by creating a node class, just as we did in the previous chapter with lists:

```
class Node:
    def __init__(self, data=None):
        self.data = data
        self.next = None
```

This should be familiar to you by now: a node holds data and a reference to the next item in a list. We are going to implement a stack instead of a list, but the same principle of nodes linked together still applies.

Now let us look at the stack class. It starts off similar to a singly linked list. We need to know the node at the top of the stack. We would also like to keep track of the number of nodes in the stack. So we will add these fields to our class:

```
class Stack:
    def __init__(self):
        self.top = None
        self.size = 0
```

Push operation

The push operation is used to add an element to the top of the stack. Here is an implementation:

```
def push(self, data):
    node = Node(data)
    if self.top:
        node.next = self.top
        self.top = node
    else:
        self.top = node
    self.size += 1
```

In the following figure, there is no existing node after creating our new node. Thus `self.top` will point to this new node. The else part of the `if` statement guarantees that this happens:

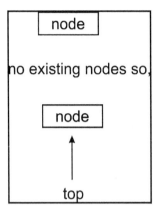

In a scenario where we have an existing stack, we move `self.top` so that it points to the newly created node. The newly created node must have its **next** pointer, pointing to the node that used to be the top node on the stack:

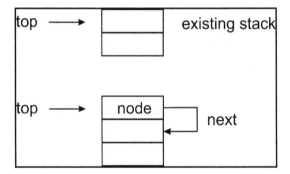

Pop operation

Now we need a `pop` method to remove the top element from the stack. As we do so, we need to return the topmost element as well. We will make the stack return `None` if there are no more elements:

```
def pop(self):
    if self.top:
        data = self.top.data
```

```
        self.size -= 1
        if self.top.next:
            self.top = self.top.next
        else:
            self.top = None
        return data
    else:
        return None
```

The thing to pay attention to here is the inner `if` statement. If the top node has its **next** attribute pointing to another node, then we must set the top of the stack to now point to that node:

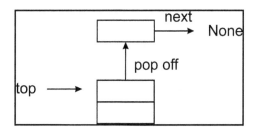

When there is only one node in the stack, the `pop` operation will proceed as follows:

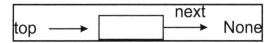

Removing such a node results in `self.top` pointing to `None`:

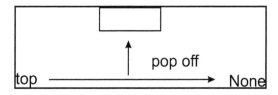

Peek

As we said earlier, we could also add a `peek` method. This will just return the top of the stack without removing it from the stack, allowing us to look at the top element without changing the stack itself. This operation is very straightforward. If there is a top element, return its data, otherwise return `None` (so that the behavior of `peek` matches that of `pop`):

```
def peek(self):
    if self.top
        return self.top.data
    else:
        return None
```

Bracket-matching application

Now let us look at an example of how we can use our stack implementation. We are going to write a little function that will verify whether a statement containing brackets--(, [, or {--is balanced, that is, whether the number of closing brackets matches the number of opening brackets. It will also ensure that one pair of brackets really is contained in another:

```
def check_brackets(statement):
    stack = Stack()
    for ch in statement:
        if ch in ('{', '[', '('):
            stack.push(ch)
        if ch in ('}', ']', ')'):
            last = stack.pop()
        if last is '{' and ch is '}':
            continue
        elif last is '[' and ch is ']':
            continue
        elif last is '(' and ch is ')':
            continue
        else:
            return False
if stack.size > 0:
    return False
else:
    return True
```

Our function parses each character in the statement passed to it. If it gets an open bracket, it pushes it onto the stack. If it gets a closing bracket, it pops the top element off the stack and compares the two brackets to make sure their types match: (should match), [should match], and { should match }. If they don't, we return `False`, otherwise we continue parsing.

Once we have got to the end of the statement, we need to do one last check. If the stack is empty, then we are fine and we can return `True`. But if the stack is not empty, then we have some opening bracket which does not have a matching closing bracket and we shall return `False`.

We can test the bracket-matcher with the following little code:

```
sl = (
    "{(foo)(bar)}[hello](((this)is)a)test",
    "{(foo)(bar)}[hello](((this)is)atest",
    "{(foo)(bar)}[hello](((this)is)a)test))"
)

for s in sl:
    m = check_brackets(s)
    print("{}: {}".format(s, m))
```

Only the first of the three statements should match. And when we run the code, we get the following output:

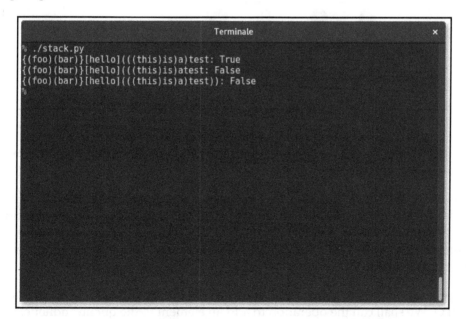

`True`, `False`, `False`. The code works. In summary, the `push` and `pop` operations of the stack data structure attract a **O**(*1*). The stack data structure is simply enough but is used to implement a whole range of functionality in the real world. The back and forward buttons on the browser are made possible by stacks. To be able to have undo and redo functionality in word processors, stacks are also used.

Queues

Another special type of list is the queue data structure. This data structure is no different from the regular queue you are accustomed to in real life. If you have stood in line at an airport or to be served your favorite burger at your neighborhood shop, then you should know how things work in a queue.

Queues are also a very fundamental and important concept to grasp since many other data structures are built on them.

The way a queue works is that the first person to join the queue usually gets served first, all things being equal. The acronym FIFO best explains this. **FIFO** stands for **first in, first out**. When people are standing in a queue waiting for their turn to be served, service is only rendered at the front of the queue. The only time people exit the queue is when they have been served, which only occurs at the very front of the queue. By strict definition, it is illegal for people to join the queue at the front where people are being served:

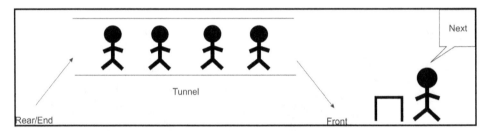

To join the queue, participants must first move behind the last person in the queue. The length of the queue does not matter. This is the only legal or permitted way by which the queue accepts new entrants.

As human as we are, the queues that we form do not conform to strict rules. It may have people who are already in the queue deciding to fall out or even have others substituting for them. It is not our intent to model all the dynamics that happen in a real queue. Abstracting what a queue is and how it behaves enables us to solve a plethora of challenges, especially in computing.

We shall provide various implementations of a queue but all will revolve around the same idea of FIFO. We shall call the operation to add an element to the queue enqueue. To remove an element from the queue, we will create a `dequeue` operation. Anytime an element is enqueued, the length or size of the queue increases by one. Conversely, dequeuing items reduce the number of elements in the queue by one.

To demonstrate the two operations, the following table shows the effect of adding and removing elements from a queue:

Queue operation	Size	Contents	Operation results
`Queue()`	0	`[]`	Queue object created
`Enqueue "Mark"`	1	`['mark']`	Mark added to queue
`Enqueue "John"`	2	`['mark', 'john']`	John added to queue
`Size()`	2	`['mark', 'john']`	Number of items in queue returned
`Dequeue()`	1	`['mark']`	John is dequeued and returned
`Dequeue()`	0	`[]`	Mark is dequeued and returned

List-based queue

To put into code everything discussed about queues to this point, let's go ahead and implement a very simple queue using Python's `list` class. This is to help us develop quickly and learn about queues. The operations that must be performed on the queue are encapsulated in the `ListQueue` class:

```
class ListQueue:
    def __init__(self):
        self.items = []
        self.size = 0
```

In the initialization method `__init__`, the `items` instance variable is set to `[]`, which means the queue is empty when created. The size of the queue is also set to `zero`. The more interesting methods are the `enqueue` and `dequeue` methods.

Enqueue operation

The `enqueue` operation or method uses the `insert` method of the `list` class to insert items (or data) at the front of the list:

```
def enqueue(self, data):
    self.items.insert(0, data)
    self.size += 1
```

Do note how we implement insertions to the end of the queue. Index 0 is the first position in any list or array. However, in our implementation of a queue using a Python list, the array index 0 is the only place where new data elements are inserted into the queue. The `insert` operation will shift existing data elements in the list by one position up and then insert the new data in the space created at index 0. The following figure visualizes this process:

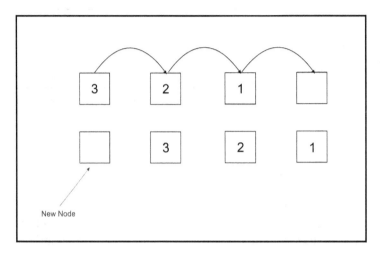

To make our queue reflect the addition of the new element, the size is increased by one:

```
self.size += 1
```

 We could have used Python's `shift` method on the list as another way of implementing the "insert at 0". At the end of the day, an implementation is the overall objective of the exercise.

Dequeue operation

The `dequeue` operation is used to remove items from the queue. With reference to the introduction to the topic of queues, this operation captures the point where we serve the customer who joined the queue first and also waited the longest:

```
def dequeue(self):
    data = self.items.pop()
    self.size -= 1
    return data
```

The Python `list` class has a method called `pop()`. The `pop` method does the following:

1. Removes the last item from the list.
2. Returns the removed item from the list back to the user or code that called it.

The last item in the list is popped and saved in the `data` variable. In the last line of the method, the data is returned.

Consider the tunnel in the following figure as our queue. To perform a `dequeue` operation, the node with data `1` is removed from the front of the queue:

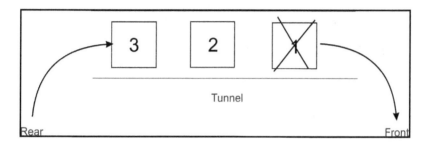

The resulting elements in the queue are as shown as follows:

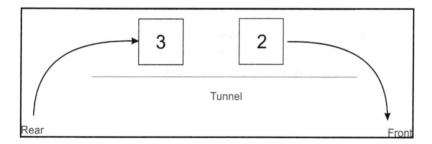

 What can we say about the `enqueue` operation? It is highly inefficient in more than one way. The method has to first shift all the elements by one space. Imagine when there are 1 million elements in a list which need to be shifted around anytime a new element is being added to the queue. This will generally make the enqueue process very slow for large lists.

Stack-based queue

Yet another implementation of a queue is to use two stacks. Once more, the Python `list` class will be used to simulate a stack:

```
class Queue:
    def __init__(self):
        self.inbound_stack = []
        self.outbound_stack = []
```

The preceding `queue` class sets the two instance variables to empty lists upon initialization. These are the stacks that will help us implement a queue. The stacks in this case are simply Python lists that allow us to call `push` and `pop` methods on them.

The `inbound_stack` is only used to store elements that are added to the queue. No other operation can be performed on this stack.

Enqueue operation

The `enqueue` method is what adds elements to the queue:

```
def enqueue(self, data):
    self.inbound_stack.append(data)
```

The method is a simple one that only receives the `data` the client wants to append to the queue. This data is then passed to the `append` method of the `inbound_stack` in the `queue` class. Furthermore, the `append` method is used to mimic the `push` operation, which pushes elements to the top of the stack.

To `enqueue` data onto the `inbound_stack`, the following code does justice:

```
queue = Queue()
queue.enqueue(5)
queue.enqueue(6)
queue.enqueue(7)
print(queue.inbound_stack)
```

A command-line output of the `inbound_stack` inside the queue is as follows:

```
[5, 6, 7]
```

Dequeue operation

The dequeue operation is a little more involved than its enqueue counterpart operation. New elements added to our queue end up in the inbound_stack. Instead of removing elements from the inbound_stack, we shift our attention to the outbound_stack. As we said, elements can be deleted from our queue only through the outbound_stack:

```
if not self.outbound_stack:
    while self.inbound_stack:
        self.outbound_stack.append(self.inbound_stack.pop())
    return self.outbound_stack.pop()
```

The if statement first checks whether the outbound_stack is empty or not. If it is not empty, we proceed to remove the element at the front of the queue by doing the following:

```
return self.outbound_stack.pop()
```

If the outbound_stack is empty instead, all the elements in the inbound_stack are moved to the outbound_stack before the front element in the queue is popped out:

```
while self.inbound_stack:
    self.outbound_stack.append(self.inbound_stack.pop())
```

The while loop will continue to be executed as long as there are elements in the inbound_stack.

The statement self.inbound_stack.pop() will remove the latest element that was added to the inbound_stack and immediately pass the popped data to the self.outbound_stack.append() method call.

Initially, our inbound_stack was filled with the elements **5**, **6** and **7**:

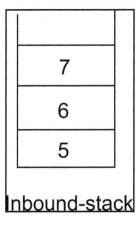

Inbound-stack

After executing the body of the `while` loop, the `outbound_stack` looks like this:

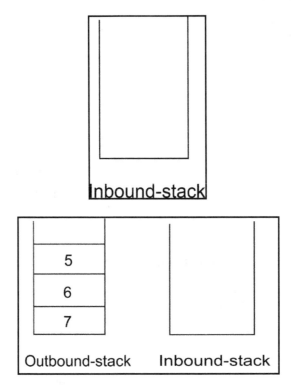

The last line in the `dequeue` method will return 5 as the result of the `pop` operation on the `outbound_stack`:

```
return self.outbound_stack.pop()
```

This leaves the `outbound_stack` with only two elements:

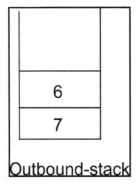

The next time the `dequeue` operation is called, the `while` loop will not be executed because there are no elements in the `outbound_stack`, which makes the outer `if` statement fail.

The `pop` operation is called right away in that case so that only the element in the queue that has waited the longest is returned.

A typical run of code to use this queue implementation is as follows:

```
queue = Queue()
queue.enqueue(5)
queue.enqueue(6)
queue.enqueue(7)
print(queue.inbound_stack)
queue.dequeue()
print(queue.inbound_stack)
print(queue.outbound_stack)
queue.dequeue()
print(queue.outbound_stack)
```

The output for the preceding code is as follows:

```
[5, 6, 7]
[]
[7, 6]
[7]
```

The code sample adds elements to a queue and prints out the elements within the queue. The `dequeue` method is called, after which a change in the number of elements is observed when the queue is printed out again.

 Implementing a queue with two stacks is a popular question posed during interviews.

Node-based queue

Using a Python list to implement a queue is a good starter to get the feel of how queues work. It is completely possible for us to implement our own queue data structure by utilizing our knowledge of pointer structures.

A queue can be implemented using a doubly linked list, and `insertion` and `deletion` operations on this data structure have a time complexity of **O(1)**.

The definition for the `node` class remains the same as the `Node` we defined when we touched on doubly linked list, The doubly linked list can be treated as a queue if it enables a FIFO kind of data access, where the first element added to the list is the first to be removed.

Queue class

The `queue` class is very similar to that of the doubly linked `list` class:

```
class Queue:
def __init__(self):
        self.head = None
        self.tail = None
        self.count = 0
```

`self.head` and `self.tail` pointers are set to `None` upon creation of an instance of the queue class. To keep a count of the number of nodes in `Queue`, the `count` instance variable is maintained here too and set to `0`.

Enqueue operation

Elements are added to a `Queue` object via the `enqueue` method. The elements in this case are the nodes:

```
def enqueue(self, data):
    new_node = Node(data, None, None)
    if self.head is None:
        self.head = new_node
        self.tail = self.head
    else:
        new_node.prev = self.tail
        self.tail.next = new_node
        self.tail = new_node

    self.count += 1
```

The `enqueue` method code is the same code already explained in the `append` operation of the doubly linked list. It creates a node from the data passed to it and appends it to the tail of the queue, or points both `self.head` and `self.tail` to the newly created node if the queue is empty. The total count of elements in the queue is increased by the line `self.count += 1`.

Dequeue operation

The other operation that makes our doubly linked list behave as a queue is the `dequeue` method. This method is what removes the node at the front of the queue.

To remove the first element pointed to by `self.head`, an `if` statement is used:

```
def dequeue(self):
current = self.head
        if self.count == 1:
            self.count -= 1
            self.head = None
            self.tail = None
        elif self.count > 1:
            self.head = self.head.next
            self.head.prev = None
            self.count -= 1
```

`current` is initialized by pointing it to `self.head`. If `self.count` is 1, then it means only one node is in the list and invariably the queue. Thus, to remove the associated node (pointed to by `self.head`), the `self.head` and `self.tail` variables are set to `None`.

If, on the other hand, the queue has many nodes, then the head pointer is shifted to point to `self.head`'s next node.

After the `if` statement is run, the method returns the node that was pointed to by `head`. `self.count` is decremented by one in either way the `if` statement execution path flows.

Equipped with these methods, we have successfully implemented a queue, borrowing heavily from the idea of a doubly linked list.

Remember also that the only things transforming our doubly linked list into a queue are the two methods, namely `enqueue` and `dequeue`.

Application of queues

Queues are used to implement a variety of functionalities in computer land. For instance, instead of providing each computer on a network with its own printer, a network of computers can be made to share one printer by queuing what each printer wants to print. When the printer is ready to print, it will pick one of the items (usually called jobs) in the queue to print out.

Operating systems also queue processes to be executed by the CPU. Let's create an application that makes use of a queue to create a bare-bones media player.

Media player queue

Most music player software allows users the chance to add songs to a playlist. Upon hitting the play button, all the songs in the main playlist are played one after the other. The sequential playing of the songs can be implemented with queues because the first song to be queued is the first song that is played. This aligns with the FIFO acronym. We shall implement our own playlist queue that plays songs in the FIFO manner.

Basically, our media player queue will only allow for the addition of tracks and a way to play all the tracks in the queue. In a full-blown music player, threads would be used to improve how the queue is interacted with, while the music player continues to be used to select the next song to be played, paused, or even stopped.

The track class will simulate a musical track:

```
from random import randint
class Track:

    def __init__(self, title=None):
        self.title = title
        self.length = randint(5, 10)
```

Each track holds a reference to the title of the song and also the length of the song. The length is a random number between 5 and 10. The random module provides the randint method to enable us generate the random numbers. The class represents any MP3 track or file that contains music. The random length of a track is used to simulate the number of seconds it takes to play a song or track.

To create a few tracks and print out their lengths, we do the following:

```
track1 = Track("white whistle")
track2 = Track("butter butter")
print(track1.length)
print(track2.length)
```

The output of the preceding code is as follows:

```
6
7
```

Your output may be different depending on the random length generated for the two tracks.

Now, let's create our queue. Using inheritance, we simply inherit from the `queue` class:

```
import time
class MediaPlayerQueue(Queue):

    def __init__(self):
        super(MediaPlayerQueue, self).__init__()
```

A call is made to properly initialize the queue by making a call to `super`. This class is essentially a queue that holds a number of track objects in a queue. To add tracks to the queue, an `add_track` method is created:

```
def add_track(self, track):
    self.enqueue(track)
```

The method passes a `track` object to the `enqueue` method of the queue `super` class. This will, in effect, create a `Node` using the `track` object (as the node's data) and point either the tail, if the queue is not empty, or both head and tail, if the queue is empty, to this new node.

Assuming the tracks in the queue are played sequentially from the first track added to the last (FIFO), then the `play` function has to loop through the elements in the queue:

```
def play(self):
    while self.count > 0:
        current_track_node = self.dequeue()
        print("Now playing {}".format(current_track_node.data.title))
        time.sleep(current_track_node.data.length)
```

`self.count` keeps count of when a track is added to our queue and when tracks have been dequeued. If the queue is not empty, a call to the `dequeue` method will return the node (which houses the `track` object) at the front of the queue. The `print` statement then accesses the title of the track through the `data` attribute of the node. To further simulate the playing of a track, the `time.sleep()` method halts program execution till the number of seconds of the track has elapsed:

```
time.sleep(current_track_node.data.length)
```

The media player queue is made up of nodes. When a track is added to the queue, the track is hidden in a newly created node and associated with the data attribute of the node. That explains why we access a node's `track` object through the data property of the node which is returned by the call to `dequeue`:

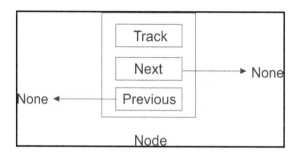

You can see, instead of our `node` object just storing just any data, it stores tracks in this case.

Let's take our music player for a spin:

```
track1 = Track("white whistle")
track2 = Track("butter butter")
track3 = Track("Oh black star")
track4 = Track("Watch that chicken")
track5 = Track("Don't go")
```

We create five track objects with random words as titles:

```
print(track1.length)
print(track2.length)
>> 8
>> 9
```

The output should be different from what you get on your machine due to the random length.

Next, an instance of the `MediaPlayerQueue` class is created:

```
media_player = MediaPlayerQueue()
```

The tracks will be added and the output of the `play` function should print out the tracks being played in the same order in which we queued them:

```
media_player.add_track(track1)
media_player.add_track(track2)
media_player.add_track(track3)
media_player.add_track(track4)
media_player.add_track(track5)
media_player.play()
```

The output of the preceding code is as follows:

```
>>Now playing white whistle
>>Now playing butter butter
>>Now playing Oh black star
>>Now playing Watch that chicken
>>Now playing Don't go
```

Upon execution of the program, it can be seen that the tracks are played in the order in which they were queued. When playing the track, the system also pauses for the number of seconds equal to that of the length of the track.

Summary

In this chapter, we used our knowledge of linking nodes together to create other data structures, namely stacks and queues. We have seen how these data structures closely mimic stacks and queues in the real world. Concrete implementations, together with their varying types, have been shown. We later applied the concept of stacks and queues to write real-life programs.

We shall consider trees in the next chapter. The major operations on a tree will be discussed, likewise the different spheres in which to apply the data structure.

6
Trees

A tree is a hierarchical form of data structure. When we dealt with lists, queues, and stacks, items followed each other. But in a tree, there is a *parent-child* relationship between items.

To visualize what trees look like, imagine a tree growing up from the ground. Now remove that image from your mind. Trees are normally drawn downward, so you would be better off imagining the root structure of the tree growing downward.

At the top of every tree is the so-called *root node*. This is the ancestor of all other nodes in the tree.

Trees are used for a number of things, such as parsing expressions, and searches. Certain document types, such as XML and HTML, can also be represented in a tree form. We shall look at some of the uses of trees in this chapter.

In this chapter, we will cover the following areas:

- Terms and definitions of trees
- Binary trees and binary search trees
- Tree traversal

Terminology

Let's consider some terms associated with trees.

To understand trees, we need to first understand the basic ideas on which they rest. The following figure contains a typical tree consisting of character nodes lettered **A** through to **M**.

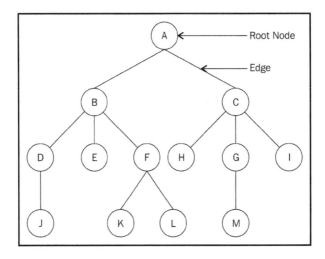

Here is a list of terms associated with a Tree:

- **Node**: Each circled alphabet represents a node. A node is any structure that holds data.
- **Root node**: The root node is the only node from which all other nodes come. A tree with an undistinguishable root node cannot be considered as a tree. The root node in our tree is the node A.
- **Sub-tree**: A sub-tree of a tree is a tree with its nodes being a descendant of some other tree. Nodes F, K, and L form a sub-tree of the original tree consisting of all the nodes.
- **Degree**: The number of sub-trees of a given node. A tree consisting of only one node has a degree of 0. This one tree node is also considered as a tree by all standards. The degree of node A is 2.
- **Leaf node**: This is a node with a degree of 0. Nodes J, E, K, L, H, M, and I are all leaf nodes.
- **Edge**: The connection between two nodes. An edge can sometimes connect a node to itself, making the edge appear as a loop.

- **Parent**: A node in the tree with other connecting nodes is the parent of those nodes. Node B is the parent of nodes D, E, and F.
- **Child**: This is a node connected to its parent. Nodes B and C are children of node A, the parent and root node.
- **Sibling**: All nodes with the same parent are siblings. This makes the nodes B and C siblings.
- **Level**: The level of a node is the number of connections from the root node. The root node is at level 0. Nodes B and C are at level 1.
- **Height of a tree**: This is the number of levels in a tree. Our tree has a height of 4.
- **Depth**: The depth of a node is the number of edges from the root of the tree to that node. The depth of node H is 2.

We shall begin our treatment of trees by considering the node in a tree and abstracting a class.

Tree nodes

Just as was the case with other data structures that we encountered, such as lists and stacks, trees are built up of nodes. But the nodes that make up a tree need to contain data about the parent-child relationship that we mentioned earlier.

Let us now look at how to build a binary tree `node` class in Python:

```
class Node:
    def __init__(self, data):
        self.data = data
        self.right_child = None
        self.left_child = None
```

Just like in our previous implementations, a node is a container for data and holds references to other nodes. Being a binary tree node, these references are to the left and the right children.

To test this class out, we first create a few nodes:

```
n1 = Node("root node")
n2 = Node("left child node")
n3 = Node("right child node")
n4 = Node("left grandchild node")
```

Next, we connect the nodes to each other. We let n1 be the root node with n2 and n3 as its children. Finally, we hook n4 as the left child to n2, so that we get a few iterations when we traverse the left sub-tree:

```
n1.left_child = n2
n1.right_child = n3
n2.left_child = n4
```

Once we have our tree structure set up, we are ready to traverse it. As mentioned previously, we shall traverse the left sub-tree. We print out the node and move down the tree to the next left node. We keep doing this until we have reached the end of the left sub-tree:

```
current = n1
while current:
    print(current.data)
    current = current.left_child
```

As you will probably have noticed, this requires quite a bit of work in the client code, as you have to manually build up the tree structure.

Binary trees

A binary tree is one in which each node has a maximum of two children. Binary trees are very common and we shall use them to build up a BST implementation in Python.

The following figure is an example of a binary tree with 5 being the root node:

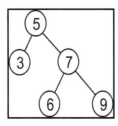

Each child is identified as being the right or left child of its parent. Since the parent node is also a node by itself, each node will hold a reference to a right and left node even if the nodes do not exist.

A regular binary tree has no rules as to how elements are arranged in the tree. It only satisfies the condition that each node should have a maximum of two children.

Binary search trees

A **binary search tree** (**BST**) is a special kind of a binary tree. That is, it is a tree that is structurally a binary tree. Functionally, it is a tree that stores its nodes in such a way to be able to search through the tree efficiently.

There is a structure to a BST. For a given node with a value, all the nodes in the left sub-tree are less than or equal to the value of that node. Also, all the nodes in the right sub-tree of this node are greater than that of the parent node. As an example, consider the following tree:

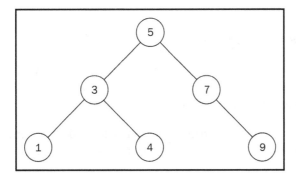

This is an example of a BST. Testing our tree for the properties of a BST, you realize that all the nodes in the left sub-tree of the root node have a value less than 5. Likewise, all the nodes in the right sub-tree have a value that is greater than 5. This property applies to all the nodes in a BST, with no exceptions:

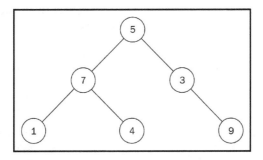

Despite the fact that the preceding figure looks similar to the previous figure, it does not qualify as a BST. Node 7 is greater than the root node 5; however, it is located to the left of the root node. Node 4 is to the right sub-tree of its parent node 7, which is incorrect.

Binary search tree implementation

Let us begin our implementation of a BST. We will want the tree to hold a reference to its own root node:

```
class Tree:
    def __init__(self):
        self.root_node = None
```

That's all that is needed to maintain the state of a tree. Let's examine the main operations on the tree in the next section.

Binary search tree operations

There are essentially two operations that are needful for having a usable BST. These are the insert and remove operations. These operations must occur with the one rule that they must maintain the principle that gives the BST its structure.

Before we tackle the insertion and removal of nodes, let's discuss some equally important operations that will help us better understand the insert and remove operations.

Finding the minimum and maximum nodes

The structure of the BST makes looking for the node with the maximum and minimum values very easy.

To find the node with smallest value, we start our traversal from the root of the tree and visit the left node each time we reach a sub-tree. We do the opposite to find the node with the biggest value in the tree:

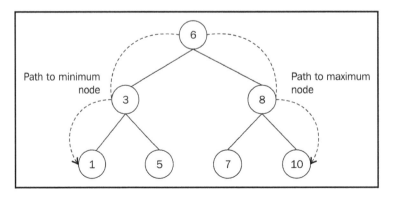

We move down from node 6 to 3 to 1 to get to the node with smallest value. Likewise, we go down 6, 8 to node 10, which is the node with the largest value.

This same means of finding the minimum and maximum nodes applies to sub-trees too. The minimum node in the sub-tree with root node 8 is 7. The node within that sub-tree with the maximum value is 10.

The method that returns the minimum node is as follows:

```
def find_min(self):
    current = self.root_node
    while current.left_child:
        current = current.left_child

    return current
```

The `while` loop continues to get the left node and visits it until the last left node points to `None`. It is a very simple method. The method to return the maximum node does the opposite, where `current.left_child` now becomes `current.right_child`.

It takes **O**(h) to find the minimum or maximum value in a BST, where h is the height of the tree.

Inserting nodes

One of the operations on a BST is the need to insert data as nodes. Whereas in our first implementation, we had to insert the nodes ourselves, here we are going to let the tree be in charge of storing its data.

In order to make a search possible, the nodes must be stored in a specific way. For each given node, its left child node will hold data that is less than its own value, as already discussed. That node's right child node will hold data greater than that of its parent node.

We are going to create a new BST of integers by starting with the data 5. To do this, we will create a node with its data attribute set to 5.

Now, to add the second node with value 3, 3 is compared with 5, the root node:

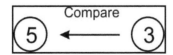

Since 5 is greater than 3, it will be put in the left sub-tree of node 5. Our BST will look as follows:

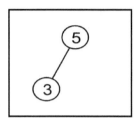

The tree satisfies the BST rule, where all the nodes in the left sub-tree are less than its parent.

To add another node of value 7 to the tree, we start from the root node with value 5 and do a comparison:

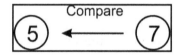

Since 7 is greater than 5, the node with value 7 is situated to the right of this root.

What happens when we want to add a node that is equal to an existing node? We will simply add it as a left node and maintain this rule throughout the structure.

If a node already has a child in the place where the new node goes, then we have to move down the tree and attach it.

Let's add another node with value 1. Starting from the root of the tree, we do a comparison between 1 and 5:

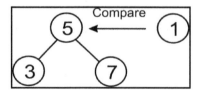

The comparison reveals that 1 is less than 5, so we move our attention to the left node of 5, which is the node with value 3:

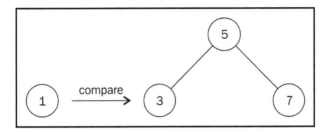

We compare 1 with 3 and since 1 is less than 3, we move a level below node 3 and to its left. But there is no node there. Therefore, we create a node with the value 1 and associate it with the left pointer of node 3 to obtain the following structure:

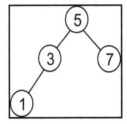

So far, we have been dealing only with nodes that contain only integers or numbers. For numbers, the idea of greater than and lesser than are clearly defined. Strings would be compared alphabetically, so there are no major problems there either. But if you want to store your own custom data types inside a BST, you would have to make sure that your class supports ordering.

Let's now create a function that enables us to add data as nodes to the BST. We begin with a function declaration:

```
def insert(self, data):
```

By now, you will be used to the fact that we encapsulate the data in a node. This way, we hide away the node class from the client code, who only needs to deal with the tree:

```
node = Node(data)
```

A first check will be to find out whether we have a root node. If we don't, the new node becomes the root node (we cannot have a tree without a root node):

```
if self.root_node is None:
    self.root_node = node
else:
```

As we walk down the tree, we need to keep track of the current node we are working on, as well as its parent. The variable `current` is always used for this purpose:

```
current = self.root_node
parent = None
while True:
    parent = current
```

Here we must perform a comparison. If the data held in the new node is less than the data held in the current node, then we check whether the current node has a left child node. If it doesn't, this is where we insert the new node. Otherwise, we keep traversing:

```
if node.data < current.data:
    current = current.left_child
    if current is None:
        parent.left_child = node
        return
```

Now we take care of the greater than or equal case. If the current node doesn't have a right child node, then the new node is inserted as the right child node. Otherwise, we move down and continue looking for an insertion point:

```
else:
    current = current.right_child
    if current is None:
        parent.right_child = node
        return
```

Insertion of a node in a BST takes $O(h)$, where h is the height of the tree.

Deleting nodes

Another important operation on a BST is the `deletion` or `removal` of nodes. There are three scenarios that we need to cater for during this process. The node that we want to remove might have the following:

- No children
- One child
- Two children

The first scenario is the easiest to handle. If the node about to be removed has no children, we simply detach it from its parent:

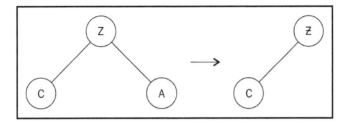

Because node A has no children, we will simply dissociate it from its parent, node Z.

On the other hand, when the node we want to remove has one child, the parent of that node is made to point to the child of that particular node:

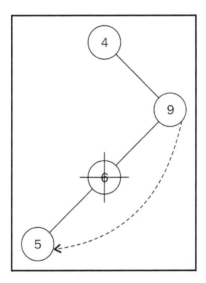

In order to remove node 6, which has as its only child, node 5, we point the left pointer of node 9 to node 5. The relationship between the parent node and child has to be preserved. That is why we need to take note of how the child node is connected to its parent (which is the node about to be deleted). The child node of the deleted node is stored. Then we connect the parent of the deleted node to that child node.

A more complex scenario arises when the node we want to delete has two children:

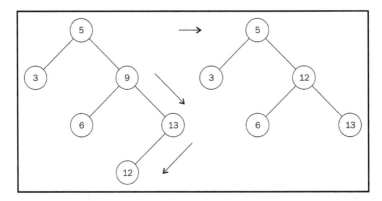

We cannot simply replace node 9 with either node 6 or 13. What we need to do is to find the next biggest descendant of node 9. This is node 12. To get to node 12, we move to the right node of node 9. And then move left to find the leftmost node. Node 12 is called the in-order successor of node 9. The second step resembles the move to find the maximum node in a sub-tree.

We replace the value of node 9 with the value 12 and remove node 12. In removing node 12, we end up with a simpler form of node removal that has been addressed previously. Node 12 has no children, so we apply the rule for removing nodes without children accordingly.

Our `node` class does not have reference to a parent. As such, we need to use a helper method to search for and return the node with its parent node. This method is similar to the `search` method:

```
def get_node_with_parent(self, data):
    parent = None
    current = self.root_node
    if current is None:
        return (parent, None)
    while True:
        if current.data == data:
            return (parent, current)
        elif current.data > data:
            parent = current
            current = current.left_child
        else:
            parent = current
            current = current.right_child

    return (parent, current)
```

The only difference is that before we update the current variable inside the loop, we store its parent with `parent = current`. The method to do the actual removal of a node begins with this search:

```
def remove(self, data):
    parent, node = self.get_node_with_parent(data)

    if parent is None and node is None:
        return False

    # Get children count
    children_count = 0

    if node.left_child and node.right_child:
        children_count = 2
    elif (node.left_child is None) and (node.right_child is None):
        children_count = 0
    else:
        children_count = 1
```

We pass the parent and the found node to `parent` and `node` respectively with the line `parent, node = self.get_node_with_parent(data)`. It is helpful to know the number of children that the node we want to delete has. That is the purpose of the `if` statement.

After this, we need to begin handling the various conditions under which a node can be deleted. The first part of the `if` statement handles the case where the node has no children:

```
if children_count == 0:
    if parent:
        if parent.right_child is node:
            parent.right_child = None
        else:
            parent.left_child = None
    else:
        self.root_node = None
```

`if parent:` is used to handle cases where there is a BST that has only one node in the whole of the three.

In the case where the node about to be deleted has only one child, the `elif` part of the `if` statement does the following:

```
elif children_count == 1:
    next_node = None
    if node.left_child:
        next_node = node.left_child
```

```
        else:
            next_node = node.right_child

    if parent:
        if parent.left_child is node:
            parent.left_child = next_node
        else:
            parent.right_child = next_node
    else:
        self.root_node = next_node
```

`next_node` is used to keep track of where the single node pointed to by the node we want to delete is. We then connect `parent.left_child` or `parent.right_child` to `next_node`.

Lastly, we handle the condition where the node we want to delete has two children:

```
    ...
    else:
        parent_of_leftmost_node = node
        leftmost_node = node.right_child
        while leftmost_node.left_child:
            parent_of_leftmost_node = leftmost_node
            leftmost_node = leftmost_node.left_child

        node.data = leftmost_node.data
```

In finding the in-order successor, we move to the right node with `leftmost_node = node.right_child`. As long as there exists a left node, `leftmost_node.left_child` will evaluate to `True` and the `while` loop will run. When we get to the leftmost node, it will either be a leaf node (meaning that it will have no child node) or have a right child.

We update the node about to be removed with the value of the in-order successor with `node.data = leftmost_node.data`:

```
    if parent_of_leftmost_node.left_child == leftmost_node:
        parent_of_leftmost_node.left_child = leftmost_node.right_child
    else:
        parent_of_leftmost_node.right_child = leftmost_node.right_child
```

The preceding statement allows us to properly attach the parent of the leftmost node with any child node. Observe how the right-hand side of the equals sign stays unchanged. That is because the in-order successor can only have a right child as its only child.

The `remove` operation takes **O**(*h*), where h is the height of the tree.

Searching the tree

Since the `insert` method organizes data in a specific way, we will follow the same procedure to find the data. In this implementation, we will simply return the data if it was found or `None` if the data wasn't found:

```
def search(self, data):
```

We need to start searching at the very top, that is, at the root node:

```
current = self.root_node
while True:
```

We may have passed a leaf node, in which case the data doesn't exist in the tree and we return `None` to the client code:

```
if current is None:
    return None
```

We might also have found the data, in which case we return it:

```
elif current.data is data:
    return data
```

As per the rules for how data is stored in the BST, if the data we are searching for is less than that of the current node, we need to go down the tree to the left:

```
elif current.data > data:
    current = current.left_child
```

Now we only have one option left: the data we are looking for is greater than the data held in the current node, which means we go down the tree to the right:

```
else:
    current = current.right_child
```

Finally, we can write some client code to test how the BST works. We create a tree and insert a few numbers between 1 and 10. Then we search for all the numbers in that range. The ones that exist in the tree get printed:

```
tree = Tree()
tree.insert(5)
tree.insert(2)
tree.insert(7)
tree.insert(9)
tree.insert(1)
```

```
for i in range(1, 10):
    found = tree.search(i)
    print("{}: {}".format(i, found))
```

Tree traversal

Visiting all the nodes in a tree can be done depth first or breadth first. These modes of traversal are not peculiar to only binary search trees but trees in general.

Depth-first traversal

In this traversal mode, we follow a branch (or edge) to its limit before recoiling upwards to continue traversal. We will be using the recursive approach for the traversal. There are three forms of depth-first traversal, namely `in-order`, `pre-order`, and `post-order`.

In-order traversal and infix notation

Most of us are probably used to this way of representing an arithmetic expression, since this is the way we are normally taught in schools. The operator is inserted (infixed) between the operands, as in `3 + 4`. When necessary, parentheses can be used to build a more complex expression: `(4 + 5) * (5 - 3)`.

In this mode of traversal, you would visit the left sub-tree, the parent node, and finally the right sub-tree.

The recursive function to return an in-order listing of nodes in a tree is as follows:

```
def inorder(self, root_node):
    current = root_node
    if current is None:
        return
    self.inorder(current.left_child)
    print(current.data)
    self.inorder(current.right_child)
```

We visit the node by printing the node and making two recursive calls with `current.left_child` and `current.right_child`.

Pre-order traversal and prefix notation

Prefix notation is commonly referred to as Polish notation. Here, the operator comes before its operands, as in + 3 4. Since there is no ambiguity of precedence, parentheses are not required: * + 4 5 - 5 3.

To traverse a tree in pre-order mode, you would visit the node, the left sub-tree, and the right sub-tree node, in that order.

Prefix notation is well known to LISP programmers.

The recursive function for this traversal is as follows:

```
def preorder(self, root_node):
    current = root_node
    if current is None:
        return
    print(current.data)
    self.preorder(current.left_child)
    self.preorder(current.right_child)
```

Note the order in which the recursive call is made.

Post-order traversal and postfix notation.

Postfix or **reverse Polish notation (RPN)** places the operator after its operands, as in 3 4 +. As is the case with Polish notation, there is never any confusion over the precedence of operators, so parentheses are never needed: 4 5 + 5 3 - *.

In this mode of traversal, you would visit the left sub-tree, the right sub-tree, and lastly the root node.

The post-order method is as follows:

```
def postorder(self, root_node):
    current = root_node
    if current is None:
        return
    self.postorder(current.left_child)
    self.postorder(current.right_child)

    print(current.data)
```

Breadth-first traversal

This kind of traversal starts from the root of a tree and visits the node from one level of the tree to the other:

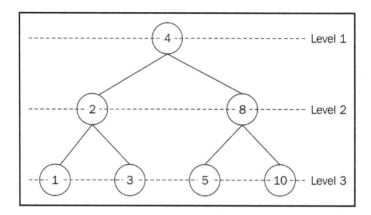

The node at level 1 is node 4. We visit this node by printing out its value. Next, we move to level 2 and visit the nodes on that level, which are nodes 2 and 8. On the last level, level 3, we visit nodes 1, 3, 5, and 10.

The complete output of such a traversal is 4, 2, 8, 1, 3, 5, and 10.

This mode of traversal is made possible by using a queue data structure. Starting with the root node, we push it into a queue. The node at the front of the queue is accessed (dequeued) and either printed and stored for later use. The left node is added to the queue followed by the right node. Since the queue is not empty, we repeat the process.

A dry run of the algorithm will enqueue the root node 4, dequeue, and access, or visit the node. Nodes 2 and 8 are enqueued as they are the left and right nodes respectively. Node 2 is dequeued in order to be visited. Its left and right nodes, 1 and 3, are enqueued. At this point, the node at the front of the queue is 8. We dequeue and visit node 8, after which we enqueue its left and right nodes. So the process continues until the queue is empty.

The algorithm is as follows:

```python
from collections import deque
class Tree:
    def breadth_first_traversal(self):
        list_of_nodes = []
        traversal_queue = deque([self.root_node])
```

We enqueue the root node and keep a list of the visited nodes in the `list_of_nodes` list. The `dequeue` class is used to maintain a queue:

```
while len(traversal_queue) > 0:
    node = traversal_queue.popleft()
    list_of_nodes.append(node.data)

    if node.left_child:
        traversal_queue.append(node.left_child)

    if node.right_child:
        traversal_queue.append(node.right_child)
return list_of_nodes
```

If the number of elements in the `traversal_queue` is greater than zero, the body of the loop is executed. The node at the front of the queue is popped off and appended to the `list_of_nodes` list. The first `if` statement will `enqueue` the left child node of the `node` provided a left node exists. The second `if` statement does the same for the right child node.

The `list_of_nodes` is returned in the last statement.

Benefits of a binary search tree

We shall now briefly look at what makes a BST a better idea than using a list for data that needs to be searched. Let us assume that we have the following dataset: 5, 3, 7, 1, 4, 6, and 9. Using a list, the worst-case scenario would require you to search through the entire list of seven elements before finding the search term:

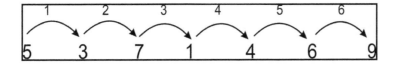

Searching for 9 requires six jumps.

With a tree, the worst-case scenario is three comparisons:

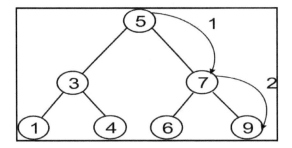

Searching for 9 requires two steps.

Notice, however, that if you insert the elements into the tree in the order 1, 2, 3, 5, 6, 7, 9, then the tree would not be more efficient than the list. We would have to balance the tree first:

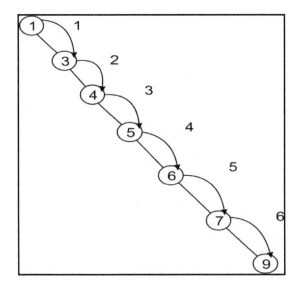

So not only is it important to use a BST but choosing a self-balancing tree helps to improve the `search` operation.

Expression trees

The tree structure is also used to parse arithmetic and Boolean expressions. For example, the expression tree for 3 + 4 would look as follows:

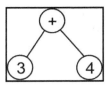

For a slightly more complex expression, (4 + 5) * (5-3), we would get the following:

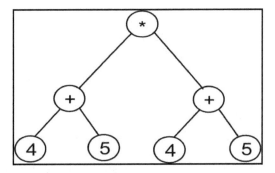

Parsing a reverse Polish expression

Now we are going to build up a tree for an expression written in postfix notation. Then we will calculate the result. We will use a simple tree implementation. To keep it really simple, since we are going to grow the tree by merging smaller trees, we only need a tree node implementation:

```
class TreeNode:
    def __init__(self, data=None):
        self.data = data
        self.right = None
        self.left = None
```

In order to build the tree, we are going to enlist the help of a stack. You will see why soon. But for the time being, let us just create an arithmetic expression and set up our stack:

```
expr = "4 5 + 5 3 - *".split()
stack = Stack()
```

Since Python is a language that tries hard to have sensible defaults, its `split()` method splits on whitespace by default. (If you think about it, this is most likely what you would expect as well.) The result is going to be that expr is a list with the values 4, 5, +, 5, 3, - and *.

Each element of the expr list is going to be either an operator or an operand. If we get an operand then we embed it in a tree node and push it onto the stack. If we get an operator, on the other hand, then we embed the operator into a tree node and pop its two operands into the node's left and right children. Here we have to take care to ensure that the first pop goes into the right child, otherwise we will have problems with subtraction and division.

Here is the code to build the tree:

```
for term in expr:
    if term in "+-*/":
        node = TreeNode(term)
        node.right = stack.pop()
        node.left = stack.pop()
    else:
        node = TreeNode(int(term))
    stack.push(node)
```

Notice that we perform a conversion from string to int in the case of an operand. You could use `float()` instead, if you wanted to support floating point operands.

At the end of this operation, we should have one single element in the stack, and that holds the full tree.

We may now want to be able to evaluate the expression. We build the following little function to help us:

```
def calc(node):
    if node.data is "+":
        return calc(node.left) + calc(node.right)
    elif node.data is "-":
        return calc(node.left) - calc(node.right)
    elif node.data is "*":
        return calc(node.left) * calc(node.right)
    elif node.data is "/":
        return calc(node.left) / calc(node.right)
    else:
        return node.data
```

This function is very simple. We pass in a node. If the node contains an operand, then we simply return that value. If we get an operator, however, then we perform the operation that the operator represents, on the node's two children. However, since one or more of the children could also contain either operators or operands, we call the `calc()` function recursively on the two child nodes (bearing in mind that all the children of every node are also nodes).

Now we just need to pop the root node off the stack and pass it into the `calc()` function and we should have the result of the calculation:

```
root = stack.pop()
result = calc(root)
print(result)
```

Running this program should yield the result 18, which is the result of `(4 + 5) * (5 - 3)`.

Balancing trees

Earlier, we mentioned that if nodes are inserted into the tree in a sequential order, then the tree behaves more or less like a list, that is, each node has exactly one child node. We normally would like to reduce the height of the tree as much as possible, by filling up each row in the tree. This process is called balancing the tree.

There are a number of types of self-balancing trees, such as red-black trees, AA trees, and scapegoat trees. These balance the tree during each operation that modifies the tree, such as insert or delete.

There are also external algorithms that balance a tree. The benefit of these is that you wouldn't need to balance the tree on every single operation, but could rather leave balancing to the point when you need it.

Heaps

At this point, we shall briefly introduce the heap data structure. A heap is a specialization of a tree in which the nodes are ordered in a specific way. Heaps are divided into max and min heaps. In a max heap, each parent node must always be greater than or equal to its children. It follows that the root node must be the greatest value in the tree. A min heap is the opposite. Each parent node must be less than or equal to both its children. As a consequence, the root node holds the lowest value.

Heaps are used for a number of different things. For one, they are used to implement priority queues. There is also a very efficient sorting algorithm, called heap sort, that uses heaps. We are going to study these in depth in subsequent chapters.

Summary

In this chapter, we have looked at tree structures and some example uses of them. We studied binary trees in particular, which is a subtype of trees where each node has at most two children.

We looked at how a binary tree can be used as a searchable data structure with a BST. We saw that, in most cases, finding data in a BST is faster than in a linked list, although this is not the case if the data is inserted sequentially, unless of course the tree is balanced.

The breadth- and depth-first search traversal modes were also implemented using queue recursion.

We also looked at how a binary tree can be used to represent an arithmetic or a Boolean expression. We built up an expression tree to represent an arithmetic expression. We showed how to use a stack to parse an expression written in RPN, build up the expression tree, and finally traverse it to get the result of the arithmetic expression.

Finally, we mentioned heaps, a specialization of a tree structure. We have tried to at least lay down the theoretical foundation for the heap in this chapter, so that we can go on to implement heaps for different purposes in upcoming chapters.

7
Hashing and Symbol Tables

We have previously looked at lists, where items are stored in sequence and accessed by index number. Index numbers work well for computers. They are integers so they are fast and easy to manipulate. However, they don't always work so well for us. If we have an address book entry, for example, with index number 56, that number doesn't tell us much. There is nothing to link a particular contact with number 56. It just happens to be the next available position in the list.

In this chapter, we are going to look at a similar structure: a dictionary. A dictionary uses a keyword instead of an index number. So, if that contact was called *James*, we would probably use the keyword *James* to locate the contact. That is, instead of accessing the contact by calling *contacts [56]*, we would use *contacts ["james"]*.

Dictionaries are often built using hash tables. As the name suggests, hash tables rely on a concept called **hashing**. That is where we are going to begin our discussion.

We will cover the following topics in this chapter:

- Hashing
- Hash tables
- Different functions with elements

Hashing

Hashing is the concept of converting data of arbitrary size into data of fixed size. A little bit more specifically, we are going to use this to turn strings (or possibly other data types) into integers. This possibly sounds more complex than it is so let's look at an example. We want to hash the expression `hello world`, that is, we want to get a numeric value that we could say *represents* the string.

By using the `ord()` function, we can get the ordinal value of any character. For example, the `ord('f')` function gives 102. To get the hash of the whole string, we could just sum the ordinal numbers of each character in the string:

```
>>> sum(map(ord, 'hello world'))
1116
```

h	e	l	l	o		w	o	r	l	d	
104	101	108	108	111	32	119	111	114	108	100	= 1116

This works fine. However, note that we could change the order of the characters in the string and get the same hash:

```
>>> sum(map(ord, 'world hello'))
1116
```

And the sum of the ordinal values of the characters would be the same for the string `gello xorld` as well, since `g` has an ordinal value which is one less than that of `h`, and `x` has an ordinal value that is one greater than that of `w`, hence:

```
>>> sum(map(ord, 'gello xorld'))
1116
```

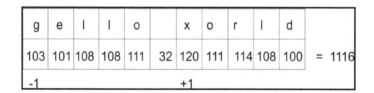

Perfect hashing functions

A perfect hashing function is one in which each string (as we are limiting the discussion to strings for now) is guaranteed to be unique. In practice, hashing functions normally need to be very fast, so trying to create a function that will give each string a unique hash value is normally not possible. Instead, we live with the fact that we sometimes get collisions (two or more strings having the same hash value), and when that happens, we come up with a strategy for resolving them.

In the meantime, we can at least come up with a way to avoid some of the collisions. We could, for example, add a multiplier, so that the hash value for each character becomes the multiplier value, multiplied by the ordinal value of the character. The multiplier then increases as we progress through the string. This is shown in the following function:

```
def myhash(s):
    mult = 1
    hv = 0
    for ch in s:
        hv += mult * ord(ch)
        mult += 1
    return hv
```

We can test this function on the strings that we used earlier:

```
for item in ('hello world', 'world hello', 'gello xorld'):
    print("{}: {}".format(item, myhash(item)))
```

Running the program, we get the following output:

```
% python hashtest.py

hello world: 6736
world hello: 6616
gello xorld: 6742
```

h	e	l	l	o		w	o	r	l	d	
104	101	108	108	111	32	119	111	114	108	100	= 1116
1	2	3	4	5	6	7	8	9	10	11	
104	202	324	432	555	192	833	888	1026	1080	1100	= 6736

Note that the last row is the result of multiplying the values in rows 2 and 3 such that 104 x 1 equals 104, as an example.

This time we get different hash values for our strings. Of course, this doesn't mean that we have a perfect hash. Let us try the strings ad and ga:

```
% python hashtest.py

ad: 297
ga: 297
```

There we still get the same hash value for two different strings. As we have said before, this doesn't have to be a problem, but we need to devise a strategy for resolving collisions. We shall look at that shortly, but first we will study an implementation of a hash table.

Hash table

A **hash table** is a form of list where elements are accessed by a keyword rather than an index number. At least, this is how the client code will see it. Internally, it will use a slightly modified version of our hashing function in order to find the index position in which the element should be inserted. This gives us fast lookups, since we are using an index number which corresponds to the hash value of the key.

We start by creating a class to hold hash table items. These need to have a key and a value, since our hash table is a key-value store:

```
class HashItem:
    def __init__(self, key, value):
        self.key = key
        self.value = value
```

This gives us a very simple way to store items. Next, we start working on the hash table class itself. As usual, we start off with a constructor:

```
class HashTable:
    def __init__(self):
        self.size = 256
        self.slots = [None for i in range(self.size)]
        self.count = 0
```

The hash table uses a standard Python list to store its elements. We could equally well have used the linked list that we developed previously, but right now our focus is on understanding the hash table, so we shall use what is at our disposal.

We set the size of the hash table to 256 elements to start with. Later, we will look at strategies for how to grow the table as we begin filling it up. We now initialize a list containing 256 elements. These elements are often referred to as slots or buckets. Finally, we add a counter for the number of actual hash table elements we have:

0	1	2	......	255
empty	empty	empty	......	empty
used slots = 0					

It is important to notice the difference between the size and count of a table. Size of a table refers to the total number of slots in the table (used or unused). Count of the table, on the other hand, simply refers to the number of slots that are filled, or put another way, the number of actual key-value pairs we have added to the table.

Now, we are going to add our hashing function to the table. It will be similar to what we evolved in the section on hashing functions, but with a slight difference: we need to ensure that our hashing function returns a value between 1 and 256 (the size of the table). A good way of doing so is to return the remainder of dividing the hash by the size of the table, since the remainder is always going to be an integer value between 0 and 255.

As the hashing function is only meant to be used internally by the class, we put an underscore(_) at the beginning of the name to indicate this. This is a normal Python convention for indicating that something is meant for internal use:

```python
def _hash(self, key):
    mult = 1
    hv = 0
    for ch in key:
        hv += mult * ord(ch)
        mult += 1
    return hv % self.size
```

For the time being, we are going to assume that keys are strings. We shall discuss how one can use non-string keys later. For now, just bear in mind that the _hash() function is going to generate the hash value of a string.

Putting elements

We add elements to the hash with the put() function and retrieve with the get() function. First, we will look at the implementation of the put() function. We start by embedding the key and the value into the HashItem class and computing the hash of the key:

```python
def put(self, key, value):
    item = HashItem(key, value)
    h = self._hash(key)
```

Now we need to find an empty slot. We start at the slot that corresponds to the hash value of the key. If that slot is empty, we insert our item there.

However, if the slot is not empty and the key of the item is not the same as our current key, then we have a collision. This is where we need to figure out a way to handle a conflict. We are going to do this by adding one to the previous hash value we had and getting the remainder of dividing this value by the size of the hash table. This is a linear way of resolving collisions and it is quite simple:

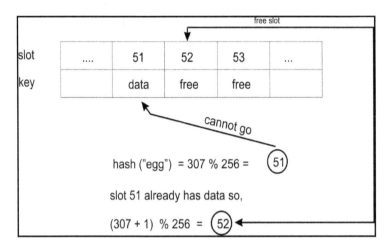

```
while self.slots[h] is not None:
    if self.slots[h].key is key:
        break
    h = (h + 1) % self.size
```

We have found our insertion point. If this is a new element (that is, it contained None previously), then we increase the count by one. Finally, we insert the item into the list at the required position:

```
if self.slots[h] is None:
    self.count += 1
self.slots[h] = item
```

Getting elements

The implementation of the get () method should return the value that corresponds to a key. We also have to decide what to do in the event that the key does not exist in the table. We start by calculating the hash of the key:

```
def get(self, key):
    h = self._hash(key)
```

Now, we simply start looking through the list for an element that has the key we are searching for, starting at the element which has the hash value of the key that was passed in. If the current element is not the correct one, then, just like in the put () method, we add one to the previous hash value and get the remainder of dividing this value by the size of the list. This becomes our new index. If we find an element that contains None, we stop looking. If we find our key, we return the value:

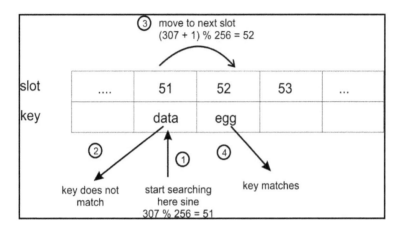

```
while self.slots[h] is not None:
    if self.slots[h].key is key:
        return self.slots[h].value
    h = (h+ 1) % self.size
```

Finally, we decide what to do if the key was not found in the table. Here we will choose to return None. Another good alternative may be to raise an exception:

```
return None
```

Testing the hash table

To test our hash table, we create a HashTable, put a few elements in it, then try to retrieve these. We will also try to get () a key that does not exist. Remember the two strings ad and ga which returned the same hash value by our hashing function? For good measure, we throw those in as well, just to see that the collision is properly resolved:

```
ht = HashTable()
ht.put("good", "eggs")
ht.put("better", "ham")
ht.put("best", "spam")
ht.put("ad", "do not")
```

```
        ht.put("ga", "collide")

        for key in ("good", "better", "best", "worst", "ad", "ga"):
            v = ht.get(key)
            print(v)
```

Running this returns the following:

```
% python hashtable.py

eggs
ham
spam
None
do not
collide
```

As you can see, looking up the key worst returns None, since the key does not exist. The keys ad and ga also return their corresponding values, showing that the collision between them is dealt with.

Using [] with the hash table

Using the put() and get() methods doesn't look very good, however. We want to be able to treat our hash table as a list, that is, we would like to be able to use ht["good"] instead of ht.get("good"). This is easily done with the special methods __setitem__() and __getitem__():

```
        def __setitem__(self, key, value):
            self.put(key, value)

        def __getitem__(self, key):
            return self.get(key)
```

Our test code can now look like this instead:

```
        ht = HashTable()
        ht["good"] = "eggs"
        ht["better"] = "ham"
        ht["best"] = "spam"
        ht["ad"] = "do not"
        ht["ga"] = "collide"

        for key in ("good", "better", "best", "worst", "ad", "ga"):
```

```
    v = ht[key]
    print(v)

print("The number of elements is: {}".format(ht.count))
```

Notice that we also print the number of elements in the hash table. This is useful for our next discussion.

Non-string keys

In most cases, it makes more sense to just use strings for the keys. However, if necessary, you could use any other Python type. If you create your own class that you want to use as a key, you will probably want to override the special __hash__() function for that class, so that you get reliable hash values.

Note that you would still have to calculate the modulo (%) of the hash value and the size of the hash table to get the slot. That calculation should happen in the hash table and not in the key class, since the table knows its own size (the key class should not know anything about the table that it belongs to).

Growing a hash table

In our example, the hash table's size was set to 256. Obviously, as we add elements to the list, we begin to fill up the empty slots. At some point, all the slots will be filled up and the table will be full. To avoid this, we can grow the table when it is getting full.

To do this, we compare the size and the count. Remember that `size` held the total number of slots and `count` the number of those slots that contained elements? Well, if `count` equals `size` then we have filled up the table.

The hash table's load factor gives us an indication of how large a portion of the available slots are being used. It is defined as follows:

$$\text{load factor} = \frac{n}{k}$$

n is the number of used slots
k is the total number of slots

As the load factor approaches 1, we need to grow the table. In fact, we should do it before it gets there in order to avoid gets becoming too slow. A value of 0.75 may be a good value in which to grow the table.

The next question is how much to grow the table by. One strategy would be to simply double the size of the table.

Open addressing

The collision resolution mechanism we used in our example, linear probing, is an example of an open addressing strategy. Linear probing is really simple since we use a fixed interval between our probes. There are other open addressing strategies as well but they all share the idea that there is an array of slots. When we want to insert a key, we check whether the slot already has an item or not. If it does, we look for the next available slot.

If we have a hash table that contains 256 slots, then 256 is the maximum number of elements in that hash. Moreover, as the load factor increases, it will take longer to find the insertion point for the new element.

Because of these limitations, we may prefer to use a different strategy to resolve collisions, such as chaining.

Chaining

Chaining is a strategy for resolving conflicts and avoiding the limit to the number of elements in a hash table. In chaining, the slots in the hash table are initialized with empty lists:

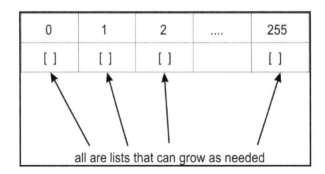

When an element is inserted, it will be appended to the list that corresponds to that element's hash value. That is, if you have two elements that both have the hash value 1167, these two elements will both be added to the list that exists in slot 1167 of the hash table:

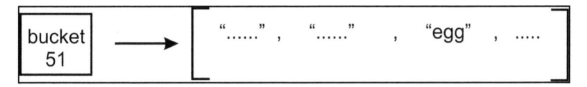

The preceding diagram shows a list of entries with hash value 51.

Chaining then avoids conflict by allowing multiple elements to have the same hash value. It also avoids the problem of insertions as the load factor increases, since we don't have to look for a slot. Moreover, the hash table can hold more values than the number of available slots, since each slot holds a list that can grow.

Of course, if a particular slot has many items, searching them can get very slow, since we have to do a linear search through the list until we find the element that has the key we want. This can slow down retrieval, which is not good, since hash tables are meant to be efficient:

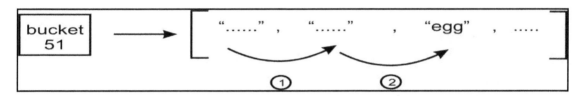

The preceding diagram demonstrates a linear search through list items until we find a match.

Instead of using lists in the table slots, we could use another structure that allows for fast searching. We have already looked at **binary search trees** (**BSTs**). We could simply put an (initially empty) BST in each slot:

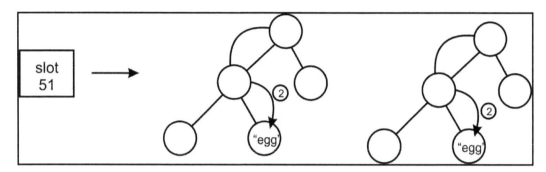

Slot 51 holds a BST which we search for the key.

But we would still have a potential problem: depending on the order in which the items were added to the BST, we could end up with a search tree that is as inefficient as a list. That is, each node in the tree has exactly one child. To avoid this, we would need to ensure that our BST is self-balancing.

Symbol tables

Symbol tables are used by compilers and interpreters to keep track of the symbols that have been declared and information about them. Symbol tables are often built using hash tables, since it is important to efficiently retrieve a symbol in the table.

Let us look at an example. Suppose we have the following Python code:

```
name = "Joe"
age = 27
```

Here we have two symbols, name and age. They belong to a namespace, which could be __main__, but it could also be the name of a module if you placed it there. Each symbol has a value; name has the value Joe and age has the value 27. A symbol table allows the compiler or the interpreter to look these values up. The symbols name and age become the keys in our hash table. All the other information associated with it, such as the value, become part of the value of the symbol table entry.

Not only variables are symbols, but functions and classes as well. They will all be added to our symbol table, so that when any one of them needs to be accessed, they are accessible from the symbol table:

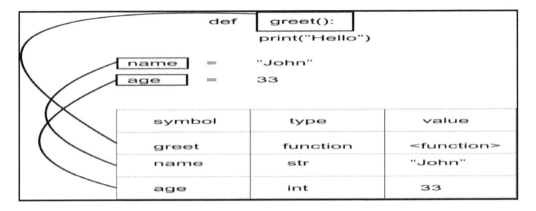

In Python, each module that is loaded has its own symbol table. The symbol table is given the name of that module. This way, modules act as namespaces. We can have multiple symbols called age, as long as they exist in different symbol tables. To access either one, we access it through the appropriate symbol table:

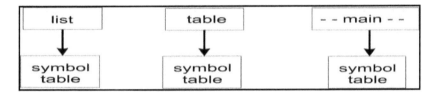

Summary

In this chapter, we have looked at hash tables. We looked at how to write a hashing function to turn string data into integer data. Then we looked at how we can use hashed keys to quickly and efficiently look up the value that corresponds to a key.

We also noticed how hashing functions are not perfect and that several strings can end up having the same hash value. This led us to look at collision resolution strategies.

We looked at growing a hash table and how to look at the load factor of the table in order to determine exactly when to grow the hash.

In the last section of the chapter, we studied symbol tables, which often are built using hash tables. Symbol tables allow a compiler or an interpreter to look up a symbol (variable, function, class, and so on) that has been defined and retrieve all information about it.

In the next chapter, we will talk about graphs and other algorithms.

8
Graphs and Other Algorithms

In this chapter, we are going to talk about graphs. This is a concept that comes from the branch of mathematics called graph theory.

Graphs are used to solve a number of computing problems. They also have much less structure than other data structures we have looked at and things like traversal can be much more unconventional, as we shall see.

By the end of this chapter, you should be able to do the following:

- Understand what graphs are
- Know the types of graphs and their constituents
- Know how to represent a graph and traverse it
- Get a fundamental idea of what priority queues are
- Be able to implement a priority queue
- Be able to determine the ith smallest element in a list

Graphs

A graph is a set of vertices and edges that form connections between the vertices. In a more formal approach, a graph G is an ordered pair of a set V of vertices and a set E of edges given as `G = (V, E)` in formal mathematical notation.

An example of a graph is given here:

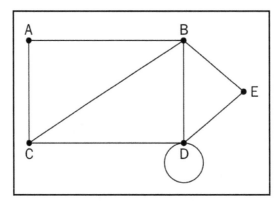

Let's now go through some definitions of a graph:

- **Node or vertex**: A point, usually represented by a dot in a graph. The vertices or nodes are A, B, C, D, and E.
- **Edge**: This is a connection between two vertices. The line connecting A and B is an example of an edge.
- **Loop**: When an edge from a node is incident on itself, that edge forms a loop.
- **Degree of a vertex**: This is the number of vertices that are incident on a given vertex. The degree of vertex B is 4.
- **Adjacency**: This refers to the connection(s) between a node and its neighbor. The node C is adjacent to node A because there is an edge between them.
- **Path**: A sequence of vertices where each adjacent pair is connected by an edge.

Directed and undirected graphs

Graphs can be classified based on whether they are undirected or directed. An undirected graph simply represents edges as lines between the nodes. There is no additional information about the relationship between the nodes than the fact that they are connected:

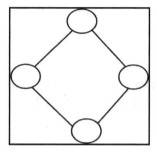

In a directed graph, the edges provide orientation in addition to connecting nodes. That is, the edges, which will be drawn as lines with an arrow, will point in which direction the edge connects the two nodes:

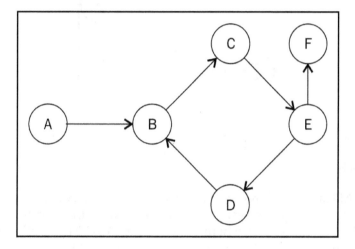

The arrow of an edge determines the flow of direction. One can only move from **A** to **B** in the preceding diagram. Not **B** to **A**.

Weighted graphs

A weighted graph adds a bit of extra information to the edges. This can be a numerical value that indicates something. Let's say, for example, that the following graph indicates different ways to get from point **A** to point **D**. You can either go straight from **A** to **D**, or choose to pass through **B** and **C**. Associated with each edge is the amount of time in minutes the journey to the next node will take:

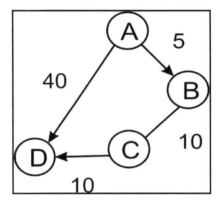

Perhaps the journey **AD** would require you to ride a bike (or walk). **B** and **C** might represent bus stops. At **B** you would have to change to a different bus. Finally, **CD** may be a short walk to reach **D**.

In this example, **AD** and **ABCD** represent two different paths. **A** path is simply a sequence of edges that you *pass through* between two nodes. Following these paths, you see that the total journey **AD** takes **40** minutes, whereas the journey **ABCD** takes **25** minutes. If your only concern is time, you would be better off traveling along **ABCD**, even with the added inconvenience of changing buses.

The fact that edges can be directed and may hold other information, such as time taken or whatever other value the move along a path is associated with, indicates something interesting. In previous data structures that we have worked with, the *lines* we have drawn between nodes have simply been connectors. Even when they had arrows pointing from a node to another, that was easy to represent in the node class by using next or previous, parent or child.

With graphs, it makes sense to see edges as objects just as much as nodes. Just like nodes, edges can contain extra information that is necessary to follow a particular path.

Graph representation

Graphs can be represented in two main forms. One way is to use an adjacency matrix and the other is to use an adjacency list.

We shall be working with the following figure to develop both types of representation for graphs:

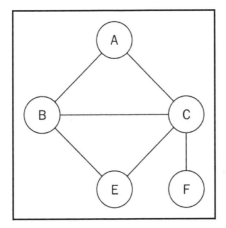

Adjacency list

A simple list can be used to present a graph. The indices of the list will represent the nodes or vertices in the graph. At each index, the adjacent nodes to that vertex can be stored:

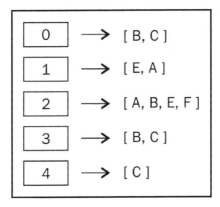

The numbers in the box represent the vertices. Index **0** represents vertex **A**, with its adjacent nodes being **B** and **C**.

Using a list for the representation is quite restrictive because we lack the ability to directly use the vertex labels. A dictionary is therefore more suited. To represent the graph in the diagram, we can use the following statements:

```
graph = dict()
graph['A'] = ['B', 'C']
graph['B'] = ['E','A']
graph['C'] = ['A', 'B', 'E','F']
graph['E'] = ['B', 'C']
graph['F'] = ['C']
```

Now we easy establish that vertex **A** has the adjacent vertices **B** and **C**. Vertex F has vertex **C** as its only neighbor.

Adjacency matrix

Another approach by which a graph can be represented is by using an adjacency matrix. A matrix is a two-dimensional array. The idea here is to represent the cells with a 1 or 0 depending on whether two vertices are connected by an edge.

Given an adjacency list, it should be possible to create an adjacency matrix. A sorted list of keys of graph is required:

```
matrix_elements = sorted(graph.keys())
cols = rows = len(matrix_elements)
```

The length of the keys is used to provide the dimensions of the matrix which are stored in `cols` and `rows`. These values in `cols` and `rows` are equal:

```
adjacency_matrix = [[0 for x in range(rows)] for y in range(cols)]
edges_list = []
```

We then set up a `cols` by `rows` array, filling it with zeros. The `edges_list` variable will store the tuples that form the edges of in the graph. For example, an edge between node A and B will be stored as (A, B).

The multidimensional array is filled using a nested for loop:

```
for key in matrix_elements:
    for neighbor in graph[key]:
        edges_list.append((key,neighbor))
```

The neighbors of a vertex are obtained by `graph[key]`. The key in combination with the `neighbor` is then used to create the tuple stored in `edges_list`.

The output of the iteration is as follows:

```
>>> [('A', 'B'), ('A', 'C'), ('B', 'E'), ('B', 'A'), ('C', 'A'),
     ('C', 'B'), ('C', 'E'), ('C', 'F'), ('E', 'B'), ('E', 'C'),
     ('F', 'C')]
```

What needs to be done now is to fill the our multidimensional array by using 1 to mark the presence of an edge with the line `adjacency_matrix[index_of_first_vertex][index_of_second_vertex] = 1`:

```
for edge in edges_list:
    index_of_first_vertex = matrix_elements.index(edge[0])
    index_of_second_vertex = matrix_elements.index(edge[1])
    adjacecy_matrix[index_of_first_vertex][index_of_second_vertex] = 1
```

The `matrix_elements` array has its `rows` and `cols` starting from A through to E with the indices 0 through to 5. The `for` loop iterates through our list of tuples and uses the `index` method to get the corresponding index where an edge is to be stored.

The adjacency matrix produced looks like so:

```
>>>
[0, 1, 1, 0, 0]
[1, 0, 0, 1, 0]
[1, 1, 0, 1, 1]
[0, 1, 1, 0, 0]
[0, 0, 1, 0, 0]
```

At column 1 and row 1, the 0 there represents the absence of an edge between A and A. On column 2 and row 3, there is an edge between C and B.

Graph traversal

Since graphs don't necessarily have an ordered structure, traversing a graph can be more involving. Traversal normally involves keeping track of which nodes or vertices have already been visited and which ones have not. A common strategy is to follow a path until a dead end is reached, then walking back up until there is a point where there is an alternative path. We can also iteratively move from one node to another in order to traverse the full graph or part of it. In the next section, we will discuss breadth and depth-first search algorithms for graph traversal.

Breadth-first search

The breadth-first search algorithm starts at a node, chooses that node or vertex as its root node, and visits the neighboring nodes, after which it explores neighbors on the next level of the graph.

Consider the following diagram as a graph:

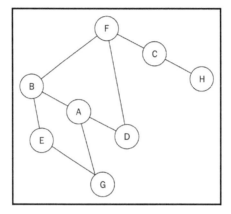

The diagram is an example of an undirected graph. We continue to use this type of graph to help make explanation easy without being too verbose.

The adjacency list for the graph is as follows:

```
graph = dict()
graph['A'] = ['B', 'G', 'D']
graph['B'] = ['A', 'F', 'E']
graph['C'] = ['F', 'H']
graph['D'] = ['F', 'A']
graph['E'] = ['B', 'G']
graph['F'] = ['B', 'D', 'C']
graph['G'] = ['A', 'E']
graph['H'] = ['C']
```

In trying to traverse this graph breadth first, we will employ the use of a queue. The algorithm creates a list to store the nodes that have been visited as the traversal process proceeds. We shall start our traversal from node A.

Node A is queued and added to the list of visited nodes. Afterward, we use a `while` loop to effect traversal of the graph. In the `while` loop, node A is dequeued. Its unvisited adjacent nodes B, G, and D are sorted in alphabetical order and queued up. The queue will now contain the nodes B, D, and G. These nodes are also added to the list of visited nodes. At this point, we start another iteration of the `while` loop because the queue is not empty, which also means we are not really done with the traversal.

Node B is dequeued. Out of its adjacent nodes A, F, and E, node A has already been visited. Therefore, we only enqueue the nodes E and F in alphabetical order. Nodes E and F are then added to the list of visited nodes.

Our queue now holds the following nodes at this point: D, G, E, and F. The list of visited nodes contains A, B, D, G, E, F.

Node D is dequeued but all of its adjacent nodes have been visited so we simply dequeue it. The next node at the front of the queue is G. We dequeue node G but we also find out that all its adjacent nodes have been visited because they are in the list of visited nodes. Node G is also dequeued. We dequeue node E too because all of its nodes have been visited. The only node in the queue now is node F.

Node F is dequeued and we realize that out of its adjacent nodes B, D, and C, only node C has not been visited. We then enqueue node C and add it to the list of visited nodes. Node C is dequeued. Node C has the adjacent nodes F and H but F has already been visited, leaving node H. Node H is enqueued and added to the list of visited nodes.

Finally, the last iteration of the `while` loop will lead to node H being dequeued. Its only adjacent node C has already been visited. Once the queue is completely empty, the loop breaks.

The output of the traversing the graph in the diagram is A, B, D, G, E, F, C, H.

The code for a breadth-first search is given as follows:

```
from collections import deque

def breadth_first_search(graph, root):
    visited_vertices = list()
    graph_queue = deque([root])
    visited_vertices.append(root)
    node = root

    while len(graph_queue) > 0:
        node = graph_queue.popleft()
        adj_nodes = graph[node]
```

```
                remaining_elements =
                    set(adj_nodes).difference(set(visited_vertices))
                if len(remaining_elements) > 0:
                    for elem in sorted(remaining_elements):
                        visited_vertices.append(elem)
                        graph_queue.append(elem)

        return visited_vertices
```

When we want to find out whether a set of nodes are in the list of visited nodes, we use the statement `remaining_elements = set(adj_nodes).difference(set(visited_vertices))`. This uses the set object's difference method to find the nodes that are in `adj_nodes` but not in `visited_vertices`.

In the worst-case scenario, each vertex or node and edge will be traversed, thus the time complexity of the algorithm is `O(|V| + |E|)`, where `|V|` is the number of vertices or nodes while `|E|` is the number of edges in the graph.

Depth-first search

As the name suggests, this algorithm traverses the depth of any particular path in the graph before traversing its breadth. As such, child nodes are visited first before sibling nodes. It works on finite graphs and requires the use of a stack to maintain the state of the algorithm:

```
    def depth_first_search(graph, root):
        visited_vertices = list()
        graph_stack = list()

        graph_stack.append(root)
        node = root
```

The algorithm begins by creating a list to store the visited nodes. The `graph_stack` stack variable is used to aid the traversal process. For continuity's sake, we are using a regular Python list as a stack.

The starting node, called `root`, is passed with the graph's adjacency matrix, graph. `root` is pushed onto the stack. `node = root` holds the first node in the stack:

```
        while len(graph_stack) > 0:

            if node not in visited_vertices:
                visited_vertices.append(node)
```

```
        adj_nodes = graph[node]


        if set(adj_nodes).issubset(set(visited_vertices)):
            graph_stack.pop()
        if len(graph_stack) > 0:
            node = graph_stack[-1]
            continue
        else:
            remaining_elements =
            set(adj_nodes).difference(set(visited_vertices))


        first_adj_node = sorted(remaining_elements)[0]
        graph_stack.append(first_adj_node)
        node = first_adj_node
            return visited_vertices
```

The body of the `while` loop will be executed provided the stack is not empty. If `node` is not in the list of visited nodes, we add it. All adjacent nodes to `node` are collected by `adj_nodes = graph[node]`. If all the adjacent nodes have been visited, we pop that node from the stack and set `node` to `graph_stack[-1]`. `graph_stack[-1]` is the top node on the stack. The `continue` statement jumps back to the beginning of the while loop's test condition.

If, on the other hand, not all the adjacent nodes have been visited, the nodes that are yet to be visited are obtained by finding the difference between the `adj_nodes` and `visited_vertices` with the statement `remaining_elements = set(adj_nodes).difference(set(visited_vertices))`.

The first item within `sorted(remaining_elements)` is assigned to `first_adj_node`, and pushed onto the stack. We then point the top of the stack to this node.

When the `while` loop exists, we will return the `visited_vertices`.

Dry running the algorithm will prove useful. Consider the following graph:

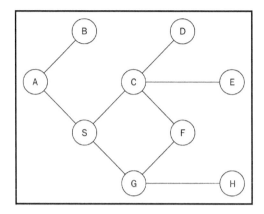

The adjacency list of such a graph is given as follows:

```
graph = dict()
graph['A'] = ['B', 'S']
graph['B'] = ['A']
graph['S'] = ['A','G','C']
graph['D'] = ['C']
graph['G'] = ['S','F','H']
graph['H'] = ['G','E']
graph['E'] = ['C','H']
graph['F'] = ['C','G']
graph['C'] = ['D','S','E','F']
```

Node A is chosen as our beginning node. Node A is pushed onto the stack and added to the `visisted_vertices` list. In doing so, we mark it as having been visited. The stack `graph_stack` is implemented with a simple Python list. Our stack now has A as its only element. We examine node A's adjacent nodes B and S. To test whether all the adjacent nodes of A have been visited, we use the if statement:

```
if set(adj_nodes).issubset(set(visited_vertices)):
    graph_stack.pop()
    if len(graph_stack) > 0:
        node = graph_stack[-1]
    continue
```

If all the nodes have been visited, we pop the top of the stack. If the stack `graph_stack` is not empty, we assign the node on top of the stack to `node` and start the beginning of another execution of the body of the `while` loop. The statement `set(adj_nodes).issubset(set(visited_vertices))` will evaluate to `True` if all the nodes in `adj_nodes` are a subset of `visited_vertices`. If the if statement fails, it means that some nodes remain to be visited. We obtain that list of nodes with `remaining_elements = set(adj_nodes).difference(set(visited_vertices))`.

From the diagram, nodes **B** and **S** will be stored in `remaining_elements`. We will access the list in alphabetical order:

```
first_adj_node = sorted(remaining_elements)[0]
graph_stack.append(first_adj_node)
node = first_adj_node
```

We sort `remaining_elements` and return the first node to `first_adj_node`. This will return B. We push node B onto the stack by appending it to the `graph_stack`. We prepare node B for access by assigning it to `node`.

On the next iteration of the `while` loop, we add node B to the list of `visited nodes`. We discover that the only adjacent node to B, which is A, has already been visited. Because all the adjacent nodes of B have been visited, we pop it off the stack, leaving node A as the only element on the stack. We return to node A and examine whether all of its adjacent nodes have been visited. The node A now has S as the only unvisited node. We push S to the stack and begin the whole process again.

The output of the traversal is A-B-S-C-D-E-H-G-F.

Depth-first searches find application in solving maze problems, finding connected components, and finding the bridges of a graph, among others.

Other useful graph methods

Very often, you are concerned with finding a path between two nodes. You may also want to find all the paths between nodes. Another useful method would be to find the shortest path between nodes. In an unweighted graph, this would simply be the path with the lowest number of edges between them. In a weighted graph, as you have seen, this could involve calculating the total weight of passing through a set of edges.

Of course, in a different situation, you may want to find the longest or shortest path.

Priority queues and heaps

A priority queue is basically a type of queue that will always return items in order of priority. This priority could be, for example, that the lowest item is always popped off first. Although it is called a queue, priority queues are often implemented using a heap, since it is very efficient for this purpose.

Consider that, in a store, customers queue in a line where service is only rendered at the front of the queue. Each customer will spend some time in the queue to get served. If the waiting times for the customers in the queue are 4, 30, 2, and 1, then the average time spent in the queue becomes (4 + 34 + 36 + 37)/4, which is 27.75. However, if we change the order of service such that customers with the least amount of waiting time are served first, then we obtain a different average waiting time. In doing so, we calculate our new average waiting time by (1 + 3 + 7 + 37)/4, which now equals 12, a better average waiting time. Clearly, there is merit to serving the customers from the least waiting time upward. This method of selecting the next item by priority or some other criterion is the basis for creating priority queues.

A heap is a data structure that satisfies the heap property. The heap property states that there must be a certain relationship between a parent node and its child nodes. This property must apply through the entire heap.

In a min heap, the relationship between parent and children is that the parent must always be less than or equal to its children. As a consequence of this, the lowest element in the heap must be the root node.

In a max heap, on the other hand, the parent is greater than or equal to its child or its children. It follows from this that the largest value makes up the root node.

As you can see from what we just mentioned, heaps are trees and, to be more specific, binary trees.

Although we are going to use a binary tree, we will actually use a list to represent it. This is possible because the heap will store a complete binary tree. A complete binary tree is one in which each row must be fully filled before starting to fill the next row:

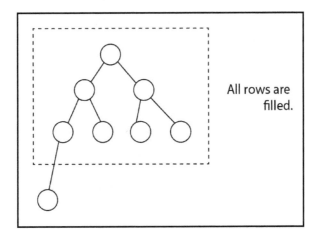

All rows are filled.

To make the math with indexes easier, we are going to leave the first item in the list (index 0) empty. After that, we place the tree nodes into the list, from top to bottom, left to right:

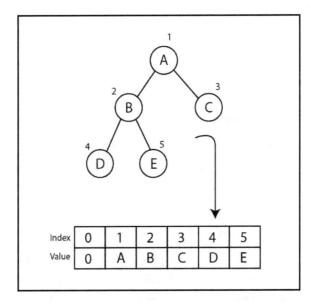

If you observe carefully, you will notice that you can retrieve the children of any node n very easily. The left child is located at $2n$ and the right child is located at $2n + 1$. This will always hold true.

We are going to look at a min heap implementation. It shouldn't be difficult to reverse the logic in order to get a max heap:

```
class Heap:
    def __init__(self):
        self.heap = [0]
        self.size = 0
```

We initialize our heap list with a zero to represent the dummy first element (remember that we are only doing this to make the math simpler). We also create a variable to hold the size of the heap. This would not be necessary as such, since we could check the size of the list, but we would always have to remember to reduce it by one. So we chose to keep a separate variable instead.

Inserting

Inserting an item is very simple in itself. We add the new element to the end of the list (which we understand to be the bottom of the tree). Then we increment the size of the heap by one.

But after each insert, we need to float the new element up if needed. Bear in mind that the lowest element in the min heap needs to be the root element. We first create a helper method called `float` that takes care of this. Let us look at how it is meant to behave. Imagine that we have the following heap and want to insert the value 2:

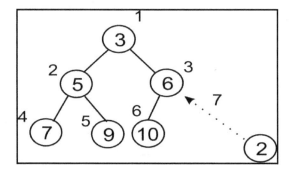

The new element has occupied the last slot in the third row or level. Its index value is **7**. Now we compare that value with its parent. The parent is at index 7/2 = 3 (integer division). That element holds **6** so we swap the **2**:

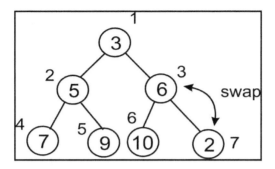

Our new element has been swapped and moved up to index **3**. We have not reached the top of the heap yet (`3 / 2 > 0`), so we continue. The new parent of our element is at index `3/2` = `1`. So we compare and, if necessary, swap again:

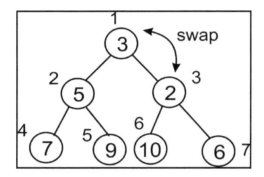

After the final swap, we are left with the heap looking as follows. Notice how it adheres to the definition of a heap:

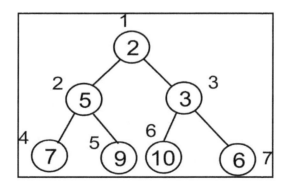

Here follows an implementation of what we have just described:

```
def float(self, k):
```

We are going to loop until we have reached the root node so that we can keep floating the element up as high as it needs to go. Since we are using integer division, as soon as we get below 2, the loop will break out:

```
while k // 2 > 0:
```

Compare parent and child. If the parent is greater than the child, swap the two values:

```
if self.heap[k] < self.heap[k//2]:
    self.heap[k], self.heap[k//2] = self.heap[k//2],
    self.heap[k]
```

Finally, let's not forget to move up the tree:

```
k //= 2
```

This method ensures that the elements are ordered properly. Now we just need to call this from our `insert` method:

```
def insert(self, item):
    self.heap.append(item)
    self.size += 1
    self.float(self.size)
```

Notice the last line in insert calls the `float()` method to reorganize the heap as necessary.

Pop

Just like insert, `pop()` is by itself a simple operation. We remove the root node and decrement the size of the heap by one. However, once the root has been popped off, we need a new root node.

To make this as simple as possible, we just take the last item in the list and make it the new root. That is, we move it to the beginning of the list. But now we might not have the lowest element at the top of the heap, so we perform the opposite of the float operation: we let the new root node sink down as required.

As we did with insert, let us have a look at how the whole operation is meant to work on an existing heap. Imagine the following heap. We pop off the `root` element, leaving the heap temporarily rootless:

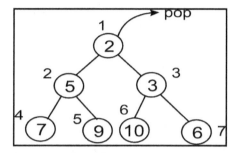

Since we cannot have a rootless heap, we need to fill this slot with something. If we choose to move up one of the children, we will have to figure out how to rebalance the entire tree structure. So instead, we do something really interesting. We move up the very last element in the list to fill the position of the `root` element:

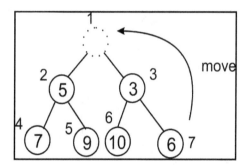

Now this element clearly is not the lowest in the heap. This is where we begin to sink it down. First we need to determine where to sink it down. We compare the two children, so that the lowest element will be the one to float up as the root sinks down:

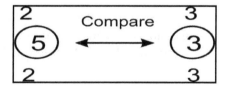

The right child is clearly less. Its index is **3**, which represents the root index `* 2 + 1`. We go ahead and compare our new root node with the value at this index:

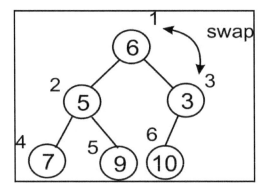

Now our node has jumped down to index **3**. We need to compare it to the lesser of its children. However, now we only have one child, so we don't need to worry about which child to compare against (for a min heap, it is always the lesser child):

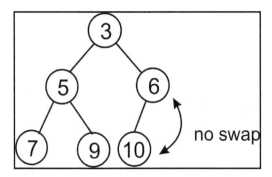

There is no need to swap here. Since there are no more rows either, we are done. Notice again how, after the `sink()` operation is completed, our heap adheres to the definition of a heap.

Now we can begin implementing this. Before we do the `sink()` method itself, notice how we need to determine which of the children to compare our parent node against. Well, let us put that selection in its own little method, just to make the code look a little simpler:

```
def minindex(self, k):
```

We may get beyond the end of the list, in which case we return the index of the left child:

```
if k * 2 + 1 > self.size:
    return k * 2
```

Otherwise, we simply return the index of the lesser of the two children:

```
elif self.heap[k*2] < self.heap[k*2+1]:
    return k * 2
else:
    return k * 2 + 1
```

Now we can create the `sink` function:

```
def sink(self, k):
```

As before, we are going to loop so that we can sink our element down as far as is needed:

```
while k * 2 <= self.size:
```

Next we need to know which of the left or the right child to compare against. This is where we make use of the `minindex()` function:

```
mi = self.minindex(k)
```

As we did in the `float()` method, we compare parent and child to see whether we need to swap:

```
if self.heap[k] > self.heap[mi]:
    self.heap[k], self.heap[mi] = self.heap[mi],
    self.heap[k]
```

And we need to make sure that we move down the tree so that we don't get stuck in a loop:

```
k = mi
```

The only thing remaining now is to implement `pop()` itself. This is very straightforward as the grunt work is performed by the `sink()` method:

```
def pop(self):
    item = self.heap[1]
    self.heap[1] = self.heap[self.size]
    self.size -= 1
    self.heap.pop()
    self.sink(1)
    return item
```

Testing the heap

Now we just need some code to test the heap. We begin by creating our heap and inserting some data:

```
h = Heap()
for i in (4, 8, 7, 2, 9, 10, 5, 1, 3, 6):
    h.insert(i)
```

We can print the heap list, just to inspect how the elements are ordered. If you redraw this as a tree structure, you should notice that it meets the required properties of a heap:

```
print(h.heap)
```

Now we will pop off the items, one at a time. Notice how the items come out in a sorted order, from lowest to highest. Also notice how the heap list changes after each pop. It is a good idea to take out a pen and paper and to redraw this list as a tree after each pop, to fully understand how the sink() method works:

```
for i in range(10):
    n = h.pop()
    print(n)
    print(h.heap)
```

In the chapter on sorting algorithms, we will reorganize the code for the heap sort algorithm.

Once you have the min heap working properly and understand how it works, it should be a simple task to implement a max heap. All you have to do is to reverse the logic.

Selection algorithms

Selection algorithms fall under a class of algorithms that seek to answer the problem of finding the ith-smallest element in a list. When a list is sorted in ascending order, the first element in the list will be the smallest item in the list. The second element in the list will be the second-smallest element in the list. The last element in the list will be the last-smallest element in the list but that will also qualify as the largest element in the list.

In creating the heap data structure, we have come to the understanding that a call to the `pop` method will return the smallest element in the heap. The first element to pop off a min heap is the first-smallest element in the list. Similarly, the seventh element to be popped off the min heap will be the seventh-smallest element in the list. Therefore, to find the ith-smallest element in a list will require us to pop the heap *i* number of times. That is a very simple and efficient way of finding the ith-smallest element in a list.

But in `Chapter 11`, *Selection Algorithms*, we will study another approach by which we can find the ith-smallest element in a list.

Selection algorithms have applications in filtering out noisy data, finding the median, smallest, and largest elements in a list, and can even be applied in computer chess programs.

Summary

Graphs and heaps have been treated in this chapter. We looked at ways to represent a graph in Python using lists and dictionaries. In order to traverse the graph, we looked at breadth-first searches and depth-first searches.

We then switched our attention to heaps and priority queues to understand their implementation. The chapter ended with using the concept of a heap to find the ith-smallest element in a list.

The subject of graphs is very complicated and just one chapter will not do justice to it. The journey with nodes will end with this chapter. The next chapter will usher us into the arena of searching and the various means by which we can efficiently search for items in lists.

9
Searching

With the data structures that have been developed in the preceding chapters, one critical operation performed on all of them is searching. In this chapter, we shall explore the different strategies that can be used to find elements in a collection of items.

One other important operation that makes use of searching is sorting. It is virtually impossible to sort without some variant of a search operation. The "how of searching" is also important as it has a bearing on how quick a sorting algorithm ends up performing.

Searching algorithms are categorized under two broad types. One category assumes that the list of items to apply the searching operation on, has already been sorted whiles the other does not.

The performance of a search operation is heavily influenced by whether the items about to be searched have already been sorted or not as we will see in the subsequent topics too.

Linear Search

Let us focus our discussions on linear search, performed on a typical Python list.

60	1	88	10	11	100
[0]	[1]	[2]	[3]	[4]	[5]

The preceding list has elements that are accessible through the list index. To find an element in the list we employ the linear searching technique. This technique traverses the list of elements, by using the index to move from the beginning of the list to the end. Each element is examined and if it does not match the search item, the next item is examined. By hopping from one item to its next, the list is traversed sequentially.

> In treating the sections in this chapter and others, we use a list with integers to enhance our understanding since integers lend themselves to easy comparison.

Unordered linear search

A list containing elements **60**, **1**, **88**, **10**, and **100** is an example of an unordered list. The items in the list have no order by magnitude. To perform a search operation on such a list, one proceeds from the very first item, compares that with the search item. If a match is not made the next element in the list is examined. This continues till we reach the last element in the list or until a match is made.

```
def search(unordered_list, term):
    unordered_list_size = len(unordered_list)
    for i in range(unordered_list_size):
        if term == unordered_list[i]:
            return i

    return None
```

The `search` function takes as parameters, the list that houses our data and the item that we are looking for called the **search term**.

The size of the array is obtained and determines the number of times the `for` loop is executed.

```
if term == unordered_list[i]:
    ...
```

On every pass of the `for` loop, we test if the search term is equal to the item that the index points to. If true, then there is no need to proceed with the search. We return the position where the match occurred.

If the loop runs to the end of the list with no match being made, `None` is returned to signify that there is no such item in the list.

In an unordered list of items, there is no guiding rule for how elements are inserted. This therefore impacts the way the search is done. The lack of order means that we cannot rely on any rule to perform the search. As such, we must visit the items in the list one after the other. As can be seen in the following image, the search for the term **66**, starts from the first element and moves to next element in the list. Thus **60** compared with **66** and if it is not equal, we compare **66** with **1, 88** and so on till we find the search term in the list.

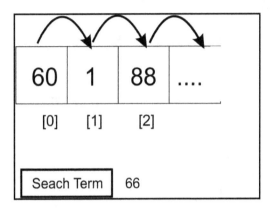

The unordered linear search has a worst case running time of O(n). All the elements may need to be visited before finding the search term. This will be the case if the search term is located at the last position of the list.

Ordered linear search

In the case where the elements of a list have been already sorted, our search algorithm can be improved. Assuming the elements have been sorted in ascending order, the search operation can take advantage of the ordered nature of the list to make search more efficient.

The algorithm is reduced to the following steps:

1. Move through the list sequentially.
2. If a search item is greater than the object or item currently under inspection in the loop, then quit and return None.

In the process of iterating through the list, if the search term is greater than the current item, then there is no need to continue with the search.

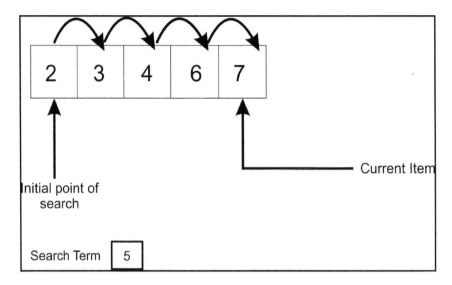

When the search operation starts and the first element is compared with (**5**), no match is made. But because there are more elements in the list the search operation moves on to examine the next element. A more compelling reason to move on is that we know the search item may match any of the elements greater than **2**.

After the 4th comparison, we come to the conclusion that the search term, can not be found in any position above where **6** is located. In other words, if the current item is greater than the search term, then it means there is no need to further search the list.

```
def search(ordered_list, term):
    ordered_list_size = len(ordered_list)
    for i in range(ordered_list_size):
        if term == ordered_list[i]:
            return i
        elif ordered_list[i] > term:
            return None

    return None
```

The `if` statement now caters for this check. The `elif` portion tests the condition where `ordered_list[i] > term`. The method returns `None` if the comparison evaluates to `True`.

The last line in the method returns `None` because the loop may go through the list and still not find any element matching the search term.

The worst case time complexity of an ordered linear search is `O(n)`. In general, this kind of search is considered inefficient especially when dealing with large data sets.

Binary search

A binary search is a search strategy used to find elements within a list by consistently reducing the amount of data to be searched and thereby increasing the rate at which the search term is found.

To use a binary search algorithm, the list to be operated on must have already been sorted.

The *binary* term carries a number of meanings and helps us put our minds in the right frame to understand the algorithm.

A binary decision has to be made at each attempt to find an item in the list. One critical decision is to guess which part of the list is likely to house the item we are looking for. Would the search term be in the first half of second half of the list, that is, if we always perceive the list as being comprised of two parts?

Instead of moving from one cell of the list to the other, if we employ the use of an educated guessing strategy, we are likely to arrive at the position where the item will be found much faster.

As an example, lets take it that we want to find the middle page of a 1000 page book. We already know that every book has its pages numbered sequentially from 1 upwards. So it figures that the 500th page should be found right at the middle of the book, instead of moving and flipping from page 1, 2 to reach the 500th page. Let's say we decide to now look for the page 250. We can still use our strategy to find the page easily. We guess that page 500 cuts the book in half. Page 250, will lay to the left of the book. No need to worry about whether we can find 250th page between page 500 and 1000 because it can never be found there. So using page 500 as reference, we can open to about half of the pages that lay between the 1st and 500th page. That brings us closer to finding the 250th page.

The following is the algorithm for conducting a binary search on an ordered list of items:

```
def binary_search(ordered_list, term):

    size_of_list = len(ordered_list) - 1

    index_of_first_element = 0
    index_of_last_element = size_of_list

    while index_of_first_element <= index_of_last_element:
```

```
mid_point = (index_of_first_element + index_of_last_element)/2

if ordered_list[mid_point] == term:
    return mid_point

if term > ordered_list[mid_point]:
    index_of_first_element = mid_point + 1
else:
    index_of_last_element = mid_point - 1

if index_of_first_element > index_of_last_element:
    return None
```

Let's assume we have to find the position where the item **10** is located in the list as follows:

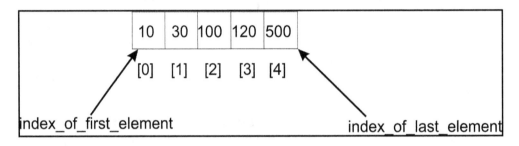

The algorithm uses a `while` loop to iteratively adjust the limits in the list within which to find a search term. So far as the difference between the starting index, `index_of_first_element` and the `index_of_last_element` index is positive, the `while` loop will run.

The algorithm first finds the mid point of the list by adding the index of the first element (**0**) to that of the last (**4**) and dividing it by **2** to find the middle index, `mid_point`.

```
mid_point = (index_of_first_element + index_of_last_element)/2
```

In this case, **10** is not found at the middle position or index in the list. If we were searching for **120**, we would have had to adjust the `index_of_first_element` to `mid_point +1`. But because **10** lies on the other side of the list, we adjust `index_of_last_element` to `mid_point-1`:

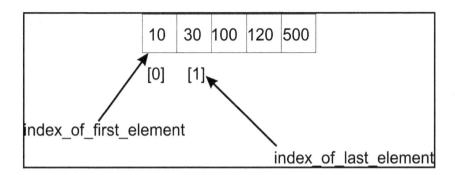

With our new index of `index_of_first_element` and `index_of_last_element` now being **0** and **1** respectively, we compute the mid `(0 + 1)/2`, which equals 0. The new midpoint is **0**, We find the middle item and compare with the search item, `ordered_list[0]` which yields the value **10**. Voila! Our search term is found.

This reduction of our list size by half, by re-adjusting the index of the `index_of_first_element` and `index_of_last_element` continues as long as `index_of_first_element` is less than `index_of_last_element`. When this fails to be the case it is most likely that our search term is not in the list.

The implementation here is an iterative one. We can also develop a recursive variant of the algorithm by applying the same principle of shifting the pointers that mark the beginning and ending of the search list.

```
def binary_search(ordered_list, first_element_index, last_element_index,
term):

    if (last_element_index < first_element_index):
        return None
    else:
        mid_point = first_element_index + ((last_element_index -
first_element_index) / 2)

        if ordered_list[mid_point] > term:
            return binary_search(ordered_list, first_element_index,
mid_point-1,term)
        elif ordered_list[mid_point] < term:
            return binary_search(ordered_list, mid_point+1,
last_element_index, term)
        else:
            return mid_point
```

A call to this recursive implementation of the binary search algorithm and its output is as follows:

```
store = [2, 4, 5, 12, 43, 54, 60, 77]
print(binary_search(store, 0, 7, 2))
```

Output:
>> 0

There only distinction between the recursive binary search and the iterative binary search is the function definition and also the way in which `mid_point` is calculated. The calculation for the `mid_point` after the `((last_element_index - first_element_index) / 2)` operation must add its result to `first_element_index`. That way we define the portion of the list to attempt the search.

The binary search algorithm has a worst time complexity of `O(log n)`. The half-ing of the list on each iteration follows a log n of the number of elements progression.

 It goes without saying that in `log` x is assumed to be referring to log base 2.

Interpolation search

There is another variant of the binary search algorithm that may closely be said to mimic more, how humans perform search on any list of items. It is still based off trying to make a good guess of where in a sorted list of items, a search item is likely to be found.

Examine the following list of items for example:

44	60	75	100	120	230	250
[0]	[1]	[2]	[3]	[4]	[5]	[6]

To find **120**, we know to look at the right hand portion of the list. Our initial treatment of binary search would typically examine the middle element first in order to determine if it matches the search term.

A more human thing would be to pick a middle element in a such a way as to not only split the array in half but to get as close as possible to the search term. The middle position was calculated for using the following rule:

```
mid_point = (index_of_first_element + index_of_last_element)/2
```

We shall replace this formula with a better one that brings us close to the search term. `mid_point` will receive the return value of the `nearest_mid` function.

```
def nearest_mid(input_list, lower_bound_index, upper_bound_index,
search_value):
    return lower_bound_index + (( upper_bound_index -lower_bound_index)/
(input_list[upper_bound_index] -input_list[lower_bound_index])) *
(search_value -input_list[lower_bound_index])
```

The `nearest_mid` function takes as arguments, the list on which to perform the search. The `lower_bound_index` and `upper_bound_index` parameters represent the bounds in the list within which we are hoping to find the search term. `search_value` represents the value being searched for.

These are used in the formula:

```
lower_bound_index + (( upper_bound_index - lower_bound_index)/
(input_list[upper_bound_index] - input_list[lower_bound_index])) *
(search_value - input_list[lower_bound_index])
```

Given our search list, **44, 60, 75, 100, 120, 230** and **250**, the `nearest_mid` will be computed with the following values:

```
lower_bound_index = 0
upper_bound_index = 6
input_list[upper_bound_index] = 250
input_list[lower_bound_index] = 44
search_value = 230
```

It can now be seen that, the `mid_point` will receive the value **5**, which is the index of the location of our search term. A binary search would have chosen **100** as the mid which will require another run of the algorithm.

A more visual illustration of how a typical binary search differs from an interpolation is given as follows. For a typical binary search finds the midpoint like so:

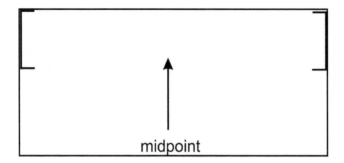

One can see that the midpoint is actually standing approximately in the middle of the preceding list. This is as a result of dividing by list 2.

An interpolation search on the other hand would move like so:

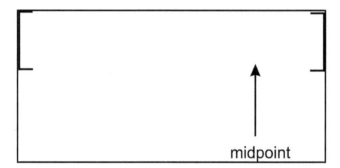

In interpolation search, our midpoint is swayed more to the left or right. This is caused by the effect of the multiplier used when dividing to obtain the midpoint. From the preceding image, our midpoint has been skewed to the right.

The remainder of the interpolation algorithm remains the same as that of the binary search except for the way the mid position is calculated for.

```
def interpolation_search(ordered_list, term):

    size_of_list = len(ordered_list) - 1

    index_of_first_element = 0
    index_of_last_element = size_of_list

    while index_of_first_element <= index_of_last_element:
```

```
        mid_point = nearest_mid(ordered_list, index_of_first_element,
index_of_last_element, term)

        if mid_point > index_of_last_element or mid_point <
index_of_first_element:
            return None

        if ordered_list[mid_point] == term:
            return mid_point

        if term > ordered_list[mid_point]:
            index_of_first_element = mid_point + 1
        else:
            index_of_last_element = mid_point - 1

    if index_of_first_element > index_of_last_element:
        return None
```

The `nearest_mid` function makes use of a multiplication operation. This can produce values that are greater than the `upper_bound_index` or lower than the `lower_bound_index`. When this occurs, it means the search term, `term`, is not in the list. `None` is therefore returned to represent this.

So what happens when `ordered_list[mid_point]` does not equal the search them? Well, we must now re-adjust the `index_of_first_element` and `index_of_last_element` such that the algorithm will focus on the part of the array that is likely to contain the search term. This is like exactly what we did in the binary search.

```
if term > ordered_list[mid_point]:
index_of_first_element = mid_point + 1
```

If the search term is greater than the value stored at `ordered_list[mid_point]`, then we only adjust the `index_of_first_element` variable to point to the index `mid_point + 1`.

The following image shows how the adjustment occurs. The `index_of_first_element` is adjusted and pointed to the index of `mid_point+1`.

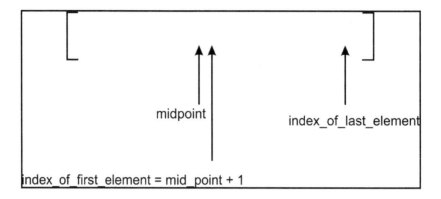

The image only illustrates the adjustment of the midpoint. In interpolation rarely does the midpoint divide the list in 2 equal halves.

On the other hand, if the search term is lesser than the value stored at `ordered_list[mid_point]`, then we only adjust the `index_of_last_element` variable to point to the index `mid_point - 1`. This logic is captured in the else part of the if statement `index_of_last_element = mid_point - 1`.

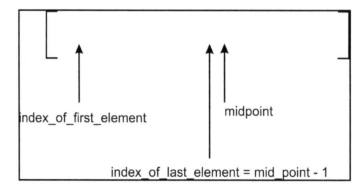

The image shows the effect of the recalculation of `index_of_last_element` on the position of the midpoint.

Let's use a more practical example to understand the inner workings of both the binary search and interpolation algorithms.

Take the list with elements:

```
[ 2, 4, 5, 12, 43, 54, 60, 77]
```

At index 0 is stored 2 and at index 7 is found the value 77. Now, assume that we want to find the element 2 in the list. How will the two different algorithms go about it?

If we pass this list to the interpolation `search` function, the `nearest_mid` function will return a value equal to 0. Just by one comparison, we would have found the search term.

On the other hand, the binary search algorithm would need three comparisons to arrive at the search term as illustrated in the following image:

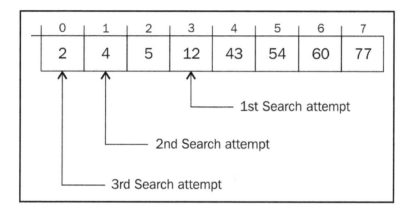

The first `mid_point` calculated is 3. The second `mid_point` is 1 and the last `mid_point` where the search term is found is 0.

Choosing a search algorithm

The binary search and interpolation search operations are better in performance than both ordered and unordered linear search functions. Because of the sequential probing of elements in the list to find the search term, ordered and unordered linear search have a time complexity of $O(n)$. This gives very poor performance when the list is large.

The binary search operation on the other hand, slices the list in two, anytime a search is attempted. On each iteration, we approach the search term much faster than in a linear strategy. The time complexity yields $O(\log n)$. Despite the speed gain in using binary search, it is most it can not be used on an unsorted list of items neither is it advised to be used for list of small sizes.

The ability to get to the portion of the list that houses a search term determines to a large extent, how well a search algorithm will perform. In the interpolation search algorithm, the mid is calculated for which gives a higher probability of obtaining our search term. The time complexity of the interpolation search is `O( log ( log n))`. This gives rise to a faster search compared to its variant, binary search.

Summary

In this chapter, we have examined two breeds of search algorithms. The implementation of both linear and binary search algorithms have been discussed and their comparisons drawn. The binary search variant, interpolation search has also been treated in this section. Knowing which kind of search operation to use will be relevant in subsequent chapters.

In our next chapter, we shall use the knowledge that we have gained to enable us perform sorting operations on a list of items.

10
Sorting

Whenever data is collected, there comes a time when it becomes necessary to sort the data. The sorting operation is common to all datasets, be it a collection of names, telephone numbers, or items on a simple to-do list.

In this chapter, we'll study a few sorting techniques, including the following:

- Bubble sort
- Insertion sort
- Selection sort
- Quick sort
- Heap sort

In our treatment of these sorting algorithms, we will take into consideration their asymptotic behavior. Some of the algorithms are relatively easy to develop but may perform poorly. Other algorithms that are a little complex to write will show impressive performance.

After sorting, it becomes much easier to conduct search operations on a collection of items. We'll start with the simplest of all sorting algorithms--the bubble sort algorithm.

Sorting algorithms

In this chapter, we will go through a number of sorting algorithms that have varying levels of difficulty of implementation. Sorting algorithms are categorized by their memory usage, complexity, recursion, whether they are comparison-based among other considerations.

Some of the algorithms use more CPU cycles and as such have bad asymptotic values. Others chew on more memory and other computing resources as they sort a number of values. Another consideration is how sorting algorithms lend themselves to being expressed recursively or iteratively or both. There are algorithms that use comparison as the basis for sorting elements. An example of this is the bubble sort algorithm. Examples of a non-comparison sorting algorithm are the buck sort and pigeonhole sort.

Bubble sort

The idea behind a bubble sort algorithm is very simple. Given an unordered list, we compare adjacent elements in the list, each time, putting in the right order of magnitude, only two elements. The algorithm hinges on a swap procedure.

Take a list with only two elements:

To sort this list, simply swap them into the right position with **2** occupying index **0** and **5** occupying index **1**. To effectively swap these elements, we need to have a temporary storage area:

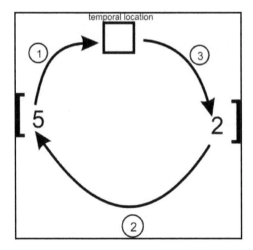

Implementation of the bubble sort algorithm starts with the swap method, illustrated in the preceding image. First, element **5** will be copied to a temporary location, `temp`. Then element **2** will be moved to index **0**. Finally, **5** will be moved from temp to index **1**. At the end of it all, the elements will have been swapped. The list will now contain the element: `[2, 5]`. The following code will swap the elements of `unordered_list[j]` with `unordered_list[j+1]` if they are not in the right order:

```
temp = unordered_list[j]
unordered_list[j] = unordered_list[j+1]
unordered_list[j+1] = temp
```

Now that we have been able to swap a two-element array, it should be simple to use this same idea to sort a whole list.

We'll run this swap operation in a double-nested loop. The inner loop is as follows:

```
for j in range(iteration_number):
    if unordered_list[j] > unordered_list[j+1]:
        temp = unordered_list[j]
        unordered_list[j] = unordered_list[j+1]
        unordered_list[j+1] = temp
```

Knowing how many times to swap is important when implementing a bubble sort algorithm. To sort a list of numbers such as `[3, 2, 1]`, we need to swap the elements a maximum of twice. This is equal to the length of the list minus 1, `iteration_number = len(unordered_list)-1`. We subtract 1 because it gives us exactly the maximum number of iterations to run:

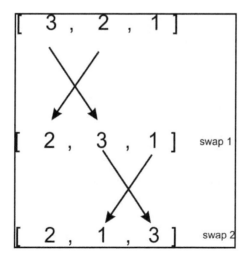

By swapping the adjacent elements in exactly two iterations, the largest number ends up at the last position on the list.

The if statement makes sure that no needless swaps occur if two adjacent elements are already in the right order. The inner for loop only causes the swapping of adjacent elements to occur exactly twice in our list.

However, you'll realize that the running of the for loop for the first time does not entirely sort our list. How many times does this swapping operation have to occur in order for the entire list to be sorted? If we repeat the whole process of swapping the adjacent elements a number of times, the list will be sorted. An outer loop is used to make this happen. The swapping of elements in the list results in the following dynamics:

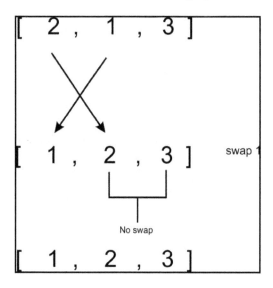

We recognize that a total of four comparisons at most were needed to get our list sorted. Therefore, both inner and outer loops have to run len(unordered_list)-1 times for all elements to be sorted:

```
iteration_number = len(unordered_list)-1
    for i in range(iteration_number):
        for j in range(iteration_number):
            if unordered_list[j] > unordered_list[j+1]:
                temp = unordered_list[j]
                unordered_list[j] = unordered_list[j+1]
                unordered_list[j+1] = temp
```

The same principle is used even if the list contains many elements. There are a lot of variations of the bubble sort too that minimize the number of iterations and comparisons.

The bubble sort is a highly inefficient sorting algorithm with a time complexity of `O(n2)` and best case of `O(n)`. Generally, the bubble sort algorithm should not be used to sort large lists. However, on relatively small lists, it performs fairly well.

There is a variant of the bubble sort algorithm where if there is no comparison within the inner loop, we simply quit the entire sorting process. The absence of the need to swap elements in the inner loop suggests the list has already been sorted. In a way, this can help speed up the generally considered slow algorithm.

Insertion sort

The idea of swapping adjacent elements to sort a list of items can also be used to implement the insertion sort. In the insertion sort algorithm, we assume that a certain portion of the list has already been sorted, while the other portion remains unsorted. With this assumption, we move through the unsorted portion of the list, picking one element at a time. With this element, we go through the sorted portion of the list and insert it in the right order so that the sorted portion of the list remains sorted. That is a lot of grammar. Let's walk through the explanation with an example.

Consider the following array:

5	1	100	2	10
0	1	2	3	4

The algorithm starts by using a `for` loop to run between the indexes **1** and **4**. We start from index **1** because we assume the sub-array with index **0** to already be in the sorted order:

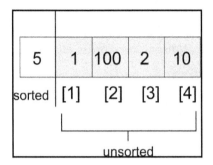

At the start of the execution of the loop, we have the following:

```
for index in range(1, len(unsorted_list)):
    search_index = index
    insert_value = unsorted_list[index]
```

At the beginning of the execution of each run of the `for` loop, the element at `unsorted_list[index]` is stored in the `insert_value` variable. Later, when we find the appropriate position in the sorted portion of the list, `insert_value` will be stored at that index or location:

```
for index in range(1, len(unsorted_list)):
    search_index = index
    insert_value = unsorted_list[index]

    while search_index > 0 and unsorted_list[search_index-1] >
            insert_value :
        unsorted_list[search_index] = unsorted_list[search_index-1]
        search_index -= 1

    unsorted_list[search_index] = insert_value
```

The `search_index` is used to provide information to the `while` loop--exactly where to find the next element that needs to be inserted in the sorted portion of the list.

The `while` loop traverses the list backwards, guided by two conditions: first, if `search_index > 0`, then it means that there are more elements in the sorted portion of the list; second, for the `while` loop to run, `unsorted_list[search_index-1]` must be greater than the `insert_value`. The `unsorted_list[search_index-1]` array will do either of the following things:

- Point to the element just before the `unsorted_list[search_index]` before the `while` loop is executed the first time
- Point to one element before `unsorted_list[search_index-1]` after the `while` loop has been run the first time

In our list example, the `while` loop will be executed because `5 > 1`. In the body of the while loop, the element at `unsorted_list[search_index-1]` is stored at `unsorted_list[search_index]`. `search_index -= 1` moves the list traversal backwards till it bears the value `0`.

Our list now looks like this:

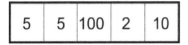

After the `while` loop exits, the last known position of `search_index` (which in this case is `0`) now helps us to know where to insert `insert_value`:

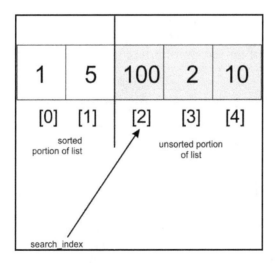

On the second iteration of the `for` loop, `search_index` will have the value **2**, which is the index of the third element in the array. At this point, we start our comparison in the direction to the left (towards index 0). **100** will be compared with **5** but because **100** is greater than **5**, the while loop will not be executed. **100** will be replaced by itself because the `search_index` variable never got decremented. As such, `unsorted_list[search_index]` = `insert_value` will have no effect.

When `search_index` is pointing at index **3**, we compare **2** with **100** and move **100** to where **2** is stored. We then compare **2** with **5** and move **5** to where **100** was initially stored. At this point, the `while` loop will break and **2** will be stored in index **1**. The array will be partially sorted with the values [1, 2, 5, 100, 10].

The preceding step will occur one last time for the list to be sorted.

The insertion sort algorithm is considered stable in that it does not change the relative order of elements that have equal keys. It also only requires no more memory than what is consumed by the list because it does the swapping in-place.

Its worst case value is $O(n^2)$ and its best case is $O(n)$.

Selection sort

Another popular sorting algorithm is the selection sort. This sorting algorithm is simple to understand, yet also inefficient, with its worst and best asymptotic values being $O(n^2)$. It begins by finding the smallest element in an array and interchanging it with data at, for instance, array index [0]. The same operation is done a second time; however, the smallest element in the remainder of the list after finding the first smallest element is interchanged with the data at index [1].

In a bid to throw more light on how the algorithm works, lets sort a list of numbers:

5	2	65	10	
0	1	2	3	

Starting at index **0**, we search for the smallest item in the list that exists between index **1** and the index of the last element. When this element has been found, it is exchanged with the data found at index **0**. We simply repeat this process until the list becomes sorted.

Searching for the smallest item within the list is an incremental process:

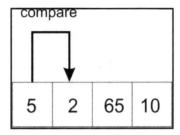

A comparison of elements **2** and **5** selects **2** as the lesser of the two. The two elements are swapped.

After the swap operation, the array looks like this:

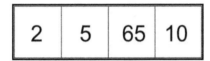

Still at index **0**, we compare **2** with **65**:

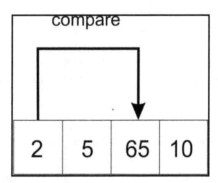

Since **65** is greater than **2**, the two elements are not swapped. A further comparison is made between the element at index **0**, which is **2**, with element at index **3**, which is **10**. No swap takes place. When we get to the last element in the list, we will have the smallest element occupying index **0**.

A new set of comparisons will begin, but this time, from index **1**. We repeat the whole process of comparing the element stored there with all the elements between index **2** through to the last index.

The first step of the second iteration will look like this:

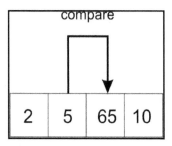

The following is an implementation of the selection sort algorithm. The argument to the function is the unsorted list of items we want to put in ascending order of magnitude:

```
def selection_sort(unsorted_list):

    size_of_list = len(unsorted_list)

    for i in range(size_of_list):
        for j in range(i+1, size_of_list):

            if unsorted_list[j] < unsorted_list[i]:
                temp = unsorted_list[i]
                unsorted_list[i] = unsorted_list[j]
                unsorted_list[j] = temp
```

The algorithm begins by using the outer `for` loop to go through the list, `size_of_list`, a number of times. Because we pass `size_of_list` to the `range` method, it will produce a sequence from **0** through to `size_of_list-1`. It is a subtle note.

The inner loop is responsible for going through the list and making the necessary swap any time that we encounter an element less than the element pointed to by `unsorted_list[i]`. Notice that the inner loop begins from `i+1` up to `size_of_list-1`. The inner loop begins its search for the smallest element between `i+1` but uses the `j` index:

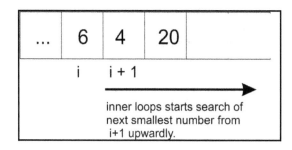

The preceding diagram shows the direction in which the algorithm searches for the next smallest item.

Quick sort

The quick sort algorithm falls under the divide and conquer class of algorithms, where we break (divide) a problem into smaller chunks that are much simpler to solve (conquer). In this case, an unsorted array is broken into sub-arrays that are partially sorted, until all elements in the list are in the right position, by which time our unsorted list will have become sorted.

List partitioning

Before we divide the list into smaller chunks, we have to partition it. This is the heart of the quick sort algorithm. To partition the array, we must first select a pivot. All the elements in the array will be compared with this pivot. At the end of the partitioning process, all elements that are less than the pivot will be to the left of the pivot, while all elements greater than the pivot will lie to the right of the pivot in the array.

Pivot selection

For the sake of simplicity, we'll take the first element in any array as the pivot. This kind of pivot selection degrades in performance, especially when sorting an already sorted list. Randomly picking the middle or last element in the array as the pivot does not improve the situation any further. In the next chapter, we will adopt a better approach to selecting the pivot in order to help us find the smallest element in a list.

Implementation

Before we delve into the code, let's run through the sorting of a list using the quick sort algorithm. The partitioning step is very important to understand so we'll tackle that operation first.

Consider the following list of integers. We shall partition this list using the partition function below:

$$[\quad 43 \quad , \quad 3 \quad , 20 \quad , \quad 89 \quad , \quad 4 \quad , 77 \quad]$$

```
def partition(unsorted_array, first_index, last_index):

    pivot = unsorted_array[first_index]
    pivot_index = first_index
    index_of_last_element = last_index

    less_than_pivot_index = index_of_last_element
    greater_than_pivot_index = first_index + 1
    . . .
```

The partition function receives the array that we need to partition as its parameters: the index of its first element and the index of its last element.

The value of the pivot is stored in the `pivot` variable, while its index is stored in `pivot_index`. We are not using `unsorted_array[0]` because when the unsorted array parameter is called with a segment of an array, index 0 will not necessarily point to the first element in that array. The index of the next element to the pivot, `first_index + 1`, marks the position where we begin to look for the element in the array that is greater than the pivot, `greater_than_pivot_index = first_index + 1`.

`less_than_pivot_index = index_of_last_element` marks the position of the last element in the list which is, where we begin the search for the element that is less than the pivot:

```
while True:

    while unsorted_array[greater_than_pivot_index] < pivot and
            greater_than_pivot_index < last_index:
        greater_than_pivot_index += 1

    while unsorted_array[less_than_pivot_index] > pivot and
            less_than_pivot_index >= first_index:
        less_than_pivot_index -= 1
```

At the beginning of the execution of the main `while` loop the array looks like this:

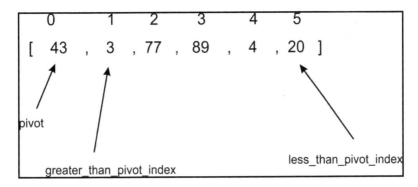

The first inner `while` loop moves one index to the right until it lands on index **2**, because the value at that index is greater than **43**. At this point, the first `while` loop breaks and does not continue. At each test of the condition in the first `while` loop, `greater_than_pivot_index += 1` is evaluated only if the `while` loop's test condition evaluates to `True`. This makes the search for the element greater than the pivot progress to the next element on the right.

The second inner `while` loop moves one index at a time to the left, until it lands on index **5**, whose value, **20**, is less than **43**:

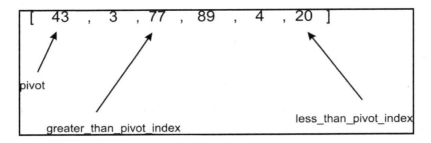

At this point, neither inner `while` loop can be executed any further:

```
if greater_than_pivot_index < less_than_pivot_index:
    temp = unsorted_array[greater_than_pivot_index]
        unsorted_array[greater_than_pivot_index] =
            unsorted_array[less_than_pivot_index]
        unsorted_array[less_than_pivot_index] = temp
else:
    break
```

Since `greater_than_pivot_index` < `less_than_pivot_index`, the body of the if statement swaps the element at those indexes. The else condition breaks the infinite loop any time `greater_than_pivot_index` becomes greater than `less_than_pivot_index`. In such a condition, it means that `greater_than_pivot_index` and `less_than_pivot_index` have crossed over each other.

Our array now looks like this:

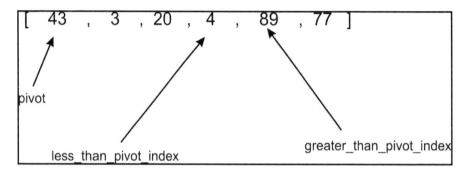

The break statement is executed when `less_than_pivot_index` is equal to 3 and `greater_than_pivot_index` is equal to 4.

As soon as we exit the `while` loop, we interchange the element at `unsorted_array[less_than_pivot_index]` with that of `less_than_pivot_index`, which is returned as the index of the pivot:

```
unsorted_array[pivot_index]=unsorted_array[less_than_pivot_index]
unsorted_array[less_than_pivot_index]=pivot
return less_than_pivot_index
```

The image below shows how the code interchanges 4 with 43 as the last step in the partitioning process:

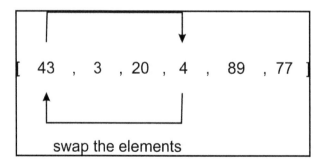

To recap, the first time the quick sort function was called, it was partitioned about the element at index **0**. After the return of the partitioning function, we obtain the array [4, 3, 20, 43, 89, 77].

As you can see, all elements to the right of element **43** are greater, while those to the left are smaller. The partitioning is complete.

Using the split point 43 with index 3, we will recursively sort the two sub-arrays [4, 30, 20] and [89, 77] using the same process we just went through.

The body of the main quick sort function is as follows:

```
def quick_sort(unsorted_array, first, last):
    if last - first <= 0:
        return
else:
    partition_point = partition(unsorted_array, first, last)
    quick_sort(unsorted_array, first, partition_point-1)
    quick_sort(unsorted_array, partition_point+1, last)
```

The quick sort function is a very simple method, no more than 6 lines of code. The heavy lifting is done by the partition function. When the partition method is called it returns the partition point. This is the point in the unsorted_array where all elements to the left are less than the pivot and all elements to its right are greater than it.

When we print the state of unsorted_array immediately after the partition progress, we see clearly how the partitioning is happening:

```
Output:
[43, 3, 20, 89, 4, 77]
[4, 3, 20, 43, 89, 77]
[3, 4, 20, 43, 89, 77]
[3, 4, 20, 43, 77, 89]
[3, 4, 20, 43, 77, 89]
```

Taking a step back, let's sort the first sub array after the first partition has happened. The partitioning of the [4, 3, 20] sub array will stop when greater_than_pivot_index is at index 2 and less_than_pivot_index is at index 1. At that point, the two markers are said to have crossed. Because greater_than_pivot_index is greater than less_than_pivot_index, further execution of the while loop will cease. Pivot 4 will be exchanged with 3, while index 1 is returned as the partition point.

The quick sort algorithm has a $O(n^2)$ worst case complexity, but it is efficient when sorting large amounts of data.

Heap sort

In Chapter 8, *Graphs and Other Algorithms*, we implemented the (binary) heap data structure. Our implementation always made sure that after an element has been removed or added to a heap, the heap order property is maintained by using the sink and float helper methods.

The heap data structure can be used to implement the sorting algorithm called the heap sort. As a recap, let's create a simple heap with the following items:

```
h = Heap()
unsorted_list = [4, 8, 7, 2, 9, 10, 5, 1, 3, 6]
for i in unsorted_list:
    h.insert(i)
print("Unsorted list: {}".format(unsorted_list))
```

The heap, h, is created and the elements in the unsorted_list are inserted. After each method call to insert, the heap order property is restored by the subsequent call to the float method. After loop has terminated, at the top of our heap will be element 4.

The number of elements in our heap is 10. If we call the pop method on the heap object h, 10 times and store the actual elements being popped, we end up with a sorted list. After each pop operation, the heap is readjusted to maintain the heap order property.

The heap_sort method is as follows:

```
class Heap:
    ...
    def heap_sort(self):
        sorted_list = []
        for node in range(self.size):
            n = self.pop()
            sorted_list.append(n)

        return sorted_list
```

The for loop simply calls the pop method self.size number of times. sorted_list will contain a sorted list of items after the loop terminates.

The insert method is called *n* number of times. Together with the float method, the insert operation takes a worst case runtime of $O(n \log n)$, as does the pop method. As such, this sorting algorithm incurs a worst case runtime of $O(n \log n)$.

Summary

In this chapter, we have explored a number of sorting algorithms. Quick sort performs much better than the other sorting algorithms. Of all the algorithms discussed, quick sort preserves the index of the list that it sorts. We'll use this property in the next chapter as we explore the selection algorithms.

11
Selection Algorithms

One interesting set of algorithms related to finding elements in an unordered list of items is selection algorithms. In doing so, we shall be answering questions that have to do with selecting the median of a set of numbers and selecting the ith-smallest or -largest element in a list, among other things.

In this chapter, we will cover the following topics:

- Selection by sorting
- Randomized selection
- Deterministic selection

Selection by sorting

Items in a list may undergo statistical enquiries such as finding the mean, median, and mode values. Finding the mean and mode values do not require the list to be ordered. However, to find the median in a list of numbers, the list must first be ordered. Finding the median requires one to find the element in the middle position of the ordered list. But what if we want to find the last-smallest item in the list or the first-smallest item in the list?

To find the ith-smallest number in an unordered list of items, the index of where that item occurs is important to obtain. But because the elements have not been sorted, it is difficult to know whether the element at index 0 in a list is really the first-smallest number.

A pragmatic and obvious thing to do when dealing with unordered lists is to first sort the list. Once the list is sorted, one is assured that the zeroth element in the list will house the first-smallest element in the list. Likewise, the last element in the list will house the last-smallest element in the list.

Assume that perhaps the luxury of sorting before performing the search cannot be afforded. Is it possible to find the ith-smallest element without having to sort the list in the first place?

Randomized selection

In the previous chapter, we examined the quick sort algorithm. The quick sort algorithm allows us to sort an unordered list of items but has a way of preserving the index of elements as the sorting algorithm runs. Generally speaking, the quick sort algorithm does the following:

1. Selects a pivot.
2. Partitions the unsorted list around the pivot.
3. Recursively sorts the two halves of the partitioned list using *step 1* and *step 2*.

One interesting and important fact is that after every partitioning step, the index of the pivot will not change even after the list has become sorted. It is this property that enables us to be able to work with a not-so-fully sorted list to obtain the ith-smallest number. Because randomized selection is based on the quick sort algorithm, it is generally referred to as quick select.

Quick select

The quick select algorithm is used to obtain the ith-smallest element in an unordered list of items, in this case, numbers. We declare the main method of the algorithm as follows:

```
def quick_select(array_list, left, right, k):

    split = partition(array_list, left, right)

    if split == k:
        return array_list[split]
    elif split < k:
        return quick_select(array_list, split + 1, right, k)
    else:
        return quick_select(array_list, left, split-1, k)
```

The `quick_select` function takes as parameters the index of the first element in the list as well as the last. The ith element is specified by the third parameter `k`. Values greater or equal to zero (0) are allowed in such a way that when `k` is 0, we know to search for the first-smallest item in the list. Others like to treat the `k` parameter so that it maps directly with the index that the user is searching for, so that the first-smallest number maps to the 0 index of a sorted list. It's all a matter of preference.

A method call to the partition function, `split = partition(array_list, left, right)`, returns the `split` index. This index of `split` array is the position in the unordered list where all elements between `right` to `split-1` are less than the element contained in the array `split`, while all elements between `split+1` to `left` are greater.

When the `partition` function returns the `split` value, we compare it with `k` to find out if the `split` corresponds to the kth items.

If `split` is less than `k`, then it means that the kth-smallest item should exist or be found between `split+1` and `right`:

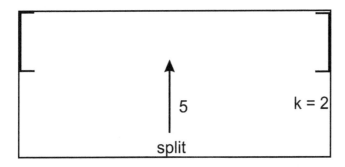

In the preceding example, a split within an imaginary unordered list occurs at index 5, while we are searching for the second-smallest number. Since 5<2 yields `false`, a recursive call to return `quick_select(array_list, left, split-1, k)` is made so that the other half of the list is searched:

If the `split` index was less than `k`, then we would make a call to `quick_select` like this:

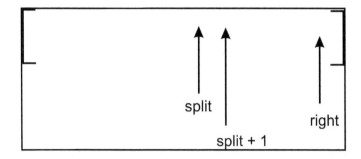

Partition step

The partition step is exactly like we had in the quick sort algorithm. There are a couple of things worthy of note:

```
def partition(unsorted_array, first_index, last_index):
    if first_index == last_index:
        return first_index

    pivot = unsorted_array[first_index]
    pivot_index = first_index
    index_of_last_element = last_index

    less_than_pivot_index = index_of_last_element
    greater_than_pivot_index = first_index + 1

    while True:

        while unsorted_array[greater_than_pivot_index] < pivot and
            greater_than_pivot_index < last_index:
            greater_than_pivot_index += 1
        while unsorted_array[less_than_pivot_index] > pivot and
            less_than_pivot_index >= first_index:
            less_than_pivot_index -= 1

        if greater_than_pivot_index < less_than_pivot_index:
            temp = unsorted_array[greater_than_pivot_index]
            unsorted_array[greater_than_pivot_index] =
                unsorted_array[less_than_pivot_index]
            unsorted_array[less_than_pivot_index] = temp
        else:
            break
```

```
unsorted_array[pivot_index] =
    unsorted_array[less_than_pivot_index]
unsorted_array[less_than_pivot_index] = pivot

return less_than_pivot_index
```

An if statement has been inserted at the beginning of the function definition to cater for situations where `first_index` is equal to `last_index`. In such cases, it means there is only one element in our sublist. We therefore simply return any of the function parameters, in this case, `first_index`.

The first element is always chosen as the pivot. This choice to make the first element the pivot is a random decision. It often does not yield a good split and subsequently a good partition. However, the ith element will eventually be found even though the pivot is chosen at random.

The `partition` function returns the pivot index pointed to by `less_than_pivot_index`, as we saw in the preceding chapter.

From this point on, you will need to follow the program execution with a pencil and paper to get a better feel of how the split variable is being used to determine the section of the list to search for the ith-smallest item.

Deterministic selection

The worst-case performance of a randomized selection algorithm is $O(n^2)$. It is possible to improve on a section of the randomized selection algorithm to obtain a worst-case performance of $O(n)$. This kind of algorithm is called **deterministic selection**.

The general approach to the deterministic algorithm is listed here:

1. Select a pivot:
    1. Split a list of unordered items into groups of five elements each.
    2. Sort and find the median of all the groups.
    3. Repeat *step 1* and *step 2* recursively to obtain the true median of the list.
2. Use the true median to partition the list of unordered items.
3. Recurse into the part of the partitioned list that may contain the ith-smallest element.

Pivot selection

Previously, in the random selection algorithm, we selected the first element as the pivot. We shall replace that step with a sequence of steps that enables us to obtain the true or approximate median. This will improve the partitioning of the list about the pivot:

```
def partition(unsorted_array, first_index, last_index):

    if first_index == last_index:
        return first_index
    else:
        nearest_median =
        median_of_medians(unsorted_array[first_index:last_index])

    index_of_nearest_median =
        get_index_of_nearest_median(unsorted_array, first_index,
                                    last_index, nearest_median)

    swap(unsorted_array, first_index, index_of_nearest_median)

    pivot = unsorted_array[first_index]
    pivot_index = first_index
    index_of_last_element = last_index

    less_than_pivot_index = index_of_last_element
    greater_than_pivot_index = first_index + 1
```

Let's now study the code for the partition function. The `nearest_median` variable stores the true or approximate median of a given list:

```
def partition(unsorted_array, first_index, last_index):

    if first_index == last_index:
        return first_index
    else:
        nearest_median =
        median_of_medians(unsorted_array[first_index:last_index])
    ....
```

If the `unsorted_array` parameter has only one element, `first_index` and `last_index` will be equal. `first_index` is therefore returned anyway.

However, if the list size is greater than one, we call the `median_of_medians` function with the section of the array, demarcated by `first_index` and `last_index`. The return value is yet again stored in `nearest_median`.

Median of medians

The `median_of_medians` function is responsible for finding the approximate median of any given list of items. The function uses recursion to return the true median:

```
def median_of_medians(elems):

    sublists = [elems[j:j+5] for j in range(0, len(elems), 5)]

    medians = []
    for sublist in sublists:
        medians.append(sorted(sublist)[len(sublist)/2])

    if len(medians) <= 5:
        return sorted(medians)[len(medians)/2]
    else:
        return median_of_medians(medians)
```

The function begins by splitting the list, `elems`, into groups of five elements each. This means that if `elems` contains 100 items, there will be 20 groups created by the statement `sublists = [elems[j:j+5] for j in range(0, len(elems), 5)]`, with each containing exactly five elements or fewer:

```
medians = []
    for sublist in sublists:
        medians.append(sorted(sublist)[len(sublist)/2])
```

An empty array is created and assigned to `medians`, which stores the medians in each of the five element arrays assigned to `sublists`.

The for loop iterates over the list of lists inside `sublists`. Each sublist is sorted, the median found, and stored in the `medians` list.

The `medians.append(sorted(sublist)[len(sublist)/2])` statement will sort the list and obtain the element stored in its middle index. This becomes the median of the five-element list. The use of an existing sorting function will not impact the performance of the algorithm due to the list's small size.

We understood from the outset that we would not sort the list in order to find the ith-smallest element, so why employ Python's sorted method? Well, since we are sorting a very small list of five elements or fewer, the impact of that operation on the overall performance of the algorithm is considered negligible.

Thereafter, if the list now contains five or fewer elements, we shall sort the `medians` list and return the element located in its middle index:

```
if len(medians) <= 5:
        return sorted(medians)[len(medians)/2]
```

If, on the other hand, the size of the list is greater than five, we recursively call the `median_of_medians` function again, supplying it with the list of the medians stored in `medians`.

Take, for instance, the following list of numbers:

[2, 3, 5, 4, 1, 12, 11, 13, 16, 7, 8, 6, 10, 9, 17, 15, 19, 20, 18, 23, 21, 22, 25, 24, 14]

We can break this list into groups of five elements each with the code statement `sublists = [elems[j:j+5] for j in range(0, len(elems), 5)]`, to obtain the following list:

[[2, 3, 5, 4, 1], [12, 11, 13, 16, 7], [8, 6, 10, 9, 17], [15, 19, 20, 18, 23], [21, 22, 25, 24, 14]]

Sorting each of the five-element lists and obtaining their medians produces the following list:

[3, 12, 9, 19, 22]

Since the list is five elements in size, we only return the median of the sorted list, or we would have made another call to the `median_of_median` function.

Partitioning step

Now that we have obtained the approximate median, the `get_index_of_nearest_median` function takes the bounds of the list indicated by the `first` and `last` parameters:

```
def get_index_of_nearest_median(array_list, first, second, median):
        if first == second:
            return first
        else:
            return first + array_list[first:second].index(median)
```

Once again, we only return the first index if there is only one element in the list. The `arraylist[first:second]` returns an array with index 0 up to the size of the `list` -1. When we find the index of the median, we lose the portion in the list where it occurs because of the new range indexing the `[first:second]` code returns. Therefore, we must add whatever index is returned by `arraylist[first:second]` to `first` to obtain the true index where the median was found:

```
swap(unsorted_array, first_index, index_of_nearest_median)
```

We then swap the first element in `unsorted_array` with `index_of_nearest_median`, using the swap function.

The utility function to swap two array elements is shown here:

```
def swap(array_list, first, second):
    temp = array_list[first]
    array_list[first] = array_list[second]
    array_list[second] = temp
```

Our approximate median is now stored at `first_index` of the unsorted list.

The partition function continues as it would in the code of the quick select algorithm. After the partitioning step, the array looks like this:

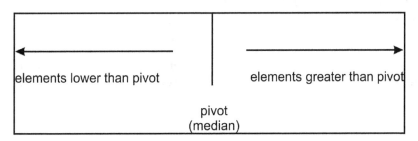

```
def deterministic_select(array_list, left, right, k):

    split = partition(array_list, left, right)


    if split == k:
        return array_list[split]
    elif split < k :
        return deterministic_select(array_list, split + 1, right, k)
    else:
        return deterministic_select(array_list, left, split-1, k)
```

As you will have already observed, the main function of the deterministic selection algorithm looks exactly the same as its random selection counterpart. After the initial `array_list` has been partitioned about the approximate median, a comparison with the kth element is made.

If `split` is less than `k`, then a recursive call to `deterministic_select(array_list, split + 1, right, k)` is made. This will look for the kth element in that half of the array. Otherwise the function call to `deterministic_select(array_list, left, split-1, k)` is made.

Summary

This chapter has examined ways to answer the question of how to find the ith-smallest element in a list. The trivial solution of simply sorting a list to perform the operation of finding the ith-smallest has been explored.

There is also the possibility of not necessarily sorting the list before we can determine the ith-smallest element. The random selection algorithm allows us to modify the quick sort algorithm to determine the ith-smallest element.

To further improve upon the random selection algorithm so that we can obtain a time complexity of $O(n)$, we embark on finding the median of medians to enable us find a good split during partitioning.

In the next chapter, we will explore the world of strings. We will learn how to efficiently store and manipulate large amounts of text. Data structures and common string operations will be covered too.

12
Design Techniques and Strategies

In this chapter, we will take a step back and look into the broader topics in computer algorithm design. As your experience with programming grows, certain patterns begin to become apparent to you. And just like with any other skilled trade, you cannot do without some techniques and principles to achieve the means. In the world of algorithms, there are a plethora of these techniques and design principles. A working knowledge and mastery of these techniques is required to tackle harder problems in the field.

We will look at the ways in which algorithms are generally classified. Other design techniques will be treated alongside implementation of some of the algorithms.

The aim of this chapter is not to make you a pro at algorithm design and strategy but to unveil the large expanse of algorithms in a few pages.

Classification of algorithms

There exist a number of classification schemes that are based on the goal that an algorithm has to achieve. In the previous chapters, we implemented a number of algorithms. One question that may arise is, do these algorithms share the same form? If yes, what are the similarities and characteristics being used as the basis? If no, can the algorithms be grouped into classes?

These are the questions we will examine as we tackle the major modes of classifying algorithms.

Classification by implementation

When translating a series of steps or processes into a working algorithm, there are a number of forms that it may take. The heart of the algorithm may employ some assets, described further in this section.

Recursion

Recursive algorithms are the ones that make calls to themselves until a certain condition is satisfied. Some problems are more easily expressed by implementing their solution through recursion. One classic example is the Towers of Hanoi. There are also different types of recursive algorithms, some of which include single and multiple recursion, indirect recursion, anonymous recursion, and generative recursion. An iterative algorithm, on the other hand, uses a series of steps or a repetitive construct to formulate a solution. This repetitive construct could be a simple `while` loop or any other kind of loop. Iterative solutions also come to mind more easily than their recursive implementations.

Logical

One implementation of an algorithm is expressing it as a controlled logical deduction. This logic component is comprised of the axioms that will be used in the computation. The control component determines the manner in which deduction is applied to the axioms. This is expressed in the form *algorithm = logic + control*. This forms the basis of the logic programming paradigm.

The logic component determines the meaning of the algorithm. The control component only affects its efficiency. Without modifying the logic, the efficiency can be improved by improving the control component.

Serial or parallel

The RAM model of most computers allows for the assumption that computing is done one instruction at a time.

Serial algorithms, also known as **sequential algorithms**, are algorithms that are executed sequentially. Execution commences from start to finish without any other execution procedure.

To be able to process several instructions at once, a different model or computing technique is required. Parallel algorithms perform more than one operation at a time. In the PRAM model, there are serial processors that share a global memory. The processors can also perform various arithmetic and logical operations in parallel. This enables the execution of several instructions at one time.

The parallel/distributed algorithms divide a problem into subproblems among its processors to collect the results. Some sorting algorithms can be efficiently parallelized, while iterative algorithms are generally parallelizable.

Deterministic versus nondeterministic algorithms

Deterministic algorithms will produce the same output without fail every time the algorithm is run with the same input. There are some sets of problems that are so complex in the design of their solutions that expressing their solution in a deterministic way can be a challenge. Nondeterministic algorithms can change the order of execution or some internal subprocess that leads to a change in the final result any time the algorithm is run. As such, with every run of a nondeterministic algorithm, the output of the algorithm is different. For instance, an algorithm that makes use of a probabilistic value will yield different outputs on successive execution depending on the value of the random number generated.

Classification by complexity

To determine the complexity of an algorithm is to try to estimate how much space (memory) and time is used overall during the computation or program execution.

Chapter 3, *Principles of Algorithm Design*, presents more comprehensive coverage of the subject matter on complexity. We will summarize what we learned there here.

Complexity curves

Now consider a problem of magnitude n. To determine the time complexity of an algorithm, we denote it with $T(n)$. The value may fall under $O(1)$, $O(log\ n)$, $O(n)$, $O(n\ log(n))$, $O(n^2)$, $O(n^3)$, or $O(2^n)$. Depending on the steps an algorithm performs, the time complexity may or may not be affected. The notation $O(n)$ captures the growth rate of an algorithm.

Let's now examine a practical scenario. By which means do we arrive at the conclusion that the bubble sort algorithm is slower than the quick sort algorithm? Or in general, how do we measure the efficiency of one algorithm against the other? Well, we can compare the Big O of any number of algorithms to determine their efficiency. It is this approach that gives us a time measure or the growth rate, which charts the behavior of the algorithm as n gets bigger.

Here is a graph of the different runtimes that an algorithm's performance may fall under:

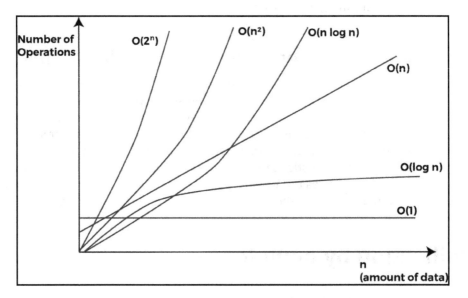

In ascending order, the list of runtimes from better to worse is given as $O(1)$, $O(\log n)$, $O(n)$, $O(n \log n)$, $O(n^2)$, $O(n^3)$, and $O(2^n)$.

Classification by design

In this section, we will present the categories of algorithms based on the design of the various algorithms used in solving problems.

A given problem may have a number of solutions. When the algorithms of these solutions are analyzed, it becomes evident that some implement a certain technique or pattern. It is these techniques that we will discuss here, and in a later section, in greater detail.

Divide and conquer

This approach to problem-solving is just as its name suggests. To solve (conquer) certain problems, this algorithm divides the problem into subproblems identical to the original problem that can easily be solved. Solutions to the subproblems are combined in such a way that the final solution is the solution of the origin problem.

The way in which the problems are broken down into smaller chunks is mostly by recursion. We will examine this technique in detail in the upcoming sections. Some algorithms that use this technique include merge sort, quick sort, and binary search.

Dynamic programming

This technique is similar to divide and conquer, in that a problem is broken down into smaller problems. In divide and conquer, each subproblem has to be solved before its results can be used to solve bigger problems. By contrast, dynamic programming does not compute the solution to an already encountered subproblem. Rather, it uses a remembering technique to avoid the recomputation.

Dynamic programming problems have two characteristics: **optimal substructure** and **overlapping subproblem**. We will talk more on this in the next section.

Greedy algorithms

For a certain category of problems, determining the best solution is really difficult. To make up for the lack of optimal solution, we resort to an approach where we select out of a bunch of options or choices the closest solution that is the most promising in obtaining a solution.

Greedy algorithms are much easier to conceive because the guiding rule is for one to always select the solution that yields the most benefit and continue doing that, hoping to reach a perfect solution.

This technique aims to find a global optimal final solution by making a series of local optimal choices. The local optimal choice seems to lead to the solution. In real life, most of those local optimal choices made are suboptimal. As such, most greedy algorithms have a poor asymptotic time complexity.

Technical implementation

Let's dig into the implementation of some of the theoretical programming techniques that we discussed previously in this chapter. We will start with dynamic programming.

Dynamic programming

As we have already described, in this approach, we divide a problem into smaller subproblems. In finding the solutions to the subprograms, care is taken not to recompute any of the previously encountered subproblems.

This sounds a bit like recursion, but things are a little broader here. A problem may lend itself to being solved by using dynamic programming but will not necessarily take the form of making recursive calls.

A property of a problem that will make it an ideal candidate for being solved with dynamic programming is that it should have an overlapping set of subproblems.

Once we realize that the form of subproblems has repeated itself during computation, we need not compute it again. Instead, we return the result of a pre-computed value of that subproblem previously encountered.

To avoid a situation where we never have to re-evaluate a subproblem, we need an efficient way in which we can store the results of each subproblem. The following two techniques are readily available.

Memoization

This technique starts from the initial problem set and divides it into small subproblems. After the solution to a subprogram has been determined, we store the result to that particular subproblem. In the future, when this subproblem is encountered, we only return its pre-computed result.

Tabulation

In tabulation, we settle on an approach where we fill a table of solutions to subproblems and then combine them to solve bigger problems.

The Fibonacci series

We will use the Fibonacci series to illustrate both memoization and tabulation techniques of generating the series.

The Memoization technique

Let's generate the Fibonacci series to the fifth term:

```
1  1  2  3  5
```

A recursive style of a program to generate the sequence is as follows:

```
def fib(n):
    if n <= 2:
        return 1
    else:
        return fib(n-1) + fib(n-2)
```

The code is very simple but a little tricky to read because of the recursive calls being made that end up solving the problem.

When the base case is met, the `fib()` function returns 1. If n is equal to or less than 2, the base case is met.

If the base case is not met, we will call the `fib()` function again and this time supply the first call with `n-1` and the second with `n-2`:

```
return fib(n-1) + fib(n-2)
```

The layout of the strategy to solve the ith term in the Fibonacci sequence is as follows:

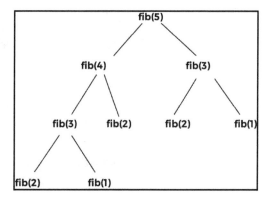

A careful observation of the preceding tree shows some interesting patterns. The call to f(1) happens twice. The call to f(1) happens thrice. Also, the call to f(3) happens twice.

The return values of the function calls to all the times that fib(2) was called never changes. The same goes for fib(1) and fib(3). The computational time is wasted since the same result is returned for the function calls with the same parameters.

These repeated calls to a function with the same parameters and output suggest that there is an overlap. Certain computations are reoccurring down in the smaller subproblems.

A better approach would be to store the results of the computation of fib(1) the first time it is encountered. This also applies to fib(2) and fib(3). Later, anytime we encounter a call to fib(1), fib(2), or fib(3), we simply return their respective results.

The diagram of our fib calls will now look like this:

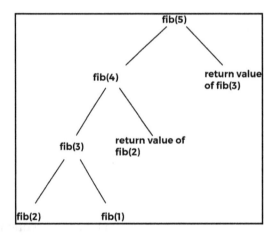

We have now completely eliminated the need to compute fib(3), fib(2), and fib(1). This typifies the memoization technique wherein breaking a problem into its subproblems, there is no recomputation of overlapping calls to functions. The overlapping function calls in our Fibonacci example are fib(1), fib(2), and fib(3):

```
def dyna_fib(n, lookup):
    if n <= 2:
        lookup[n] = 1

    if lookup[n] is None:
        lookup[n] = dyna_fib(n-1, lookup) + dyna_fib(n-2, lookup)

    return lookup[n]
```

To create a list of 1,000 elements, we do the following and pass it to the lookup parameter of the `dyna_fib` function:

```
map_set = [None]*(10000)
```

This list will store the value of the computation of the various calls to the `dyna_fib()` function:

```
if n <= 2:
    lookup[n] = 1
```

Any call to the `dyna_fib()` with n being less than or equal to 2 will return 1. When `dyna_fib(1)` is evaluated, we store the value at index 1 of `map_set`:

Write the condition for `lookup[n]`, as the following:

```
if lookup[n] is None:
    lookup[n] = dyna_fib(n-1, lookup) + dyna_fib(n-2, lookup)
```

We pass lookup so that it can be referenced when evaluating the subproblems. The calls to `dyna_fib(n-1, lookup)` and `dyna_fib(n-2, lookup)` are stored in `lookup[n]`. When we run our updated implementation of the function to find the ith term of the Fibonacci series, we realize that there is considerable improvement. This implementation runs much faster than our initial implementation. Supply the value 20 to both implementations and witness the difference in the execution speed. The algorithm sacrificed space complexity for time because of the use of memory in storing the result to the function calls.

The tabulation technique

There is a second technique in dynamic programming, which involves the use of a table of results or matrix in some cases to store results of computations for later use.

This approach solves the bigger problem by first working out a route to the final solution. In the case of the `fib()` function, we will develop a table with the values of `fib(1)` and `fib(2)` predetermined. Based on these two values, we will work our way up to `fib(n)`:

```
def fib(n):

    results = [1, 1]

    for i in range(2, n):
        results.append(results[i-1] + results[i-2])

    return results[-1]
```

The `results` variable is at index 0, and 1 the values, 1 and 1. This represents the return values of `fib(1)` and `fib(2)`. To calculate the values of the `fib()` function for higher than 2, we simply call the `for` loop appends the sum of the `results[i-1] + results[i-2]` to the list of results.

Divide and conquer

This programming approach to problem-solving emphasizes the need to break down a problem into smaller problems of the same type or form of the original problem. These subproblems are solved and combined to solve the original problem. The following three steps are associated with this kind of programming.

Divide

To divide means to break down an entity or problem. Here, we devise the means to break down the original problem into subproblems. We can achieve this through iterative or recursive calls.

Conquer

It is impossible to continue to break the problems into subproblems indefinitely. At some point, the smallest indivisible problem will return a solution. Once this happens, we can reverse our thought process and say that if we know the solution to the smallest problem possible, we can obtain the final solution to the original problem.

Merge

To obtain the final solution, we need to combine the smaller solutions to the smaller problems in order to solve the bigger problem.

There are other variants to the divide and conquer algorithm, such as merge and combine, and conquer and solve.

Algorithms that make use of the divide and conquer principle include merge sorting, quick sort, and Strassen's matrix multiplication. We will go through an implementation of the merge sort as we started earlier in `Chapter 3`, *Principles of Algorithm Design*.

Merge sort

The merge sort algorithm is based on the divide and conquer rule. Given a list of unsorted elements, we split the list into approximately two halves. We continue to divide the two halves recursively. After a while, the sublists created as a result of the recursive call will contain only one element. At that point, we begin to merge the solutions in the conquer or merge step:

```
def merge_sort(unsorted_list):
    if len(unsorted_list) == 1:
        return unsorted_list

    mid_point = int((len(unsorted_list))/2)

    first_half = unsorted_list[:mid_point]
    second_half = unsorted_list[mid_point:]

    half_a = merge_sort(first_half)
    half_b = merge_sort(second_half)

    return merge(half_a, half_b)
```

Our implementation starts by accepting the list of unsorted elements into the `merge_sort` function. The `if` statement is used to establish the base case, where if there is only one element in the `unsorted_list`, we simply return that list again. If there is more than one element in the list, we find the approximate middle using `mid_point = int((len(unsorted_list))/2)`.

Using this `mid_point`, we divide the list into two sublists, namely `first_half` and `second_half`:

```
first_half = unsorted_list[:mid_point]
second_half = unsorted_list[mid_point:]
```

A recursive call is made by passing the two sublists to the `merge_sort` function again:

```
half_a = merge_sort(first_half)
half_b = merge_sort(second_half)
```

Enter the merge step. When `half_a` and `half_b` have been passed their values, we call the merge function that will merge or combine the two solutions stored in `half_a` and `half_b`, which are lists:

```
def merge(first_sublist, second_sublist):
    i = j = 0
    merged_list = []
```

```
    while i < len(first_sublist) and j < len(second_sublist):
        if first_sublist[i] < second_sublist[j]:
            merged_list.append(first_sublist[i])
            i += 1
        else:
            merged_list.append(second_sublist[j])
            j += 1

    while i < len(first_sublist):
        merged_list.append(first_sublist[i])
        i += 1

    while j < len(second_sublist):
        merged_list.append(second_sublist[j])
        j += 1

    return merged_list
```

The merge function takes the two lists we want to merge together, `first_sublist` and `second_sublist`. The `i` and `j` variables are initialized to 0 and are used as pointers to tell us where in the two lists we are with respect to the merging process. The final `merged_list` will contain the merged list:

```
    while i < len(first_sublist) and j < len(second_sublist):
        if first_sublist[i] < second_sublist[j]:
            merged_list.append(first_sublist[i])
            i += 1
        else:
            merged_list.append(second_sublist[j])
            j += 1
```

The `while` loop starts comparing the elements in `first_sublist` and `second_sublist`. The `if` statement selects the smaller of the two, `first_sublist[i]` or `second_sublist[j]`, and appends it to `merged_list`. The `i` or `j` index is incremented to reflect the point we are at with the merging step. The `while` loop only when either sublist is empty.

There may be elements left behind in either `first_sublist` or `second_sublist`. The last two `while` loops make sure that those elements are added to the `merged_list` before it is returned.

The last call to `merge(half_a, half_b)` will return the sorted list.

Let's give the algorithm a dry run by playing the last step of merging the two sublists `[4, 6, 8]` and `[5, 7, 11, 40]`:

Step	first_sublist	second_sublist	merged_list
Step 0	[**4** 6 8]	[**5** 7 11 40]	[]
Step 1	[**6** 8]	[**5** 7 11 40]	[4]
Step 2	[**6** 8]	[**7** 11 40]	[4 5]
Step 3	[**8**]	[**7** 11 40]	[4 5 6]
Step 4	[**8**]	[**11** 40]	[4 5 6 7]
Step 5	[ ]	[**11** 40]	[4 5 6 7 8]

Note that the text in bold represents the current item referenced in the loops `first_sublist` (which uses the index i) and `second_sublist` (which uses the index j).

At this point in the execution, the third `while` loop in the merge function kicks in to move 11 and 40 into the `merged_list`. The returned `merged_list` will contain the fully sorted list.

Greedy algorithms

As we said earlier, greedy algorithms make decisions that yield the largest benefit in the interim. It is the hope of this technique that by making these high yielding benefit choices, the total path will lead to an overall good solution or end.

Examples of greedy algorithms include **Prim's algorithm** for finding the minimum spanning trees, the **Knapsack problem**, and the **Travelling Salesman problem**, just to mention a few.

Coin-counting problem

Let's examine a very simple use of this greedy technique. In some arbitrary country, we have the denominations 1 GHC, 5 GHC, and 8 GHC. Given an amount such as 12 GHC, we may want to find the least possible number of denominations needed to provide change. Using the greedy approach, we pick the largest value from our denomination to divide 12 GHC. We use 8 because it yields the best possible means by which we can reduce the amount 12 GHC into lower denominations.

The remainder, 4 GHC, cannot be divided by 5, so we try the 1 GHC denomination and realize that we can multiply it by 4 to obtain 4 GHC. At the end of the day, the least possible number of denominations to create 12 GHC is to get a one 8 GHC and four 1 GHC notes.

So far, our greedy algorithm seems to be doing pretty well. A function that returns the respective denominations is as follows:

```
def basic_small_change(denom, total_amount):
    sorted_denominations = sorted(denom, reverse=True)

    number_of_denoms = []

    for i in sorted_denominations:
        div = total_amount / i
        total_amount = total_amount % i
        if div > 0:
            number_of_denoms.append((i, div))

    return number_of_denoms
```

This greedy algorithm always starts by using the largest denomination possible. `denom` is a list of denominations. `sorted(denom, reverse=True)` will sort the list in reverse so that we can obtain the largest denomination at index 0. Now, starting from index 0 of the sorted list of denominations, `sorted_denominations`, we iterate and apply the greedy technique:

```
for i in sorted_denominations:
    div = total_amount / i
    total_amount = total_amount % i
    if div > 0:
        number_of_denoms.append((i, div))
```

The loop will run through the list of denominations. Each time the loop runs, it obtains the quotient, `div`, by dividing the `total_amount` by the current denomination, `i`. `total_amount` is updated to store the remainder for further processing. If the quotient is greater than 0, we store it in `number_of_denoms`.

Unfortunately, there are instances where our algorithm fails. For instance, when passed 14 GHS, our algorithm returns one 8 GHC and four 1 GHS. This output is, however, not the optimal solution. The right solution will be to use two 5 GHC and two 1 GHC denominations.

A better greedy algorithm is presented here. This time, the function returns a list of tuples that allow us to investigate the better results:

```
def optimal_small_change(denom, total_amount):

    sorted_denominations = sorted(denom, reverse=True)

    series = []
    for j in range(len(sorted_denominations)):
        term = sorted_denominations[j:]

        number_of_denoms = []
        local_total = total_amount
        for i in term:
            div = local_total / i
            local_total = local_total % i
            if div > 0:
                number_of_denoms.append((i, div))

        series.append(number_of_denoms)

    return series
```

The outer `for` loop enables us to limit the denominations from which we find our solution:

```
for j in range(len(sorted_denominations)):
    term = sorted_denominations[j:]
    . . .
```

Assuming that we have the list [5, 4, 3] in `sorted_denominations`, slicing it with `[j:]` helps us obtain the sublists [5, 4, 3], [4, 3], and [3], from which we try to get the right combination to create the change.

Dijkstra's shortest path algorithm

We introduce and study Dijkstra's algorithm. This algorithm is an example of a greedy algorithm. It finds the shortest distance from a source to all other nodes or vertices in a graph. By the end of this section, you will come to understand why it is classified as a greedy algorithm.

Consider the following graph:

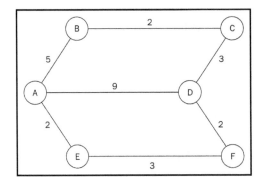

By inspection, the first answer to the question of finding the shortest path between node **A** and node **D** that comes to mind is the edge with value or distance 9. From the diagram, it would seem that the straight path from node **A** to **D** would also yield the shortest route between the two nodes. But the assumption that the edge connecting the two nodes is the shortest route does not always hold true.

This shortsighted approach of selecting the first option when solving a problem is what gives the algorithm its name and class. Having found the supposed shortest route or distance, the algorithm continues to refine and improve its results.

Other paths from node **A** to node **D** prove to be shorter than our initial pick. For instance, travelling from node **A** to node **B** to node **C** will incur a total distance of 10. But the route through node **A** to **E**, **F**, and **D** is even shorter.

We will implement the shortest path algorithm with a single source. Our result should help us determine the shortest path from the origin, which in this case is **A**, to any other node in the graph.

The shortest path from node **A** to node **C** is 7 through node **B**. Likewise, the shortest path to **F** is through node **E** with a total distance of 5.

In order to come up with an algorithm to help us find the shortest path in a graph, let's solve the problem by hand. Thereafter, we will present the working solution in Python.

In the chapter on graphs, we saw how we could represent a graph with an adjacency list. We will use it with a slight modification to enable us capture the distance on every edge. A table will be used to also keep track of the shortest distance from the source in the graph to any other node. A Python dictionary will be used to implement this table. Here is one such table:

Node	Shortest distance from source	Previous node
A	0	None
B	∞	None
C	∞	None
D	∞	None
E	∞	None
F	∞	None

The adjacency list for the diagram and table is as follows:

```
graph = dict()
graph['A'] = {'B': 5, 'D': 9, 'E': 2}
graph['B'] = {'A': 5, 'C': 2}
graph['C'] = {'B': 2, 'D': 3}
graph['D'] = {'A': 9, 'F': 2, 'C': 3}
graph['E'] = {'A': 2, 'F': 3}
graph['F'] = {'E': 3, 'D': 2}
```

The nested dictionary holds the distance and adjacent nodes.

This table forms the basis for our effort as we try to solve the problem at hand. When the algorithm starts, we have no idea what the shortest distance from the source (**A**) to any of the nodes is. To play it safe, we set the values in that column to infinity with the exception of node **A**. From the starting node, the distance covered from node **A** to node **A** is 0. So we can safely use this value as the shortest distance from node **A** to itself. No prior nodes have been visited when the algorithm begins. We therefore mark the previous node column of node as None.

In step 1 of the algorithm, we start by examining the adjacent nodes of node **A**. To find the shortest distance from node **A** to node **B**, we need to find the distance from the start node to the previous node of node B, which happens to be node **A**, and add it to the distance from node **A** to node **B**. We do this for other adjacent nodes of **A**, which are **B**, **E**, and **D**.

Using the adjacent node **B** as an example, the distance from the start node to the previous node is 0. The distance from the previous node to the current node (**B**) is 5. This sum is compared with the data in the shortest distance column of node B. Since 5 is less than infinity(∞), we replace ∞ with the smallest of the two, which is 5.

Any time the shortest distance of a node is replaced by a lesser value, we need to update the previous node column too. At the end of the first step, our table looks as follows:

Node	Shortest distance from source	Previous node
A*	0	None
B	5	A
C	∞	None
D	9	A
E	2	A
F	∞	None

At this point, node **A** is considered visited. As such, we add node **A** to the list of visited nodes. In the table, we show that node **A** has been visited by making the text bold and appending an asterisk sign to it.

In the second step, we find the node with the shortest distance using our table as a guide. Node **E** with its value 2 has the shortest distance. This is what we can infer from the table about node **E**. To get to node **E**, we must visit node **A** and cover a distance of 2. From node A, we cover a distance of 0 to get to the starting node, which is node **A** itself.

The adjacent nodes of node **E** are **A** and **F**. But node **A** has already been visited, so we only consider node **F**. To find the shortest route or distance to node **F**, we must find the distance from the starting node to node **E** and add it to the distance between node **E** and **F**. We can find the distance from the starting node to node **E** by looking at the shortest distance column of node **E**, which has the value 2. The distance from node **E** to **F** can be obtained from the adjacency list we developed in Python earlier in this section. This distance is 3. These two sum up to 5, which is less than infinity. Remember we are on examining the adjacent node **F**. Since there are more adjacent nodes of node **E**, we mark node **E** as visited. Our updated table will have the following values:

Node	Shortest distance from source	Previous node
A*	0	None
B	5	A
C	∞	None
D	9	A
E*	2	A
F	5	E

At this point, we initiate another step. The smallest value in the shortest distance column is 5. We choose **B** instead of **F** purely on an alphabetical basis. The adjacent nodes of **B** are **A** and **C**, but node **A** has already been visited. Using the rule we established earlier, the shortest distance from **A** to **C** is 7. We arrive at this number because the distance from the starting node to node **B** is 5, while the distance from node **B** to **C** is 2. Since the sum, 7, is less than infinity, we update the shortest distance to 7 and update the previous node column with node **B**. Now **B** is also marked as visited. The new state of the table is as follows:

Node	Shortest distance from source	Previous node
A*	0	None
B*	5	A
C	7	B
D	9	A
E*	2	A
F	5	E

The node with the shortest distance yet unvisited is node **F**. The adjacent nodes of **F** are nodes **D** and **E**. But node **E** has already been visited. As such, we focus on finding the shortest distance from the starting node to node **D**. We calculate this distance by adding the distance from node **A** to **F** to the distance from node **F** to **D**. This sums up to 7, which is less than 9. Thus, we update the 9 with 7 and replace **A** with **F** in node **D**'s previous node column. Node **F** is now marked as visited. Here is the updated table up to this point:

Node	Shortest distance from source	Previous node
A*	0	None
B*	5	A
C	7	B
D	7	F
E*	2	A
F*	5	E

Now, the two unvisited nodes are **C** and **D**. In alphabetical order, we choose to examine **C** because both nodes have the same shortest distance from the starting node **A**.

However, all the adjacent nodes of **C** have been visited. Thus, we have nothing to do but mark node C as visited. The table remains unchanged at this point.

Lastly, we take node **D** and find out that all its adjacent nodes have been visited too. We only mark it as visited. The table remains unchanged:

Node	Shortest distance from source	Previous node
A*	0	None
B*	5	A
C*	7	B
D*	7	F
E*	2	A
F*	5	E

Let's verify this table with our graph. From the graph, we know that the shortest distance from **A** to **F** is 5. We will need to go through **E** to get to node **F**. According to the table, the shortest distance from the source column for node **F** is the value 5. This is true. It is also tells us that to get to node **F**, we need to visit node **E**, and from **E**, node **A**, which is our starting node. This is actually the shortest path.

We begin the program for finding the shortest distance by representing the table that enables us to track the changes in our graph. For the given diagram we used, here is a dictionary representation of the table:

```
table = dict()
table = {
    'A': [0, None],
    'B': [float("inf"), None],
    'C': [float("inf"), None],
    'D': [float("inf"), None],
    'E': [float("inf"), None],
    'F': [float("inf"), None],
}
```

The initial state of the table uses `float("inf")` to represent infinity. Each key in the dictionary maps to a list. At the first index of the list is stored the shortest distance from the source A. At the second index is the stored the previous node:

```
DISTANCE = 0
PREVIOUS_NODE = 1
INFINITY = float('inf')
```

To avoid the use of magic numbers, we use the preceding constants. The shortest path column's index is referenced by `DISTANCE`. The previous node column's index is referenced by `PREVIOUS_NODE`.

Now all is set for the main function. It will take the graph, represented by the adjacency list, the table, and the starting node as parameters:

```
def find_shortest_path(graph, table, origin):
    visited_nodes = []
    current_node = origin
    starting_node = origin
```

We keep the list of visited nodes in the list, `visited_nodes`. The `current_node` and `starting_node` variables will both point to the node in the graph we choose to make our starting node. The `origin` value is the reference point for all other nodes with respect to finding the shortest path.

The heavy lifting of the whole process is accomplished by the use of a `while` loop:

```python
while True:
    adjacent_nodes = graph[current_node]
    if set(adjacent_nodes).issubset(set(visited_nodes)):
        # Nothing here to do. All adjacent nodes have been visited.
        pass
    else:
        unvisited_nodes =
            set(adjacent_nodes).difference(set(visited_nodes))

        for vertex in unvisited_nodes:

            distance_from_starting_node =
                get_shortest_distance(table, vertex)
            if distance_from_starting_node == INFINITY and
                current_node == starting_node:
                total_distance = get_distance(graph, vertex,
                                                  current_node)
            else:
                total_distance = get_shortest_distance (table,
                current_node) + get_distance(graph, current_node,
                                                  vertex)

            if total_distance < distance_from_starting_node:
                set_shortest_distance(table, vertex,
                                         total_distance)
                set_previous_node(table, vertex, current_node)

    visited_nodes.append(current_node)

    if len(visited_nodes) == len(table.keys()):
        break

    current_node = get_next_node(table,visited_nodes)
```

Let's break down what the `while` loop is doing. In the body of the `while` loop, we obtain the current node in the graph we want to investigate with the line `adjacent_nodes = graph[current_node]`. `current_node` should have been set prior. The `if` statement is used to find out whether all the adjacent nodes of `current_node` have been visited. When the `while` loop is executed the first time, `current_node` will contain A and `adjacent_nodes` will contain nodes B, D, and E. `visited_nodes` will be empty too. If all nodes have been visited, we only move on to the statements further down the program. Else, we begin a whole other step.

The statement `set(adjacent_nodes).difference(set(visited_nodes))` returns the nodes that have not been visited. The loop iterates over this list of unvisited nodes:

```
distance_from_starting_node = get_shortest_distance(table, vertex)
```

The helper method `get_shortest_distance(table, vertex)` will return the value stored in the shortest distance column of our table using one of the unvisited nodes referenced by `vertex`:

```
if distance_from_starting_node == INFINITY and current_node ==
    starting_node:
total_distance = get_distance(graph, vertex, current_node)
```

When we are examining the adjacent nodes of the starting node, `distance_from_starting_node == INFINITY and current_node == starting_node` will evaluate to True, in which case we only have to get the distance between the starting node and vertex by referencing the graph:

```
total_distance = get_distance(graph, vertex, current_node)
```

The `get_distance` method is another helper method we use to obtain the value (distance) of the edge between `vertex` and `current_node`.

If the condition fails, then we assign `total_distance` the sum of the distance from the starting node to `current_node` and the distance between `current_node` and `vertex`.

Once we have our total distance, we need to check whether this `total_distance` is less than the existing data in the shortest distance column in our table. If it is less, then we use the two helper methods to update that row:

```
if total_distance < distance_from_starting_node:
    set_shortest_distance(table, vertex, total_distance)
set_previous_node(table, vertex, current_node)
```

At this point, we add the `current_node` to the list of visited nodes:

```
visited_nodes.append(current_node)
```

If all nodes have been visited, then we must exit the `while` loop. To check whether all the nodes have been visited, we compare the length of the `visited_nodes` list to the number of keys in our table. If they have become equal, we simply exit the `while` loop.

The helper method, `get_next_node`, is used to fetch the next node to visit. It is this method that helps us find the minimum value in the shortest distance column from the starting nodes using our table.

The whole method ends by returning the updated table. To print the table, we use the following statements:

```
shortest_distance_table = find_shortest_path(graph, table, 'A')
for k in sorted(shortest_distance_table):
    print("{} - {}".format(k, shortest_distance_table[k]))
```

Output for the preceding statement:

```
>>>
A - [0, None]
B - [5, 'A']
C - [7, 'B']
D - [7, 'F']
E - [2, 'A']
F - [5, 'E']
```

For the sake of completeness, let's find out what the helper methods are doing:

```
def get_shortest_distance(table, vertex):
    shortest_distance = table[vertex][DISTANCE]
    return shortest_distance
```

The `get_shortest_distance` function returns the value stored in the zero[th] index of our table. At that index, we always store the shortest distance from the starting node up to vertex. The `set_shortest_distance` function only sets this value by the following:

```
def set_shortest_distance(table, vertex, new_distance):
    table[vertex][DISTANCE] = new_distance
```

When we update the shortest distance of a node, we update its previous node using the following method:

```
def set_previous_node(table, vertex, previous_node):
    table[vertex][PREVIOUS_NODE] = previous_node
```

Remember that the constant, `PREVIOUS_NODE`, equals 1. In the table, we store the value of the `previous_node` at `table[vertex][PREVIOUS_NODE]`.

To find the distance between any two nodes, we use the `get_distance` function:

```
def get_distance(graph, first_vertex, second_vertex):
    return graph[first_vertex][second_vertex]
```

The last helper method is the `get_next_node` function:

```
def get_next_node(table, visited_nodes):
    unvisited_nodes =
        list(set(table.keys()).difference(set(visited_nodes)))
    assumed_min = table[unvisited_nodes[0]][DISTANCE]
    min_vertex = unvisited_nodes[0]
    for node in unvisited_nodes:
        if table[node][DISTANCE] < assumed_min:
            assumed_min = table[node][DISTANCE]
            min_vertex = node

    return min_vertex
```

The `get_next_node` function resembles a function to find the smallest item in a list.

The function starts off by finding the unvisited nodes in our table by using `visited_nodes` to obtain the difference between the two sets of lists. The very first item in the list of `unvisited_nodes` is assumed to be the smallest in the shortest distance column of `table`. If a lesser value is found while the `for` loop runs, the `min_vertex` will be updated. The function then returns `min_vertex` as the unvisited vertex or node with the smallest shortest distance from the source.

The worst-case running time of Dijkstra's algorithm is $O(|E| + |V| \log |V|)$, where $|V|$ is the number of vertices and $|E|$ is the number of edges.

Complexity classes

The problems that computer algorithms try to solve fall within a range of difficulty by which their solutions are arrived at. In this section, we will discuss the complexity classes N, NP, NP-complete, and NP-hard problems.

P versus NP

The advent of computers has sped up the rate at which certain tasks are performed. In general, computers are good at perfecting the art of calculation and all problems that can be reduced to a set of mathematical computations. However, this assertion is not entirely true. There are some nature or classes of problems that just take an enormous amount of time for the computer to make a sound guess, let alone find the right solution.

In computer science, the class of problems that computers can solve within polynomial time using a step-wise process of logical steps is called P-type problems, where P stands for polynomial. These are relatively easy to solve.

Then there is another class of problems that is considered very hard to solve. The word "hard problem" is used to refer to the way in which problems increase in difficulty when trying to find a solution. However, the good thing is that despite the fact that these problems have a high growth rate of difficulty, it is possible to determine whether a proposed solution solves the problem in polynomial time. These are the NP-Type problems. NP here stands for nondeterministic polynomial time.

Now the million dollar question is, does N = NP?

The proof for $N = NP$ is one of the Millennium Prize Problems from the Clay Mathematics Institute that attract a $1,000,000 prize for a correct solution. These problems number 7 in number.

The Travelling Salesman problem is an example of an NP-Type problem. The problem statement says: given that there are n number of cities in some country, find the shortest route between all the cities, thus making the trip a cost-effective one. When the number of cities is small, this problem can be solved in a reasonable amount of time. However, when the number of cities is above any two-digit number, the time taken by the computer is remarkably long.

A lot of computer systems and cybersecurity is based on the RSA encryption algorithm. The strength of the algorithm and its security is due to the fact that it is based on the integer factoring problem, which is an NP-Type problem.

Finding the prime factors of a prime number composed of many digits is very difficult. When two large prime numbers are multiplied, a large non-prime number is obtained with only two large prime factors. Factorization of this number is where many cryptographic algorithms borrow their strength:

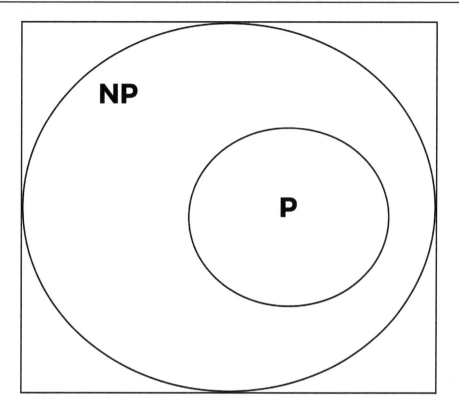

All P-type problems are subsets of NP problems. This means that any problem that can be solved in polynomial time can also be verified in polynomial time.

But the question, is P = NP? investigates whether problems that can be verified in polynomial time can also be solved in polynomial time. In particular, if they are equal, it would mean that problems that are solved by trying a number of possible solutions can be solved without the need to actually try all the possible solutions, invariably creating some sort of shortcut proof.

The proof, when finally discovered, will definitely have serious consequences in the fields of cryptography, game theory, mathematics, and many other fields.

NP-Hard

A problem is NP-Hard if all other problems in NP can be polynomial time reducible or mapped to it.

NP-Complete

A problem is considered an NP-complete problem if it is first of all an NP hard and is also found in the NP class.

Summary

In this last chapter, we looked at the theories that support the computer science field. Without the use of too much mathematical rigor, we saw some of the main categories into which algorithms are classified. Other design techniques in the field, such as the divide and conquer, dynamic programming, and greedy algorithms, were also discussed, along with sample implementations.

Lastly, one of the outstanding problems yet to be solved in the field of mathematics was tackled. We saw how the proof for P = NP? will definitely be a game-changer in a number of fields, if such a proof is ever discovered.

13
Implementations, Applications, and Tools

Learning about algorithms without any real-life application remains a purely academic pursuit. In this chapter, we will explore data structures and algorithms that are shaping our world.

One of the golden nuggets of this age is the abundance of data. E-mails, phone numbers, text, and image documents contain large amounts of data. In this data is found valuable information that makes the data become more important. But to extract this information from the raw data, we will have to use data structures, processes, and algorithms specialized for this task.

Machine learning employs a significant number of algorithms to analyze and predict the occurrence of certain variables. Analyzing data on a purely numerical basis still leaves much of the latent information buried in the raw data. Presenting data visually thus enables one to understand and gain valuable insights too.

By the end of this chapter, you should be able to do the following:

- Prune and present data accurately
- Use both supervised and unsupervised learning algorithms for the purposes of prediction
- Visually represent data in order to gain more insight

Tools of the trade

In order to proceed with this chapter, you will need to install the following packages. These packages will be used to preprocess and visually represent the data being processed. Some of the packages also contain well-written and perfected algorithms that will operate on our data.

Preferably, these modules should be installed within a virtual environment such as `pip`:

```
% pip install numpy
% pip install scikit-learn
% pip install matplotlib
% pip install pandas
% pip install textblob
```

These packages may require other platform-specific modules to be installed first. Take note and install all dependencies:

- **Numpy**: A library with functions to operate on n-dimensional arrays and matrices.
- **Scikit-learn**: A highly advanced module for machine learning. It contains a good number of algorithms for classification, regression, and clustering, among others.
- **Matplotlib**: This is a plotting library that makes use of NumPy to graph a good variety of charts, including line plots, histograms, scatter plots, and even 3D graphs.
- **Pandas**: This library deals with data manipulation and analysis.

Data preprocessing

Collection of data from the real world is fraught with massive challenges. The raw data collected is plagued with a lot of issues, so much so that we need to adopt ways to sanitize the data to make it suitable for use in further studies.

Why process raw data?

Raw data as collected from the field is rigged with human error. Data entry is a major source of error when collecting data. Even technological methods of collecting data are not spared. Inaccurate reading of devices, faulty gadgetry, and changes in environmental factors can introduce significant margins of errors as data is collected.

The data collected may also be inconsistent with other records collected over time. The existence of duplicate entries and incomplete records warrant that we treat the data in such a way as to bring out hidden and buried treasure. The raw data may also be shrouded in a sea of irrelevant data.

To clean the data up, we can totally discard irrelevant data, better known as noise. Data with missing parts or attributes can be replaced with sensible estimates. Also, where the raw data suffers from inconsistency, detecting and correcting them becomes necessary.

Let us explore how we can use NumPy and pandas for data preprocessing techniques.

Missing data

Data collection is tedious and, as such, once data is collected, it should not be easily discarded. Just because a dataset has missing fields or attributes does not mean it is not useful. Several methods can be used to fill up the nonexistent parts. One of these methods is by either using a global constant, using the mean value in the dataset, or supplying the data manually. The choice is based on the context and sensitivity of what the data is going to be used for.

Take, for instance, the following data:

```
import numpy as np
data = pandas.DataFrame([
    [4., 45., 984.],
    [np.NAN, np.NAN, 5.],
    [94., 23., 55.],
])
```

As we can see, the data elements data[1][0] and data[1][1] have values being np.NAN, representing the fact that they have no value. If the np.NAN values are undesired in a given dataset, they can be set to some constant figure.

Let's set data elements with the value np.NAN to 0.1:

```
print(data.fillna(0.1))
```

The new state of the data becomes the following:

```
     0     1      2
0   4.0  45.0  984.0
1   0.1   0.1    5.0
2  94.0  23.0   55.0
```

To apply the mean values instead, we do the following:

```
print(data.fillna(data.mean()))
```

The mean value for each column is calculated and inserted in those data areas with the `np.NAN` value:

```
     0     1      2
0   4.0   45.0   984.0
1  49.0   34.0     5.0
2  94.0   23.0    55.0
```

For the first column, column 0, the mean value was obtained by $(4 + 94)/2$. The resulting `49.0` is then stored at `data[1][0]`. A similar operation is carried out for columns 1 and 2.

Feature scaling

The columns in a data frame are known as its features. The rows are known as records or observations. Now examine the following data matrix. This data will be referenced in subsections so please do take note:

```
[[ 58.    1.   43.]
 [ 10.  200.   65.]
 [ 20.   75.    7.]]
```

Feature 1, with data 58, 10, 20, has its values lying between `10` and `58`. For feature 2, the data lies between `1` and `200`. Inconsistent results will be produced if we supply this data to any machine learning algorithm. Ideally, we will need to scale the data to a certain range in order to get consistent results.

Once again, a closer inspection reveals that each feature (or column) lies around different mean values. Therefore, what we would want to do is to align the features around similar means.

One benefit of feature scaling is that it boosts the learning parts of machine learning.

The `scikit` module has a considerable number of scaling algorithms that we shall apply to our data.

Min-max scalar

The min-max scalar form of normalization uses the mean and standard deviation to box all the data into a range lying between a certain min and max value. For most purposes, the range is set between 0 and 1. At other times, other ranges may be applied but the 0 to 1 range remains the default:

```
scaled_values = preprocessing.MinMaxScaler(feature_range=(0,1))
results = scaled_values.fit(data).transform(data)
print(results)
```

An instance of the MinMaxScaler class is created with the range (0,1) and passed to the variable scaled_values. The fit function is called to make the necessary calculations that will be used internally to change the dataset. The transform function effects the actual operation on the dataset, returning the value to results:

```
[[ 1.          0.          0.62068966]
 [ 0.          1.          1.        ]
 [ 0.20833333  0.3718593   0.        ]]
```

We can see from the preceding output that all the data is normalized and lies between 0 and 1. This kind of output can now be supplied to a machine learning algorithm.

Standard scalar

The mean values for the respective features in our initial dataset or table are 29.3, 92, and 38. To make all the data have a similar mean, that is, a zero mean and a unit variance across the data, we shall apply the standard scalar algorithm:

```
stand_scalar =  preprocessing.StandardScaler().fit(data)
results = stand_scalar.transform(data)
print(results)
```

data is passed to the fit method of the object returned from instantiating the StandardScaler class. The transform method acts on the data elements in the data and returns the output to the results:

```
[[ 1.38637564 -1.10805456  0.19519899]
 [-0.93499753  1.31505377  1.11542277]
 [-0.45137812 -0.2069992  -1.31062176]]
```

Examining the results, we observe that all our features are now evenly distributed.

Binarizing data

To binarize a given feature set, we make use of a threshold. If any value within a given dataset is greater than the threshold, the value is replaced by 1. If the value is less than the threshold 1, we will replace it:

```
results = preprocessing.Binarizer(50.0).fit(data).transform(data)
print(results)
```

An instance of `Binarizer` is created with the argument 50.0. 50.0 is the threshold that will be used in the binarizing algorithm:

```
[[ 1.   0.   0.]
 [ 0.   1.   1.]
 [ 0.   1.   0.]]
```

All values in the data that are less than 50 will have 0 in their stead. The opposite also holds true.

Machine learning

Machine learning is a subfield of artificial intelligence. We know that we can never truly create machines that actually "think" but we can supply machines with enough data and models by which sound judgment can be reached. Machine learning focuses on creating autonomous systems that can continue the process of decision making, with little or no human intervention.

In order to teach the machine, we need data drawn from the real world. For instance, to shift through which e-mails constitute spam and which ones don't, we need to feed the machine with samples of each. After obtaining this data, we have to run the data through models (algorithms) that will use probability and statistics to unearth patterns and structure from the data. If this is properly done, the algorithm by itself will be able to analyze e-mails and properly categorize them. Sorting e-mails is just one example of what machines can do if they are "trained".

Types of machine learning

There are three broad categories of machine learning, as follows:

- **Supervised learning**: Here, an algorithm is fed a set of inputs and their corresponding outputs. The algorithm then has to figure out what the output will be for an unfamiliar input. Examples of such algorithms include naive Bayes, linear regression, and decision tree algorithms.
- **Unsupervised learning**: Without using the relationship that exists between a set of input and output variables, the unsupervised learning algorithm uses only the inputs to unearth groups, patterns, and clusters within the data. Examples of such algorithms include hierarchical clustering and k-means clustering.
- **Reinforcement learning**: The computer in this kind of learning dynamically interacts with its environment in such a way as to improve its performance.

Hello classifier

To invoke the blessing of the programming gods in our quest to understand machine learning, we begin with an hello world example of a text classifier. This is meant to be a gentle introduction to machine learning.

This example will predict whether a given text carries a negative or positive connotation. Before this can be done, we need to train our algorithm (model) with some data.

The naive Bayes model is suited for text classification purposes. Algorithms based on naive Bayes models are generally fast and produce accurate results. The whole model is based on the assumption that features are independent from each other. To accurately predict the occurrence of rainfall, three conditions need to be considered. These are wind speed, temperature, and the amount of humidity in the air. In reality, these factors do have an influence on each other to tell the likelihood of rainfall. But the abstraction in naive Bayes is to assume that these features are unrelated in any way and thus independently contribute to chances of rainfall. Naive Bayes is useful in predicting the class of an unknown dataset, as we will see soon.

Now back to our hello classifier. After we have trained our mode, its prediction will fall into either the positive or negative category:

```
from textblob.classifiers import NaiveBayesClassifier
train = [
    ('I love this sandwich.', 'pos'),
    ('This is an amazing shop!', 'pos'),
    ('We feel very good about these beers.', 'pos'),
```

```
            ('That is my best sword.', 'pos'),
            ('This is an awesome post', 'pos'),
            ('I do not like this cafe', 'neg'),
            ('I am tired of this bed.', 'neg'),
            ("I can't deal with this", 'neg'),
            ('She is my sworn enemy!', 'neg'),
            ('I never had a caring mom.', 'neg')
    ]
```

First, we will import the `NaiveBayesClassifier` class from the `textblob` package. This classifier is very easy to work with and is based on the Bayes theorem.

The `train` variable consists of tuples that each holds the actual training data. Each tuple contains the sentence and the group it is associated with.

Now, to train our model, we will instantiate a `NaiveBayesClassifier` object by passing the train to it:

```
    cl = NaiveBayesClassifier(train)
```

The updated naive Bayesian model `cl` will predict the category that an unknown sentence belongs to. Up to this point, our model knows of only two categories that a phrase can belong to, `neg` and `pos`.

The following code runs the following tests using our model:

```
    print(cl.classify("I just love breakfast"))
    print(cl.classify("Yesterday was Sunday"))
    print(cl.classify("Why can't he pay my bills"))
    print(cl.classify("They want to kill the president of Bantu"))
```

The output of our test is as follows:

```
pos
pos
neg
neg
```

We can see that the algorithm has had some degree of success in classifying the input phrases into their categories well.

This contrived example is overly simplistic but it does show promise that if given the right amounts of data and a suitable algorithm or model, it is possible for a machine to carry out tasks without any human help.

The specialized class `NaiveBayesClassifier` also did some heavy lifting for us in the background so we could not appreciate the innards by which the algorithm arrived at the various predictions. Our next example will use the `scikit` module to predict the category that a phrase may belong to.

A supervised learning example

Assume that we have a set of posts to categorize. As with supervised learning, we need to first train the model in order for it to accurately predict the category of an unknown post.

Gathering data

The `scikit` module comes with a number of sample data we will use for training our model. In this case, we will use the newsgroups posts. To load the posts, we will use the following lines of code:

```
from sklearn.datasets import fetch_20newsgroups
training_data = fetch_20newsgroups(subset='train',
    categories=categories, shuffle=True, random_state=42)
```

After we have trained our model, the results of a prediction must belong to one of the following categories:

```
categories = ['alt.atheism',
              'soc.religion.christian','comp.graphics', 'sci.med']
```

The number of records we are going to use as training data is obtained by the following:

```
print(len(training_data))
```

Machine learning algorithms do not mix well with textual attributes so the categories that each post belongs to are presented as numbers:

```
print(set(training_data.target))
```

The categories have integer values that we can map back to the categories themselves with `print(training_data.target_names[0])`.

Here, 0 is a numerical random index picked from `set(training_data.target)`.

Now that the training data has been obtained, we must feed the data to a machine learning algorithm. The bag of words model will break down the training data in order to make it ready for the learning algorithm or model.

Bag of words

The bag of words is a model that is used for representing text data in such a way that it does not take into consideration the order of words but rather uses word counts to segment words into regions.

Take the following sentences:

```
sentence_1 = "As fit as a fiddle"
sentence_2 = "As you like it"
```

The bag of words enables us to decompose text into numerical feature vectors represented by a matrix.

To reduce our two sentences into the bag of words model, we need to obtain a unique list of all the words:

```
set((sentence_1 + sentence_2).split(" "))
```

This set will become our columns in the matrix. The rows in the matrix will represent the documents that are being used in training. The intersection of a row and column will store the number of times that word occurs in the document. Using our two sentences as examples, we obtain the following matrix:

	As	Fit	A	Fiddle	You	Like	it
Sentence 1	2	1	1	1	0	0	0
Sentence 2	1	0	0	0	1	1	1

The preceding data alone will not enable us to predict accurately the category that new documents or articles will belong to. The table has some inherent flaws. There may be situations where longer documents or words that occur in many of the posts reduce the precision of the algorithm. Stop words can be removed to make sure only relevant data is analyzed. Stop words include is, are, was, and so on. Since the bag of words model does not factor grammar into its analysis, the stop words can safely be dropped. It is also possible to add to the list of stop words that one feels should be exempted from final analysis.

To generate the values that go into the columns of our matrix, we have to tokenize our training data:

```
from sklearn.feature_extraction.text import CountVectorizer
from sklearn.feature_extraction.text import TfidfTransformer
from sklearn.naive_bayes import MultinomialNB
count_vect = CountVectorizer()
training_matrix = count_vect.fit_transform(training_data.data)
```

The `training_matrix` has a dimension of (2257, 35788). This means that 2257 corresponds to the dataset while 35788 corresponds to the number of columns that make up the unique set of words in all posts.

We instantiate the `CountVectorizer` class and pass the `training_data.data` to the `fit_transform` method of the `count_vect` object. The result is stored in `training_matrix`. The `training_matrix` holds all the unique words and their respective frequencies.

To mitigate the problem of basing prediction on frequency count alone, we will import the `TfidfTransformer` that helps to smooth out the inaccuracies in our data:

```
matrix_transformer = TfidfTransformer()
tfidf_data = matrix_transformer.fit_transform(training_matrix)

print(tfidf_data[1:4].todense())
```

`tfidf_data[1:4].todense()` only shows a truncated list of a three rows by 35,788 columns matrix. The values seen are the term frequency--inverse document frequency that reduce the inaccuracy resulting from using a frequency count:

```
model = MultinomialNB().fit(tfidf_data, training_data.target)
```

`MultinomialNB` is a variant of the naive Bayes model. We pass the rationalized data matrix, `tfidf_data` and categories, `training_data.target`, to its `fit` method.

Prediction

To test whether our model has learned enough to predict the category that an unknown post is likely to belong to, we have the following sample data:

```
test_data = ["My God is good", "Arm chip set will rival intel"]
test_counts = count_vect.transform(test_data)
new_tfidf = matrix_transformer.transform(test_counts)
```

The list `test_data` is passed to the `count_vect.transform` function to obtain the vectorized form of the test data. To obtain the term frequency--inverse document frequency representation of the test dataset, we call the `transform` method of the `matrix_transformer` object.

To predict which category the docs may belong to, we do the following:

```
prediction = model.predict(new_tfidf)
```

The loop is used to iterate over the prediction, showing the categories they are predicted to belong to:

```
for doc, category in zip(test_data, prediction):
    print('%r => %s' % (doc, training_data.target_names[category]))
```

When the loop has run to completion, the phrase, together with the category that it may belong to, is displayed. A sample output is as follows:

```
'My God is good' => soc.religion.christian
'Arm chip set will rival intel' => comp.graphics
```

All that we have seen up to this point is a prime example of supervised learning. We started by loading posts whose categories are already known. These posts were then fed into the machine learning algorithm most suited for text processing based on the naive Bayes theorem. A set of test post fragments were supplied to the model and the category was predicted.

To explore an example of an unsupervised learning algorithm, we shall study the k-means algorithm for clustering some data.

An unsupervised learning example

A category of learning algorithms is able to discover inherent groups that may exist in a set of data. An example of these algorithms is the k-means algorithm.

K-means algorithm

The k-means algorithm uses the mean points in a given dataset to cluster and discover groups within the dataset. K is the number of clusters that we want and are hoping to discover. After the k-means algorithm has generated the groupings, we can pass it additional but unknown data for it to predict to which group it will belong.

Note that in this kind of algorithm, only the raw uncategorized data is fed to the algorithm. It is up to the algorithm to find out if the data has inherent groups within it.

To understand how this algorithm works, we will examine 100 data points consisting of x and y values. We will feed these values to the learning algorithm and expect that the algorithm will cluster the data into two sets. We will color the two sets so that the clusters are visible.

Let's create a sample data of 100 records of *x* and *y* pairs:

```
import numpy as np
import matplotlib.pyplot as plt
original_set = -2 * np.random.rand(100, 2)
second_set = 1 + 2 * np.random.rand(50, 2)
original_set[50: 100, :] = second_set
```

First, we create 100 records with `-2 * np.random.rand(100, 2)`. In each of the records, we will use the data in it to represent x and y values that will eventually be plotted.

The last 50 numbers in `original_set` will be replaced by `1 + 2 * np.random.rand(50, 2)`. In effect, what we have done is to create two subsets of data, where one set has numbers in the negative while the other set has numbers in the positive. It is now the responsibility of the algorithm to discover these segments appropriately.

We instantiate the `KMeans` algorithm class and pass it `n_clusters=2`. That makes the algorithm cluster all its data under only two groups. It is through a series of trial and error that this figure, 2, is obtained. But for academic purposes, we already know this number. It is not at all obvious when working with unfamiliar datasets from the real world:

```
from sklearn.cluster import KMeans
kmean = KMeans(n_clusters=2)

kmean.fit(original_set)

print(kmean.cluster_centers_)

print(kmean.labels_)
```

The dataset is passed to the `fit` function of `kmean`, `kmean.fit(original_set)`. The clusters generated by the algorithm will revolve around a certain mean point. The points that define these two mean points are obtained by `kmean.cluster_centers_`.

The mean points when printed appear as follows:

```
[[ 2.03838197  2.06567568]
 [-0.89358725 -0.84121101]]
```

Each data point in `original_set` will belong to a cluster after our k-means algorithm has finished its training. The k-mean algorithm represents the two clusters it discovers as 1s and 0s. If we had asked the algorithm to cluster the data into four, the internal representation of these clusters would have been 0, 1, 2, and 3. To print out the various clusters that each dataset belongs to, we do the following:

```
print(kmean.labels_)
```

This gives the following output:

```
[1 1 1 1 1 1 1 1 1 1 1 1 1 1 1 1 1 1 1 1 1 1 1 1 1 1 1 1 1 1 1 1 1 1 1
 1 1 1 1 1 1 1 1 1 1 1 1 1 1 0 0 0 0 0 0 0 0 0 0 0 0 0 0 0 0 0 0 0 0 0 0
 0 0 0 0 0 0 0 0 0 0 0 0 0 0 0 0 0 0 0 0 0 0 0 0 0 0 0 0 0]
```

There are 100 1s and 0s. Each shows the cluster that each data point falls under. By using `matplotlib.pyplot`, we can chart the points of each group and color it appropriately to show the clusters:

```
import matplotlib.pyplot as plt
for i in set(kmean.labels_):
    index = kmean.labels_ == i
    plt.plot(original_set[index,0], original_set[index,1], 'o')
```

`index = kmean.labels_ == i` is a nifty way by which we select all points that correspond to the group i. When i=0, all points belonging to the group 0 are returned to index. It's the same for `index =1, 2 ...`, and so on.

`plt.plot(original_set[index,0], original_set[index,1], 'o')` then plots these data points using o as the character for drawing each point.

Next, we will plot the centroids or mean values around which the clusters have formed:

```
plt.plot(kmean.cluster_centers_[0][0],kmean.cluster_centers_[0][1],
        '*', c='r', ms=10)
plt.plot(kmean.cluster_centers_[1][0],kmean.cluster_centers_[1][1],
        '*', c='r', ms=10)
```

Lastly, we show the whole graph with the two means illustrated by a star:

```
plt.show()
```

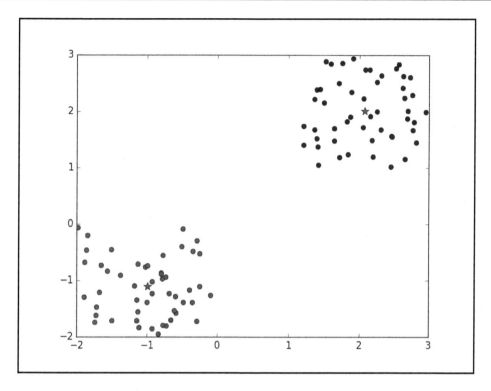

The algorithm discovers two distinct clusters in our sample data. The two mean points of the two clusters are denoted with the red star symbol.

Prediction

With the two clusters that we have obtained, we can predict the group that a new set of data might belong to.

Let's predict which group the points `[[-1.4, -1.4]]` and `[[2.5, 2.5]]` will belong to:

```
sample = np.array([[-1.4, -1.4]])
print(kmean.predict(sample))

another_sample = np.array([[2.5, 2.5]])
print(kmean.predict(another_sample))
```

The output is seen as follows:

```
[1]
[0]
```

At the barest minimum, we can expect the two test datasets to belong to different clusters. Our expectation is proved right when the `print` statement prints 1 and 0, thus confirming that our test data does indeed fall under two different clusters.

Data visualization

Numerical analysis does not sometimes lend itself to easy understanding. Indeed, a single image is worth 1,000 words and in this section, an image would be worth 1,000 tables comprised of numbers only. Images present a quick way to analyze data. Differences in size and lengths are quick markers in an image upon which conclusions can be drawn. In this section, we will take a tour of the different ways to represent data. Besides the graphs listed here, there is more that can be achieved when chatting data.

Bar chart

To chart the values 25, 5, 150, and 100 into a bar graph, we will store the values in an array and pass it to the `bar` function. The bars in the graph represent the magnitude along the y-axis:

```
import matplotlib.pyplot as plt

data = [25., 5., 150., 100.]
x_values = range(len(data))
plt.bar(x_values, data)

plt.show()
```

`x_values` stores an array of values generated by `range(len(data))`. Also, `x_values` will determine the points on the x-axis where the bars will be drawn. The first bar will be drawn on the x-axis where x is 0. The second bar with data 5 will be drawn on the x-axis where x is 1:

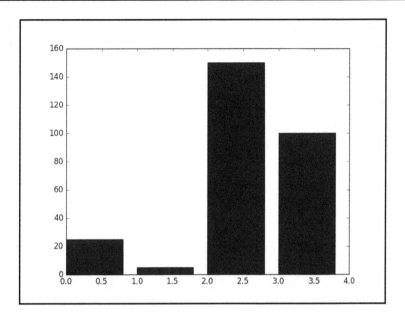

The width of each bar can be changed by modifying the following line:

```
plt.bar(x_values, data, width=1.)
```

This should produce the following graph:

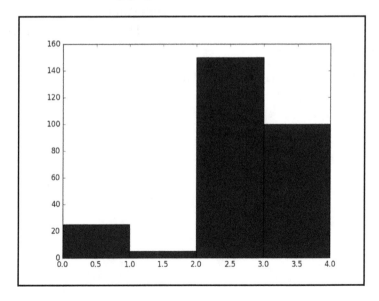

However, this is not visually appealing because there is no space anymore between the bars, which makes it look clumsy. Each bar now occupies one unit on the *x*-axis.

Multiple bar charts

In trying to visualize data, stacking a number of bars enables one to further understand how one piece of data or variable varies with another:

```
data = [
        [8., 57., 22., 10.],
        [16., 7., 32., 40.],
        ]

import numpy as np
x_values = np.arange(4)
plt.bar(x_values + 0.00, data[0], color='r', width=0.30)
plt.bar(x_values + 0.30, data[1], color='y', width=0.30)

plt.show()
```

The y values for the first batch of data are [8., 57., 22., 10.]. The second batch is [16., 7., 32., 40.]. When the bars are plotted, 8 and 16 will occupy the same x position, side by side.

x_values = np.arange(4) generates the array with values [0, 1, 2, 3]. The first set of bars are drawn first at position x_values + 0.30. Thus, the first x values will be plotted at 0.00, 1.00, 2.00 and 3.00.

The second batch of x_values will be plotted at 0.30, 1.30, 2.30 and 3.30:

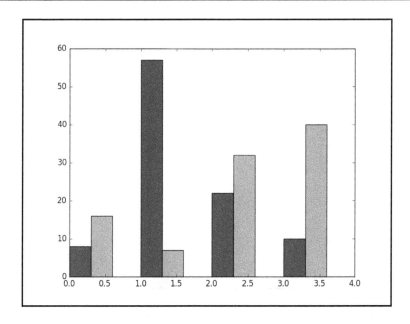

Box plot

The box plot is used to visualize the median value and low and high ranges of a distribution. It is also referred to as a box and whisker plot.

Let's chart a simple box plot.

We begin by generating 50 numbers from a normal distribution. These are then passed to `plt.boxplot(data)` to be charted:

```
import numpy as np
import matplotlib.pyplot as plt

data = np.random.randn(50)

plt.boxplot(data)
plt.show()
```

The following figure is what is produced:

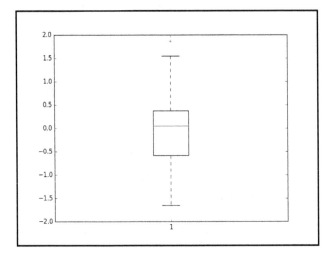

A few comments on the preceding figure: the features of the box plot include a box spanning the interquartile range, which measures the dispersion; the outer fringes of the data are denoted by the whiskers attached to the central box; the red line represents the median.

The box plot is useful to easily identify the outliers in a dataset as well as determining in which direction a dataset may be skewed.

Pie chart

The pie chart interprets and visually presents data as if to fit into a circle. The individual data points are expressed as sectors of a circle that add up to 360 degrees. This chart is good for displaying categorical data and summaries too:

```
import matplotlib.pyplot as plt
data = [500, 200, 250]

labels = ["Agriculture", "Aide", "News"]

plt.pie(data, labels=labels,autopct='%1.1f%%')
plt.show()
```

The sectors in the graph are labeled with the strings in the labels array:

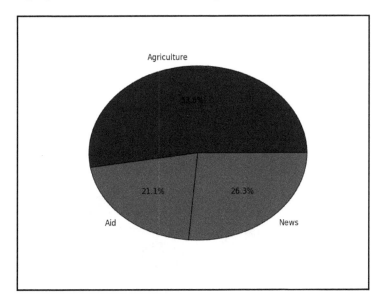

Bubble chart

Another variant of the scatter plot is the bubble chart. In a scatter plot, we only plot the x, y points of the data. Bubble charts add another dimension by illustrating the size of the points. This third dimension may represent sizes of markets or even profits:

```
import numpy as np
import matplotlib.pyplot as plt


n = 10
x = np.random.rand(n)
y = np.random.rand(n)
colors = np.random.rand(n)
area = np.pi * (60 * np.random.rand(n))**2

plt.scatter(x, y, s=area, c=colors, alpha=0.5)
plt.show()
```

With the variable n, we specify the number of randomly generated x and y values. This same number is used to determine the random colors for our x and y coordinates. Random bubble sizes are determined by area = np.pi * (60 * np.random.rand(n))**2.

The following figure shows this bubble chart:

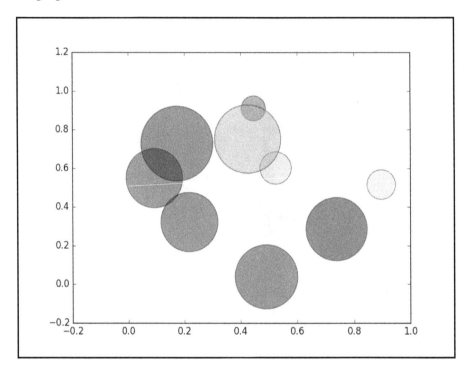

Summary

In this chapter, we have explored how data and algorithms come together to aid machine learning. Making sense of huge amounts of data is made possible by first pruning our data through normalization processes. Feeding this data to specialized algorithms, we are able to predict the categories and sets that our data will fall into.

Lastly, charting and plotting the condensed data helps to better understand and make insightful discoveries.

Index

S

scikit-learn 266
search algorithm
  selecting 207
search term 196
selection algorithms 192
selection by sorting 227
selection sort 216, 217, 218
sequences 38
sequential algorithms 238
serial algorithms 238
sets
  about 45
  example 47
  methods 45
  operations 45
siblings 135
singly linked list class 94
singly linked lists
  about 93
  append operation 94
size
  obtaining, of list 96
sorting algorithms
  about 209
  bubble sort 210, 211, 212, 213
  insertion sort 213, 214, 215, 216
  quick sort 219
  selection sort 216, 217, 218
special methods 28
stack-based queue
  about 122
  dequeue operation 123, 124, 125
  enqueue operation 122
stacks
  about 111
  bracket-matching application 116
  implementing 113
  operations 112
  peek method 116
  pop operation 114
  push operation 113
  usage 112
static methods 29

strings
  about 14
  examples 16, 17
  methods 15
sub tree 134
supervised learning 271
supervised learning example
  about 273
  bag of words model 274
  data, gathering 273
  prediction 275
symbol tables 168

T

tabulation 242
technical implementation
  about 242
  divide and conquer 246
  dynamic programming 242
  Fibonacci series 243
  greedy algorithms 249
text classifier
  example 271
Theta notation 83
tight lower bound 83
tight upper bound 80
time complexity 81
Travelling Salesman Problem 249
tree nodes 135
tree traversal
  about 148
  depth first traversal 148
trees
  about 133
  balancing 155
tuples 39
Turing machine 63
type 14

U

undirected graph 172
unordered linear search 196, 197
unsupervised learning 271
unsupervised learning example
  about 276

www.ingramcontent.com/pod-product-compliance
Lightning Source LLC
Chambersburg PA
CBHW062109050326
40690CB00016B/3262